Grace Always Comes
Daily Devotionals Through the Bible

Lyn Robbins

Grace Always Comes:
Daily Devotionals Through the Bible

Author: Lyn Robbins

Published by Austin Brothers Publishing
Fort Worth, Texas

www.abpbooks.com
ISBN 978-0-9845366-7-2
Copyright © 2016 by Lyn Robbins

All scripture quotations taken from the New International Version (NIV) unless otherwise indicated.

ALL RIGHTS RESERVED. *No part of this book may be reproduced in any form without permission in writing from the publisher, except in the case of brief quotations embodied in critical reviews or articles.*

Austin Brothers
Publishing

Books are available in quantity for promotional or educational use. Contact Austin Brothers Publishing for information at 3616 Sutter Ct., Fort Worth, TX 76137 or wterrya@gmail.com.

This and other books published by Austin Brothers Publishing can be purchased at www.abpbooks.com.

Printed in the United States of America
2016 -- First Edition

*"Tis grace has brought me safe thus far,
and grace will lead me home."*
– John Newton

*"And God raised us up with Christ and seated us
with Him in the heavenly realms in Christ Jesus,
in order that in the coming ages He might show the
incomparable riches of His grace, expressed in His
kindness to us in Christ Jesus. For it by grace you
have been saved…"*
– Ephesians 2:6-8

"Lyn Robbins is a pure practitioner of the Christian faith. From a ringside seat as his former pastor to a regular reader of his writing, I marvel at his crisp and vibrant writing style along with his precise understanding of theological concepts. *Grace Always Comes* is not your typical devotional guide. Each day, the discovery of a spiritual truth emerges from Lyn's exposition of the chosen texts. It is my honor to recommend *Grace Always Comes*!"

Dr. Dan R. Francis
Pastor, Latonia Baptist Church, Covington, Kentucky

"In this day of biblical illiteracy, Lyn Robbins has done us all a superb favor: he has written a basic primer to the Bible story for a general readership presented in a digestible format. *Grace Always Comes* is an educational—as well as devotional—resource that will give the reader an overview of the Bible in a year's schedule of readings and applications. This material is relevant for both newcomers to the Bible and those who have read Holy Scripture their entire lives. But, no pabulum here. Lyn's interpretations of the 'old, old story' are lively, engaging, and sure to provoke the reader's own flights of spiritual discovery. An indispensable tool for pastors in helping shape disciples of Christ of any age."

Rev. Charles Foster Johnson
Pastor, Bread Fellowship, Fort Worth, Texas

"Lyn Robbins has a deep faith that is reflected in each of the daily devotions in *Grace Always Comes*. A lawyer by training, Robbins is a gifted Bible Study teacher who communicates truth in a thought provoking and grace-filled way. Each devotion is intended to help the Christ follower remember that God always has the last redeeming word. You will be encouraged by the daily grace you re-discover as you journey with Lyn through God's grace-filled narrative one Bible story after another."

Dr. Frank R. Lewis
Senior Pastor, First Baptist Church, Nashville, Tennessee

"Lyn is a master writer and wordsmith. Through this inspiring daily devotional, you will grow stronger in your personal faith journey, and Lyn's insights will draw you deeper into God's greater Story. I highly recommend this book for all who desire a richness and depth in their relationship with God."

Rev. Jeff Simmons
Lead Pastor, Rolling Hills Community Church
Franklin and Nolensville, Tennessee

"For generations, Christians have practiced reading the Bible in manageable, daily-sized pieces. Lyn Robbins presents us with an invitation to find inspiration in all of Scripture. In these pages, he calls us to do more than just read an ancient text; he invites us to reflect on the God who is present to us in it. He teases out connections, even from the tedium, that illuminate the God-filled ordinary moments in our lives, and he gives us the gift of helping us find our story in the broader narrative that begins in creation and points us toward new creation to come. Such a journey can only be taken one step, one day, one passage at a time. Robbins has given us a guide on that journey, and it is one worth taking."

Rev. Monty Stallins
Pastor, Second Avenue Baptist Church, Rome, Georgia

Grace Always Comes is a fresh and innovative way to travel through the Bible from cover to cover in only one year. Mr. Robbins' stories are captivating and engaging as we daily travel through the story of God's loving plan for His people and His glory. A definite must-have for any devotional library."

Rev. John Parker
Associate Pastor of Music and Worship
Austin Baptist Church, Austin, Texas

Bible Reading Plan

Foreword

Having attempted to read the Bible through numerous times, and having failed more times than I have succeeded, I wish that I could have had *Grace Always Comes* next to my Bible. This daily devotion is a guide through the Bible, from Genesis to Revelation, which is readable, insightful, and personally applicable.

Finding a consistent theme throughout the Bible is a challenge, both in theological accuracy and in literary craftsmanship, but Lyn nails it. *Grace Always Comes* is the right thread to pull that runs from Genesis to Revelation. Lyn manages to identify that thread without mishandling the Old Testament, pointing to Jesus where appropriate, and connecting it all to God's grace that is made perfectly clear in the New Testament. For readers of all types, this helps tie the whole Bible together.

For those who become mired in "less exciting" portions of the Old Testament, the devotionals not only help the reader through, but they actually enliven these portions and connect them with both God's work throughout the Bible and lives today. Not a simple task, but Lyn works as easily with Leviticus as with Luke. For example, on Day 38, which covers Leviticus 23, we find instructions about leaving grain at the edges of the fields for the poor. Well, I don't own a field, and most other readers don't either. But Lyn helps us discover the principle that God is teaching which does apply to us today.

One of the characteristic things I appreciated most was the variety of the final application in each day's reading. Some were uplifting encouragements. Some were a convicting question or a thoughtful reflection. Others were a challenge to action in everyday life. This variety helps the reader avoid the sameness and staleness that can easily appear after Day 200 of reading the same devotional author.

Christmas is coming, and then New Year's Day, along with the handful of assorted commitments I always attempt. This year I am going to try again to read the Bible through, but this time, with the help of *Grace Always Comes*, I have a feeling I am going to make it to Revelation 22. I hope you do too.

Dr. David E. Benjamin
Pastor, Winfree Memorial Baptist Church
Midlothian, Virginia
Former Professor
Hong Kong Baptist Theological Seminary
August 2, 2016

Introduction and Dedication

Grace always comes…

As I wrote this book, I had at least three purposes in mind:

1. To help those who want to launch a yearlong daily practice
    of reading the Bible, front to back, by offering both a bit of
    motivation to keep reading every day and some explanation
    of stories, poems, prophecies, and hard-to-decipher items
    in scripture they would encounter along the way. I imagine
    among my readers both the committed Christ-follower who
    has never quite made it all the way through a Read-The-Bi-
    ble-In-A-Year plan and the Christ-seeker who is encounter-
    ing scripture for the first time and wondering how best to
    approach the task. And if there is among the readers a true
    unbeliever or skeptic who is willing to pick up a Bible and
    see what all the fuss is about, I would be honored for this
    book to be used as guide for the effort.

2. To provide a daily devotional for those who do not want to
    tackle reading the entire Bible, but who nonetheless would
    be intrigued by and interested in devotionals that follow the
    Bible story and build upon each other as scripture does.

3. To give some new perspective to the dedicated disciple who has read the Bible through many times before and is looking for a new companion piece as she reads through yet again.

However you use this book, I hope you will see, as I have discovered, the repeated them of grace throughout scripture. Grace is classically defined as the "unmerited favor" of God, and I find that favor given and displayed in virtually every chapter of the Bible.

I wrote the book just as you will read it. What I mean is this: On January 1, 2015, I read Genesis 1-3. I then chose one idea from those chapters and wrote 250 words about that idea. On January 2, I started with Genesis 4 and read that day's chapters, and then I wrote that day's devotional. And so I continued all year, finishing my first draft on December 31, 2015. I decided that the best way to write a year-long devotional was to take a year to do it, writing on February 5 what you read on February 5, and on October 16 what you will read on October 16. That way, I was encountering the unfolding stories and themes of scripture just as you will if you choose to use this book while reading through the Bible. I then took several months of 2016 to edit and to polish.

Some words of explanation are in order:

*   I limited each day's entry to 250 words, both to make sure that there would be only one page per day (The book is long enough as it is!) and to communicate only the message that I heard God giving me on each day. Fashioning each piece to be exactly the same number of words was a discipline for me both as I wrote and as I edited. I take some pride that each devotional is exactly 250 words, for that means you know exactly what you will get every day if you choose to take this journey with me.

- On some days, I picked the "obvious" lesson—the most famous story from the chapters for that day—as the basis for the day's devotion. On other days, I chose not to write about what others might find to be the clear lesson in favor of an idea that struck me uniquely during my 2015 travels through scripture. Titles like "Strange Fire" and "Bring Me a Witch," just to name two, come from that choice.

- I am well aware that I have defaulted to masculine forms in many places.

  ◊ Masculine pronouns and generic terms are not meant to exclude women or to indicate a hierarchy of importance between the genders, for I fully believe that "in Christ, there is no male or female." I use them because the English language flows more clearly, most of the time, when we avoid awkward usages like "he or she" or "forefathers and foremothers" and instead agree with the longstanding social contract that the generic "he" and references to "man" or "mankind" are intended to communicate no more and no less than a reference to a single human being or a collective group of people of both genders. If that usage offends you, I apologize and beg your indulgence. I promise it is not meant to demean or trivialize any female.

  ◊ I also use the masculine when referring to God. I do not believe that God is an old man with a white beard, has Y chromosomes, or is otherwise more male than female in characteristics. I believe that God—Creator, Sustainer, and Spirit—is genderless; more precisely, if you will allow me to make up a word, I believe that God is "genderful," possessing and displaying the very best of both

men and women, mothers and fathers, priests and priest-
esses, queens and kings, and prophets and prophetesses.
I do, however, respect scripture's use of the masculine
pronoun in reference to God. I resonate with the Bible's
repeated reference to God as "Father," not because God
does not possess maternal qualities but rather because
God as "Father" has for millennia meant something crucial to the world without implying anything male. I thus
use the masculine references to God for the same reason, for it is the best way I know to discuss Him.

My late uncle, Dr. Charles Wellborn, whom my father has called
the best preacher he ever heard, entitled one of his books *Grits,
Grace, and Goodness*. His title comes from the story of the traveler
making his first visit to the South, eating breakfast at a diner in Georgia. When the plate came, there was a side dish he could not identify.
Told by the waitress that it was grits, he responded that he had not
ordered grits. Her response—a truism any Southerner would understand without being told—was, "Oh, you don't have to order 'em.
Grits just come."

Compelled by the universality of the image, Uncle Charles
wrote that grace, like grits with your ham and eggs south of the
Mason Dixon line, "just comes" whether we order it or not. It is
with deep appreciation for his insights, scholarship, ministry, and life
that I dedicate this book to the memory of Uncle Charles—pastor,
teacher, uncle, and friend.

There is, of course, Grace with a capital G. It is the "Amazing
Grace" that saves us, the "marvelous, infinite, matchless Grace" that
is greater than all our sin. We do not order, request, or earn saving

Grace. It just comes, offered freely to all. It is up to us to respond to it.

There are many other kinds of grace, ranging from the small to the mighty, from the (almost) unnoticed to the obvious, and from the natural to the miraculous. In scripture, grace begins with the provision of a garden to the homeless and an outfit to the naked and ends with an invitation and a benediction. In between, we see grace coming to us as an ark, in the belly of a big fish, out of a rock in the desert, in hair that grows back, as flour from an empty pot, by healings, through words, and in countless other places and avenues. This grace comes often, and it comes to point the way to Grace.

As you read through scripture with the help of these individual little devotionals, it is my prayer that you see both Grace and grace. God repeatedly sends Grace our way to give us every possible chance to accept the free gift of eternal life; and grace comes every day—God's mercies are new every morning—because the kingdom of God is at hand, and God loves us so much that He lavishes His unmerited favor on us in ways too numerous to quantify.

Grace continues to come to you and to me. We do not put in a request for it… Grace always comes.

January

Sin Makes Them Naked; God Makes Them Clothes — Genesis 3:21

In the beginning, God.

The first critical lessons scripture teaches us are that (1) God is our Creator and (2) there are consequences for breaking God's rules. Adam and Eve give in to temptation, and they forfeit Paradise, the Garden of Eden.

There is another lesson in the beginning: God is a God of grace.

While the words "love" and "grace" do not appear in these verses, we nonetheless discover God's lovingkindness in scripture from the beginning. Chapter 1 describes each created thing as "good" — God has created a good world for us. Chapter 2 details God's compassion for Adam in creating a companion for him so that he will not be alone.

Perhaps the most subtle and yet the most profound early statement of God's grace happens as the crunch of the forbidden fruit still echoes. Having sinned, Adam and Eve are suddenly ashamed of how they look. They have always been unclothed, but now they know they are naked. They hide from God.

God is a God of grace, always. While Adam and Eve will indeed lose Eden, notice what happens first. In Verse 21 of Chapter 3, God makes garments of skin for Adam and Eve and clothes them. Even in the midst of punishment and disappointment, God's grace reaches out to their most basic need. Sin makes them naked, so God makes clothes for them. Even before the basics of sin and obedience are explained or understood, "in the beginning," God is in the grace business!

Day 2/January 2 – Genesis 4-7

Go into the Ark
Genesis 7:1

S in is everywhere. Sin is alluring. Sin is powerful. Discontent and jealousy lead to the world's first murder, and the flood-waters are unleashed. We learn in Chapter 5 that "every inclination" of humanity is "only evil…all the time." What began in the garden has mushroomed so that God Himself regrets creating the world.

Our own experience confirms this theme. What starts as a simple choice–a lustful look here, a dishonest moment there–spirals into a lifestyle that we would never have considered mere weeks before but that has now become our routine. We look around and see immorality rampant outside our windows, on our airwaves, and across the worldwide web. In our time, everyone's inclination seems only evil all the time.

Fortunately, God always responds with grace. As in yesterday's reading, we still do not see words like "love," yet the character of God is already being laid out for us. Abel receives God's favor. Cain receives God's mark of protection.

And then we get to Noah, a "righteous, blameless" man who "walks with God." We will learn from the prophet that Noah defines what the Lord requires: to do justice, to love kindness, and to walk humbly with God. (Micah 6:8) Even in the midst of regret, knowing that the depravity has to be eliminated, God is looking for a way to shower grace. He chooses Noah, and when the rain comes, the ark of grace is ready.

And Noah is ready to go into that ark.

Come out of the Ark
Genesis 8:15

In yesterday's scripture, God tells Noah, "Go into the ark." Now, the command is "Come out of the ark." Sometimes, God calls us to reverse.

We often grow content with routine. We heard God speak once, and we followed, and it felt good. So now we keep on doing what gave us that satisfaction. The idea that God has something new may never occur to us.

Our Christian life is one of movement. God calls Moses from the palace to the wilderness back to his people to the road toward the Promised Land and to a new wilderness. He calls Elijah to preach, and then to talk to kings, and then to tutor a young prophet. He calls Peter to fish, and then to follow, and then to preach, and then to write.

What if Noah were so satisfied with building the ark and gathering the animals and getting on board with his family that he either chooses to ignore or misses completely the new, opposite command? What if Nehemiah is so satisfied with his job as the king's cupbearer that he misses the call to leave and rebuild Jerusalem? What if Paul so enjoys his first missionary journey that he decides to continue it forever?

What if Abe Lincoln had been content to stay a fine Christian lawyer or C. S. Lewis had just worked on teaching literature?

Are you obeying an obsolete call? Has God's call changed to something new? What is God calling you to do today?

Leave… and Go to the Land I Will Show You – Genesis 12:1

God's call to Abram models how Jesus leads us today. Abram is not told where he is going. He is called to leave where he is. The offer is to trust what God has in store, whatever that may be.

There is more clarity about where Abram is to leave than about where he will end up. The promise is not a specific destination; the promises are (1) that God will show Abram a new land; (2) that God–the Promiser–will travel with and before Abram; and (3) that God knows the way.

Abram believes that God does not say "go to the land I will show you" without being ahead on the path that He intends Abram to take, whether it leads through the dark, by the sea, or into Egypt.

Jesus calls Peter, James, and John to leave their fishermen's nets. Matthew is called to leave his tax collector's booth. Jesus is unmistakable about what is to be abandoned but not so plain concerning what happens next.

"Walking by faith" means following God when there is no stated destination and no exit strategy.

Like God with Abram, Jesus does not always show us the whole plan; instead, He promises to lead us on our paths. He makes straight the crooked path and lights the road ahead.

Jesus is not the target; He is the way. We learn from Abram that faith does not need to know the destination; faith knows the Promiser. Following needs only a leader.

Walk Before Me and Be Blameless
Genesis 17:1

Now that Abram has had time to get to know God better, and now that he has experienced God's reliability, the covenant matures into something much more complex. God's covenant given to Noah was one-sided; it was a promise from God. Now, God is ready to ask Abram for something in return: the covenant is to be sealed with circumcision.

Like many of God's commands, circumcision is one that modern science has validated, but cleanliness is not the primary point. The reason God commands it is to mark the people as God's. That is reason enough.

You may not always understand God's commands. Ultimately, they are for your best, but in the moment, you obey not because the command is "good for you" but simply because it is God's command.

To be sure, God has already shown that He demands obedience, but now the call is far more complex: "I am God Almighty; walk before me and be blameless." (Genesis 17:1)

We all sin. We all miss the mark. Even so, God calls us to be blameless, to be holy. (Leviticus 19:2) Even to be perfect. (Matthew 5:48) Each time we are faced with a choice, we have the free will to choose rightly. We do not have to sin in that moment. We can be perfect. We can walk blamelessly.

Compliance with God because He is God is the heart of a covenant relationship with God. And yes, it is "good for you" too.

Today, walk blamelessly before God.

Day 6 / January 6 – Genesis 18-21

Sarah Laughs
Genesis 18:12

When Sarah overhears that she will bear a child, she laughs. Do not judge Sarah harshly. We might have laughed too. Her husband laughs when he first hears the same promise. (Genesis 17:17)

Sarah's laughter comes from momentary bewilderment. If your neighbor told you that she was about to sprout wings and fly away, you would laugh.

Sarah laughs because God has told a funny joke – "Did you hear the one about the 90-year-old pregnant lady?"

Sarah's is nervous laughter. God is going to involve her in a supernatural event. Is she worthy? Can she do it? Has God picked the right person? Why in the world has God chosen her?

Sarah laughs because of relief. Her lifetime's prayer is being answered. Will she really lay down the burden of barrenness and become a mother?

Sarah's laughter is a reaction to the unexpected. Groucho Marx says: "One morning I shot an elephant in my pajamas... How he got in my pajamas, I'll never know;" the surprising turn in the conversation tickles our funny bone.

The child's name is "Isaac," which means laughter. Sarah laughs again, this time with pure joy, as her "laughter" is born in her old age.

And, maybe God laughs too, just a little. We are, after all, made in the image of God. If laughter is uttered in joy and relief and unexpected twist, maybe God, a twinkle in His divine eye, chuckles when He says "Sarah will have a child."

Did God Really Say That?
Genesis 22:2

Following God is not easy.

God is not mean or sadistic, but He is demanding. The parable of the pearl of great price (Matthew 13:45-46) teaches us to give up all that we have to gain the kingdom of God. That is not easy.

It would be sadistic for God actually to expect, and to allow, Abraham to kill his son, but the story does not turn out that way. One point of this story is that God decidedly does not want child sacrifice. The test is about obedience when we do not understand God. The test is about trusting God.

That command is difficult, not mean. God is demanding, but He is not sadistic. We know God better than that.

Small children stand on the side of the pool and hear their father call them to jump in. The father does not explain that his arms are strong enough. He just asks them to trust him and jump. Reasonable humans who cannot swim fear drowning; trusting children learn to jump into water because they know their father will provide protection.

The ram in the thicket foreshadows the role of Jesus, the Lamb of God who takes our place. If the call were not there to sacrifice Isaac, the shedding of that ram's blood would mean far less.

Does God really expect Abraham to be willing to kill his own child? Yes. Is God that demanding? Yes. Is it a hard story? Yes.

Does it teach us much? Oh yes.

Day 8/January 8 – Genesis 24:28-26

The First Grasp
Genesis 25:29-34

Pay attention to Jacob. He will become "Israel," and the life of Israel comprises the rest of the Old Testament. Through these stories of how God deals with Israel, we learn how God deals with us.

Jacob's story is our story. Pay attention.

Jacob, born clutching his twin brother's foot, is a grasper, literally. His parents name him Jacob, meaning "he grasps the heel." The name, a Hebrew euphemism for "deceiver," fits.

When Esau, home from a particularly exhausting hunt, smells Jacob's homemade stew and asks for a bowlful, Jacob concocts an outrageous offer that only his dimwit brother would accept–his birthright in exchange for a dollop of gumbo! In ancient times, the birthright included double inheritance rights and long-term family authority. Its worth was incalculable. For the price of a bowl of pea soup, Esau lays his most valuable asset on the table.

Put simply, Jacob decides to see if he can take advantage of Esau, and Esau falls for it. Jacob the Grasper has his chance to clutch what is not his. He exploits the opening.

Jacob does not stop with taking the birthright. One successful grasping leads to another. Jacob is about to set out on a life of deceit, double-dealing, and manipulation.

What opportunity to grasp will present itself today? You won't steal or lie… still, those with less ability will cross your path, and there will be something for you to gain by taking advantage of their shortsightedness.

Pay attention. This is our story.

Stairway to Heaven
Genesis 28:12

Jacob's story, our story, progresses. Jacob, in for a penny in for a pound, by now has no problem with outright lies, even to his own father, to get what he wants.

Jacob meets Laban, and the Grasper becomes the target of a double-cross. In a classic bait and switch, sober Jacob is promised Rachel, then drunken Jacob is given Leah. The worm has turned: Jacob is now the victim of deceit.

Between these tales of trickery, both by Jacob and at his expense, we find Jacob's dream: angels on a stairway ("Jacob's ladder"), with God at the top. God speaks to Jacob and renews the covenant first made with Abraham–a promise of descendants, blessings, and God's protecting presence.

This is an amazing scene. Not only has Jacob done nothing to earn it, he has gone out of his way to live a life of dishonesty and selfish scheming. Yet, the creator of the world seeks him in the desert with a covenant promise.

To his credit, Jacob knows something sacred has happened. He declares "surely the Lord is in this place." Jacob calls the place Bethel, the "house of God."

Remember, this is our story. As our sins multiply, God seeks—and finds—us in the most unlikely of places. The question is whether we recognize the presence of God. Do we hear Him speak to us? Do we notice that we are in an awesome place, none other than the house of God?

Pay attention.

Day 10/January 10 – Genesis 30 – 32:21

Seeking Reconciliation
Genesis 32:3-5

There are many places in the Old Testament where sweeping history gives way to individual stories of basic human interaction. The emotion of everyday encounters is not all that different in these ancient stories than it is today.

Jacob is returning home after more than twenty years away. Recall that Jacob left because he had wronged Esau yet again, so returning to Esau's territory presents a problem. Now, finally, Jacob the Grasper, the Supplanter, the deceiver, has to act like an adult and face his past.

Jacob cannot know whether Esau has matured into a man ready to forgive, but Jacob does know that he was in the wrong. Twenty years of trading swindles and double-crosses with Laban have been a constant reminder of Jacob's own unfairness to his brother. Now, he seeks to reconcile.

Jacob recognizes his own unworthiness, and he fears his brother – that is a frightening combination. Jacob has the presence of mind, first, to pray and, second, to prepare gifts for his brother. Hoping to show he has changed, he sends offerings for Esau's good (for a change) and sends messages ahead that demonstrate his humility.

Seeking reconciliation when we have been in the wrong is not easy. Taking the steps of prayer, of showing humility, and approaching the one we have wronged are the right ways to begin the process. Jacob cannot know how Esau will react, but he knows that it is incumbent upon him to try.

Do you need to do the same?

Your Name Will No Longer Be Jacob
Genesis 32:28

This story—not creation, not the flood, not the initial covenant with Abram, but this one, Jacob's wrestling match with God—is the high point of the book of Genesis.

Why? Because Jacob's story is our story.

God comes to each of us, seeking us despite our hypocrisy, our wandering, our dishonesty, and our feeble self-reliance. Most of us are not ready for God, and we react defensively, so meeting God is a struggle.

God touches us, and we are forever different.

There are two key changes in Jacob after this struggle with God that are with him the rest of his life:

- He leaves with a new walk: Jacob has a permanent limp. We leave our encounter with God walking differently—either we are walking as servants, seeking the places where we can be God's eyes and hands in the world, or we walk as nomads, wandering like Cain, alienated and alone. Either way, we cannot strive with God and act the same afterwards. Our walk will always be different.

- He leaves with a new name: He is hereafter Israel, translated "he who struggles with God." God gives him a new name to go with his new walk.

Believers were first called Christians—"little Christs"—because their new walk justified a new name. (Acts 11:26) God has a new name for you, a name to show that you are blessed, that God delights in you. (Isaiah 62:1-4) How will you walk after you struggle with God?

Day 12/January 12 – Genesis 35-37

Go Back to Bethel
Genesis 35:1

Israel is in trouble. His sons (the apple does not far fall from this tree) have created havoc. Life is unsure.

Suddenly, the word from God comes: Go back to Bethel, to the place of Jacob's ladder, where he has first recognized God's presence and heard the covenant of God. Bethel reminds Israel not only that God is with him but that God has blessed and protected him.

When Jacob arrives again at Bethel, God reminds him of both his name change and the covenant. Jacob's nature has changed—he is no longer the "Grasper" or "Supplanter;" he is now Israel, the "Struggler." God's covenant still is sure, and God's plans are not changed.

In *Les Miserables*, Jean Valjean steals costly silver candlesticks from the bishop, who, in a life-changing act, forgives him, giving him the candlesticks as a sign the bishop has "bought your soul for God." In the stage version, the director always makes sure that, for the rest of the play, the candlesticks remain prominent for Valjean, and the audience, to see. These reminders of the sacrifice made and the time when Valjean first understood the presence of God are never far away.

We all have markers in our walks, places and times in our journeys that have signified the presence of God to us. When we are in trouble, we need to find that marker, to look at our candlesticks. We often need to go back to Bethel, for surely the Lord is in that place.

Day 13/January 13 – Genesis 38-39

How Could I Do Such a Wicked Thing and Sin Against God? – Genesis 39:9

Joseph, saved from the pit and working as a servant in an important man's house, is confronted with a quandary—his master's wife tries to seduce him. Unlike his brother in the previous chapter, Joseph resists sexual temptation. Joseph's refusal, though, comes with great cost, for the scorned woman trumps up an outrageous charge of attempted rape, and Joseph winds up in jail.

Joseph's reaction to temptation is amazing. Among ancient peoples whose morality is not at all developed, Joseph appreciates the higher issue at play. To be sure, his refusal of her advances is based on loyalty to Potipher ("My master has withheld nothing from me except you"), but there is more to it than that for Joseph.

Joseph says, "How then could I do such a wicked thing and sin against God?" At this time before God has laid down specific laws or even yet given the Ten Commandments, for Joseph to understand the "sinful" nature of what she suggests shows uncommon insight. Joseph knows that this action would create a rift between himself and God.

Later in the Old Testament, having committed adultery, David says to God, "Against you, you only, have I sinned." (Psalm 51:4) The point is not that wickedness does not hurt others—of course it does. David's sin leads to his murder of his paramour's husband, and to chaos in his own family. The point, however, is that sin is a matter between us and God above.

Joseph's response is "How could I?"

Day 14/January 14 — Genesis 40-42

God Saves a Nation through Joseph
Genesis 41:40

Is it coincidence?

Joseph's interpretations of his own dreams made him unpopular as a child. Now, a series of events—his brothers sell him into slavery, a false rape accusation lands him in jail, a cupbearer remembers his dream interpretation, then Joseph is called to interpret Pharaoh's dreams—has resulted in Joseph's position as second in command in Egypt. Joseph implements a plan to store enough food during the years of plenty so that Egypt can survive the coming famine.

Can anyone say that God's hand was not in the events that led to Joseph being in that place? We do not have to conclude God "caused" his brothers to act despicably or Potipher's wife to lie in order to understand that God works through what happens in the world.

What has happened to Joseph is terrible, but God redeems it. God works through dreams, dungeons, memories, and the king of Egypt himself to allow Joseph to save a nation.

How can God redeem the tragedies of your life? What positions are you in now to help and to serve? Are you able to look back and see how what seemed disastrous at the time was in fact preparing you for greater things?

You do not have to blame God for tragedies in order to see His hand in play. God is in the business of meeting us where we are and blessing others through us. In Joseph's case, an entire nation is saved. What can God do through you?

God Saves a Family through Joseph
Genesis 45:5-7

God's work through Joseph is not only on a national scale; it is personal. Yesterday, we read how Joseph is able to save a nation. Today, we see how he saves his own family. God's hand is seen in addressing regional famine and in healing relationships.

Joseph's words are so important to people of faith: "Do not be distressed and do not be angry with yourselves for selling me here, because it was to save lives that God sent me ahead of you."

For some, it is easier to believe that God works to affect entire nations than it is to see personal work of God in individual lives. The great joy of scripture like this is in seeing God concerned with and involved in our personal problems. Yes, Joseph's position allows God to save many people from famine, but how critical it is to see that God also works through Joseph to save Israel and his sons.

God's care for you and your needs is no different than his care for the nations. The hymn "His Eye Is on the Sparrow, so I Know He Watches Me" is based on the gospel. Jesus says that God knows and loves each of us individually.

Joseph has more than his share of personal tragedy, of course, and God saves him from that and elevates him to a position he could never have imagined. More than that, God uses him to save his family from starvation.

God never forgets any individual. Ever.

Day 16 / January 16 – Genesis 46-48

I Will Go to Egypt with You
Genesis 46:4

Israel, having survived his youthful errors, is comfortable. But life throws him a curve ball. Israel has to leave home, Canaan, the land God has given to his grandfather Abraham. There is famine in the land, and the only food is in Egypt. Israel is old, and he knows that once he leaves, he will not see his home again.

We know, because we know our history and what follows this story in the Old Testament, that Israel's stay will turn into over 400 years of slavery for his family and descendants. This famine will have consequences that last for generations.

Curve balls can have unpleasant, unexpected results. We find ourselves alone, strangers in a strange land.

God does not solve all of those problems. He does not prevent the famine, and He does not immediately end the slavery.

He does not prevent every disease or bankruptcy or drunk driver that comes our way either. Yet again, Israel's story is our story.

What God does promise is His presence. The Psalmist calls God an "ever present help in trouble." (Psalm 46:1) When the apostles are caught in a storm and are paralyzed with fear, Jesus appears to them, but He does not immediately calm the storm. What He does do is assure them of His presence: "Take courage. It is I. Do not be afraid." (Matthew 14:27)

The nearness of God is our good. (Psalm 78:23)

Even if we have to go to Egypt, God promises that He will go with us.

Day 17/January 17 – Genesis 49–Exodus 1

Some People Do Not Know and Do Not Care – Exodus 1:8

Are you ready for Exodus?

The language here of the King James Version—there arose a new king in Egypt who "knew not Joseph"—is one of the great political statements of all literature, not just of the Bible. The stories of the Hebrew who had saved his nation and of his God are ancient history to this new pharaoh, who sees only the threat of a growing group of foreigners in his land. His solution is to make slaves of them.

Israel is in trouble. There is no leader, there have been no recent appearances of God, and no new patriarch has risen up. The king has ordered the murder of their sons.

We are always closer than we know to being surrounded by those who do not know God or his people. In fact, if we are honest, we know that we do not even have to look into the future to find that reality. If our world and our nation were ever "Christian" in any sense, they certainly are not now.

This is the real world. Our ancient stories of arks, patriarchs, covenants, and dreams are true and meaningful; but they do not keep the evil away in the here and now. In life, there arise circumstances—cancer, divorce, job loss, distress, depression, betrayal—that "know not Joseph."

Exodus is the story of how God leads Israel out of Egypt. Remember, Israel's story is our story. Our world does not know Joseph. Are you ready?

Day 18 / January 18 – Exodus 2-4

The Excuses of Moses
Exodus 3:11, 13; 4:1, 10, 13

When mighty Moses, hero of the faith, meets God at the burning bush, his faith is overwhelming, and we see a model for the ages. Right?

No. Instead, what we find is a man of doubt and excuses.

Called to lead God's people out of Egypt, Moses has five responses–excuses really, some questions and some exclamations, each more desperate than the one before–for God. Some of these may sound familiar to you.

"Who am I?" (3:11) God, I am not able to do what you ask. I am just a shepherd in my father-in-law's service. You have the wrong man.

"Who are you?" (3:13) God, if I tell them you have sent me, why will that matter? Who are you? What is your name? Why will anybody care?

"What if they don't believe me?" (4:1) What if I do exactly what you tell me to do, and it doesn't work? What if Pharaoh says "no?" What if the people don't follow me? What if I am just not good enough?

"I don't know how." (4:10) Moses says "I am slow of speech and slow of tongue." The implication is God does not know what He is doing, that God has made a mistake.

"Please send some else." (4:13)

Moses sounds a lot like us, and therein is a word of encouragement. Your doubts are no different than his are, and yet look what God does through him.

What can God do through you?

Day 19/January 19 – Exodus 5-8

The Promise of Deliverance
Exodus 6:6

This story of the plagues is full of potential distractions: blood, frogs, gnats, and flies. These troubling details can block the key lesson from our view. We can get caught up in questions like "How did the staff turn into a snake?" and "What is all this stuff about hardening hearts?"

Those questions are valid and deserve attention, but the overarching message here—what we most need to see—is a promise that will sustain God's people forevermore: God will deliver.

"I will bring you out from under the yoke of the Egyptians. I will free you from being slaves. I will redeem you."

It is the message God continues to bring, and it is a promise on which God's people continue to rely.

A yoke is a burden, and you know what that feels like. Hardship, limitation, disability, poverty, and the basic requirements of making a living can encumber us, dragging us down. We all, sometimes, are in our own Egypt.

Jesus tells us that when we sin, we are enslaved by sin. (John 8:34) Paul writes that slavery is the clear illustration for our lives without Christ. (Romans 6)

People needing redemption are people who owe a debt they cannot pay. A coupon is just a worthless piece of paper until it is redeemed, when a store gives value for what was valueless. We, too, need redemption.

The promise of God is that the yoke, the slavery, the worthlessness is gone. God, the Redeemer, will deliver us.

Day 20/ January 20 – Exodus 8-12

Passover
Exodus 12:13

Much in the story of the plagues, culminating with the deaths of the firstborn throughout Egypt, is disquieting. The sins of Egypt, and the consequences of those sins, are great. Without question, the point is that God is holy and expects obedience; and when people are neither holy nor obedient, their choices often lead to disastrous results. Floods come. Plagues come. God will be known.

Regardless of how complete the tales of the plagues are in terms of describing God, there is no way to read the story without seeing the grace of God. Just as God has clothed Adam and Eve, marked Cain, and sent Noah plans for a big boat, God once again steps in with unmistakable grace in the face of catastrophe. This time, the grace is the Passover.

God's grace is for those homes marked by lamb's blood. "When I see the blood, I will pass over." Sin has a price, and without the shedding of blood, there is no remission of sins, no forgiveness. (Hebrews 9:22) Yet, grace means we need not pay that price. Do not miss the foreshadowing here of the work of Christ for each of us.

God's design for His people is longer in view than even 430 years in Egypt. God will accomplish His plan, and when the Pharaohs of the world interfere, destruction often results. But Jesus has shed His blood for us, and when God sees that blood, He passes over us.

Let us commemorate. Grace always comes.

Day 21/January 21 – Exodus 13-14

A Strong East Wind
Exodus 14:21

God is in control of the nature He has created. The moon, the stars, and the waves of the sea are subject to His command. (Jeremiah 31:35) Likewise, the lightning, wind, and rain are His. (Psalm 135:7)

The parting of the Red Sea is a famous story. Many picture Charlton Heston in front of the Cecil B. DeMille backdrop and imagine a miraculous divine hand holding back the waters. In reality, scripture teaches that God uses natural forces to achieve His supernatural end. God uses the wind to part the sea.

When Israel reaches the shore, the people are ready to return to slavery. Hail and boils and the Angel of Death are mere memories now, and their present dilemma is at the forefront of their minds. The sea is in front of them, and the Egyptian army, with chariots and armor and Pharaoh himself, is approaching rapidly from the rear. They are cornered.

Their memories of their delivering God have faded. There is no way out, at least that they can see.

Moses sees more. His words ring in our ears today; "Do not be afraid. Stand firm and you will see the deliverance the LORD will bring you today. The Egyptians you see today you will never see again." (Exodus 14:13)

God is aware of what traps you. Before you is the immovable object. Behind you, the irresistible force is bearing down. There is no way out.

But there is God. And the wind is in His hand.

Day 22/January 22 – Exodus 15-17

Grumbling
Exodus 15:24

Do you ever find yourself so caught up in the problems that have presented themselves today that you cannot remember what God did for you yesterday?

The Israelites have seen incredible acts of God, all done for their benefit. They do not have to rely on teachings or even faith—they have seen with their own eyes the plagues that led Pharaoh to let them go. They are within a week of having seen the very sea parted so that they could walk through on dry ground.

So, what is it that now makes them grumble? It is not a major crisis. It is not something so terrible or complex that they must draw back in fear. No... it is something so natural and basic that they grumble without thinking.

They are thirsty.

Do not be too hard on Israel. We too grumble when our stomach aches. We need to ask ourselves whether we remember to trust God with the basics. If we have seen God perform tremendous miracles in our own lives, and we have, surely we can trust Him with the little things. Freed from our bondage, set free from our burdens, we know that God is the source of everything good.

At Marah in Chapter 15, and again at Meribah in Chapter 17, God hears the grumbles and provides water... still more grace from God.

We get thirsty, and we grumble. And God sends grace.

Where you see only a rock, God sees water. Grace always comes.

Commandments
Exodus 20:2-17

The Ten Commandments come hurtling across time.

Reading the Ten Commandments, you notice some patterns. The first four concern our relationship with God–worship only God, have nothing to do with idols, honor God's name, protect the Sabbath. The last six are about our relationships with each other–valuing family, human life, marriage, property, truth, and boundaries.

When Jesus is asked what is the greatest commandment, His answer reflects these patterns: "Love the Lord your God ... and love your neighbor." (Matthew 23:37-39)

Viewing the Ten Commandment as a set of "don'ts" misses the point. God gives them to us as beginning guides for living life to the fullest. When we do well with these, we are ready to move on to the next steps of life.

Start by honoring God. Worship God and God alone, and worship respectfully and intentionally.

Love others as you love yourself. Treat people as you want to be treated. See them in the light in which the person who loves you best sees you. Love them with your thoughts, with your words, and with your deeds.

Many people wonder what the will of God is for their lives. Some aspects of His plan may be hard to discern, but some parts are not. If God is not spelling everything out for you, perhaps you should ask yourself, "How well am I doing with what I already know God wants for me? How am I doing on the Ten Commandments?"

Love God. Love your neighbor.

Day 24/January 24 – Exodus 21-23

Eye for an Eye
Exodus 21:24

These words—eye for eye, tooth for tooth, hand for hand, foot for foot—have been misused to justify all sorts of evil and abuse through the ages. Why does God give this command?

In these verses of Exodus, God is talking to a most primitive people, men and women who have been slaves, a nation that for generations has served a pagan king and his taskmasters. At this point in ancient history, justice, mercy, and forgiveness are not part of any code, anywhere. God is starting with a lesson of fairness: the punishment should fit the crime. No more, no less.

God's revelation of Himself and His plan will progress until we get the full picture in Jesus, but now, still on the mountain where the Ten Commandments have been given, we are seeing the most rudimentary beginnings. Pay for what you break. Replace what you cause to be lost.

Fifteen hundred or so years later, Jesus teaches in the Sermon on the Mount that the time for these rudimentary teachings is over. You have heard that it was said, 'eye for eye, and tooth for tooth.' But I tell you, do not resist an evil person. If someone strikes you on the right cheek, turn to him the other also." (Matthew 5:38-39)

God's teachings grow with us. Understand why God starts with basics, just as we teach our toddlers with unnuanced absolutes. We then learn to move to the complete explanation—love—shown to us by Jesus.

A Promise of Absolute Obedience
Exodus 24:3

It is a noble promise: "Everything the Lord has said we will do." It is repeated four verses later: "We will do everything the Lord has said; we will obey." (Exodus 24:7)

This is not the first time Israel has made such a sweeping promise. We have seen it already in Chapter 19. And once again, it will not last long. Soon will come grumbling and disobedience, in turn leading to outright rebellion.

Still, in the moment, the sentiment is admirable: "If God has said it, we will obey it." The fact that history will disprove Israel's steadfastness, obedience, and consistency does not mean their intent is bad or their honesty is lacking.

Making a commitment when you have just seen God is often what will carry you later, when you cannot see God and the mountaintop seems far away. Even when you have been disobedient, the echo of a past full-throated promise to God of absolute obedience can renew your energy to follow His commands.

We have already read enough about Israel to know that God's chosen people are wildly variable, moving from commitments to dissatisfaction, from energy to despair, from following to turning away.

That description applies just as well to contemporary humans, both believers and non-believers. We have our worshipful times of commitment, and we have our frustrated times of giving up. It does us well to look back to these words, to renew our commitments to obedience.

Everything the Lord has said will we do.

Amen.

Day 26/January 26 – Exodus 27-29

Sacrifices
Exodus 29:42-43

The intricate instructions and regulations that God sets out during this section of Exodus deal primarily with the priests and the altar. These rules of worship culminate in the Old Testament priests' most important duty: sacrifice.

There are blood sacrifices, food offerings, wave offerings, grain offerings, peace offerings, trespass offerings, and sin offerings. The priest acts as the people's spokesman before God, confessing their sins and offering their gifts.

These verses make it clear that God is carefully setting up this entire system. Details about the clothes of the priest and the raw materials to be used for meat forks demonstrate the infinitesimal specifics of the Lord's plan.

Why does God call for such detail?

God is asking His people to follow what appear to us to be minuscule niceties to make the point that they will do what God asks, down to the finest point. Viewing these chapters as irrelevant or trivial misses the message that God has a plan and wants His people to follow.

If we follow in the little things, we will follow in the big plans.

In the sacrificial system, the people find deeper truths: (1) the creator and giver of all things deserves to be remembered as we use and consume those creations; and (2) our sin offends God and thus requires us to acknowledge our failings and seek His forgiveness.

The sacrificial system is not permanent, but the underlying messages are. Acknowledge the giver and creator, and know that your sin requires atonement.

Quick to Turn Away
Exodus 32:8

The tragic story of the golden calf is in many ways the most offensive in scripture. Building an idol in the shadow of the very mountain where the Ten Commandments have been given is nasty enough. That Aaron would try to cloak this idolatry as part of a "festival to the Lord" (Exodus 32:5) is insulting. Aaron's weak attempt at excuse ("They gave me this gold, and I threw it into the fire, and out came this calf!" –Exodus 32:24) would be comical if it were not so distasteful.

More odious is the reaction the people's creation and worship of the calf provokes in Moses, who orders the Levites to go throughout the camp, killing their brothers and friends. Israel loses thousands as a result.

But if we are honest, the truly disgusting aspect of this story is how it hits home. As much as we do not want to admit it, we identify all too well with Aaron and his cronies. We are suckers for shiny things and substitutes for God.

We experience the presence of God, see His miracles, benefit from His deliverance, and receive His promises… and we are quick to turn away. We are Israel, and we act like Israel. Once again, Israel's story is our story.

How can Israel do this? Why do we do this?

Sin is powerful. Its hold on us is mighty. We see God and make holy promises, and we, like Israel, soon find ourselves acting the fool.

God forgive us.

Day 28/January 28 – Exodus 33-35

In the Cleft of the Rock
Exodus 33:22

Despite adages to the contrary, God often sends us more than we can handle. Fortunately, grace always comes along.

Moses prays to see God, but actually seeing the Almighty would be fatal to him, so God provides a shield. God agrees to pass in front of Moses, but He will cover the man with His hand as a means of protection.

Jonah gets more than he is ready to handle. He disobeys God, running to Tarshish instead of Nineveh as God has commanded. At sea, Jonah's boat is tossed by a powerful storm, and Jonah ends up overboard. He does not drown, however, because God sends a mighty fish to swallow him and then spit him up on dry land.

The grace of God comes in many shapes and sizes. As we have already seen, it can be clothes for Adam and Eve, a distinctive mark for Cain, an ark for Noah, a sacrificial ram for Abraham and Isaac, a wrestling match for Jacob, a dream for Joseph, or even a big fish. It can be a prayer answered "no." Moses asks, and God says "no." That is grace.

God's "no" is followed with a "but." "No, you are not able to stand what you think you want… but I will do this for you. My glory will be here, but I will place you in the cleft of the rock and cover you with My hand so that you will live."

A sheltering hand. A big fish. It's all grace.

Skilled to Follow the Call
Exodus 36:2

Bezalel and Oholiab are not household names. They are not heroes of the Old Testament. Yet, as we read through these detailed sections of Exodus, their names keep appearing.

God calls them to very specific tasks: creating and decorating, jobs that require patience and detail and artistic flair and substantial competence.

Moses is called to lead the people, judge their disputes, and represent them before God. When Moses needs help, Aaron is called to speak to Pharaoh. But Moses and Aaron are not called to what they cannot do. God does not call Moses to fashion a breastplate or sew a robe, nor is Aaron to build the Ark of the Covenant or construct the tabernacle. When God needs artisans and builders, He calls Bezalel and Oholiab.

There is a crucial lesson here for our own lives. While it can be true that "God does not call the equipped… He equips the called," it is far more often true that God prepares us ahead of time for the call He will give to us. Our talents, skills, likes and dislikes, and experience are all clues to the call. God is not in the business of playing tricks on us; what you are good at, like to do, and prepared for by experience is likely your call.

God calls Bezalel and Oholiab "and has filled them with the Spirit of God, with skill, ability and knowledge in all kinds of crafts…." (Exodus 35:30-31) For what call is God preparing you?

Day 30/January 30 – Exodus 39-Leviticus 1

Cloud and Fire
Exodus 40:38

How does God make Himself known to you?

Moses has been in the presence of God, hearing His voice. At times, the people have seen evidence of God through miracles and plagues and storms. They have the stone tablets etched by the finger of God.

But there is something else that they have all the time: the presence of God seen as a cloud during the day and a pillar of fire at night. God has started leading them like this back at the Red Sea (Exodus 13:21), and Israel continues to move only when the cloud moves.

Today, you and I do not have a cloud or a fiery pillar. So what is our evidence of the presence of God?

For some, it is the beauty found in nature or music. For others, it is an inner peace. Some hear an audible voice. Others see God in the people around them. To many, God speaks through sermons, hymns, and scripture.

Do not discount the daily miracles you see that give God away—sunrise, childbirth, a butterfly emerging from a cocoon, a bee pollinating a flower, the turning of the seasons. And of course do not miss the periodic miracles that rival anything in scripture—healings, answered prayers, interventions to prevent catastrophe.

In this scripture, God provides a visible form for Himself to Israel. In today's world, we walk by faith, not by sight. Still, the message is the same. God is here, and God will not leave us alone.

Day 31/January 31 – Leviticus 2-4

Offering Your Best
Leviticus 2:1

See what you notice particularly about these verses: Chapter 2, verses 1, 4, and 7; Chapter 3, verses 1 and 6; Chapter 4, verses 3, 23, 28, and 32.

Grain offerings are to be from the "finest of the flour." Animals chosen for the sacrifice must be "without defect."

When God's people make an offering to God, we should bring our best. Your tithe, calculated on your total gross earnings, comes first out of your paycheck, before you pay your bills. Your time offering to God is time when you are at your best, awake and alert.

The principle applies to prayer as well. There are times of hurt or anguish or exhaustion where we can offer nothing more than inarticulate grunts, and God honors those. But to make a true prayer offering requires more.

We all have moments where circumstances combine to force us to give less than our best to God, but whatever else happens as we go, we must find the opportunities to plan and give offerings of our best. We want to create an "aroma pleasing to the Lord." We want our offering to be from the best of what we have, like Abel's offering; we should not follow the example of Cain and toss an afterthought to God. (Genesis 4:3-5)

These Leviticus passages can be difficult to read. Stay with them; in their detail are keys to the nature of God. In today's reading, the message is clear: God demands and deserves our best.

February

Restitution and Atonement
Leviticus 6:5-7

When we have sinned by hurting another person, we have two duties: both to make up to the person we have wronged and to seek again the face of God.

Whether we have swindled, injured, stolen, cheated, or lied, we have hurt another person. We must restore what was lost, replace what we have stolen, or otherwise do what we can to compensate and make the injured person whole. The Biblical word for that restoration—also a word used by the law today—is "restitution." We make restitution by paying back what we have caused the person to lose. Restitution is horizontal—person to person—and is a necessary part of the process when we recognize that we have sinned.

Separate and apart from restitution is "atonement." This word is also one that is used in everyday life: we think of atoning for our wrongs in much the same way we talk about restitution. If my son throws a ball and breaks a neighbor's window, my son is expected to "atone for" his mistake by paying for a new window.

Scripturally, however, atonement is vertical—between us and God—because sin is against God. After restitution is made, the person who has sinned by hurting another still needs the priest to make atonement for him "before the Lord."

Ultimately, our atonement comes from the work of Jesus.

Make restitution to those you have harmed, but do not forget that you have also sinned against God. Like Israel, we need atonement.

Day 33/February 2 – Leviticus 8-10

Strange Fire
Leviticus 10:1

Have you found yourself skipping verses yet? Some call this section of Leviticus "the place where daily Bible reading commitments go to die." These detailed verses about a kind of worship that we no longer practice seem, at best, tedious and, at worst, unnecessarily boring.

That perception is not just a twenty-first century phenomenon.

Despite all of the careful instructions that God has given through Moses, Nadab and Abihu cannot be bothered with reading the tedious details, the fine print. They consequently have not learned how properly to approach the altar, so they dare show up haphazardly with "strange fire," also translated as "unauthorized fire," in a way and with a sacrifice that are not what God has laid out.

They are breaking the rules: they are approaching the holy with the unholy. They have recklessly ignored God's details.

Have you ever asked yourself why the wages of sin is death? (Romans 6:23) The reason has everything to do with the holiness of God. Once we sin, we are stained and impure: everything that God is not. Being uniquely pure, God cannot commune with the unholy.

This lesson is taught clearly and tragically through Nadab and Abihu, who carelessly bring the unholy into the presence of the holy. The presence of God literally consumes the strange fire.

The work of Jesus is necessary because we cannot approach the holy God with our sinful ways. We must be wiped clean, made holy. Otherwise, we bring nothing to God but strange fire.

Day 34/February 3 – Leviticus 11-13

Keeping Kosher
Leviticus 11:47

The vast majority of Christians today do not follow the dietary laws set out in Leviticus 11, the purification rules of chapter 12, or the disease regulations of chapter 13. Biblical revelation progresses from these chapters, culminating in key New Testament proclamations like Jesus' words that it is not what goes into the mouth, but rather what comes out, that defiles a person (Matthew 15:17-20), and Peter's vision in which God tells him that He has made all animals clean to eat. (Acts 10:10-15)

Why, then, is the Kosher code of these Leviticus passages relevant to any but current orthodox Jews?

First, these instructions show the love and care of God for His people. Israel, in the ancient time of Leviticus, is a primitive people traveling across a desert. Refrigeration is nonexistent; what and how they eat has significant physical effects. Medical care—more than 3,000 years before even bloodletting by leeches will become state-of-the-art—needs divine guidance if the people are to survive.

Second, these passages continue the theme of Israel's setting itself apart from the other peoples Israel encounters. God wants His people (1) identifiable by their uniqueness and (2) answerable to Him alone. This "holiness code" of Leviticus is God's initial conversation with His still newly-minted chosen people, and establishing Israel's God-given identity and God's rightful authority are matters of first priority.

Do your actions, choices, and differences mark you as God's child? Is your decision-making rooted in God's authority, following what He asks you to do?

Day 35 / February 4 – Leviticus 14-15

Clean and Unclean
Leviticus 15:31

These are perhaps the two grossest chapters in Scripture. Skin infections, mold, dead birds, bodily discharge, and the details of menstruation are not typically the subjects of anyone's chosen reading. Like yesterday, we discover insights in the words of God, crucial information that science will not comprehend for centuries about topics like contagious disease, fungal infestation, and the spread of germs.

There is a fundamental spiritual principle amidst these distasteful details: living in this world makes us unclean. No one can escape it. Whether you get sick, interact with someone else who is affected, or simply go into a house were a mold has been, you are unclean. Regular physical processes, personal relationships, and unintentional automatic bodily functions result in uncleanness. Nobody is exempt.

The message for life, of course, cannot be clearer: we are all unclean. There is none of us righteous, no, not one of us. (Romans 3:10) When the Psalmist asks, "Who shall ascend to the hill of the Lord? Who shall stand in His holy place?," the answer is "He who has clean hands and a pure heart." (Psalm 24:3-4) That is a bleak outlook, for none of us has clean hands or a pure heart.

The people of Israel must be aware of their uncleanness because of mold and skin diseases, but they are more conscious of their rebellion, their golden calf, and their cries of "Why did you lead us out of Egypt?" Israel is unclean. Israel needs purification.

Israel's story is our story.

Day 36/February 5 – Leviticus 16-18

Scapegoat
Leviticus 16:21-22

"Scapegoat" is a term that has survived from ancient times to modern usage. In today's parlance, a scapegoat is an innocent on whom the crimes of others are wrongly blamed. When bullies are confronted or criminal masterminds are close to conviction for their wrongs, they look for someone else to take the fall for them. That someone else is a scapegoat.

The concept of the scapegoat goes all the way back to Leviticus. Among the discussions of animals that are to be sacrificed, curiously, one goat is to be set free (allowed to escape, as it were) into the wilderness. This goat, over whose head all the sins of the people are confessed, escapes to the wilderness, taking the nation's sins—all their iniquities—with it. It is, literally, the scapegoat.

The scapegoat is a foreshadowing of—perhaps even an appearance of—Jesus within the ancient terms of the Torah. Jesus is the innocent, the only one ever in whom there is no sin, and all of our sins are placed on Him. Isaiah says that we have all gone astray, and the Lord has laid on Him the iniquity of us all. (Isaiah 53:6)

The Leviticus scapegoat runs to the wilderness. Jesus has a journey through the wilderness of death itself because of our sins laid on Him. For our sake, Jesus, who knows no sin, becomes sin so that we may return to a state of righteousness. (2 Corinthians 5:21)

Thank God for sending the perfect, ultimate scapegoat.

Day 37 / February 6 – Leviticus 19-21

Be Holy
Leviticus 19:2, 20:7

It is an awesome challenge to which God calls Israel. It is not simply to come close, try hard, or be better than the other people.

No, God says, "Be holy."

Holiness is the critical first aspect of the character of God. The seraphim in Isaiah 6 describe God has "holy, holy, holy." In Hebrew writing, this double-repetition is the extreme form of emphasis, the superlative. In English, we might call God "holiest" or "very, very holy." Holiness is God's defining characteristic.

To be holy is to be pure, set apart, perfect, unstained. Holiness is unsurpassable moral excellence.

God's holiness is unique. Holiness is ascribed by scripture to God's nature, God's name, God's dwelling place, and God's righteous actions. God's holiness is why sin is fatal, for the purity of God cannot coexist with the imperfect. Holiness requires forgiveness… cleansing… some supernatural slate-clearing so that we who sin may be with God.

We all sin, yet God tells us to "be holy." This is not an out-of-date thought just appearing in Leviticus; in fact, it is a major theme of scripture. Jesus calls us to "be perfect." (Matthew 5:48) Paul tells us to present ourselves "holy" to God. (Romans 12:1) The image of the church offering itself to God as the bride of Christ calls us to be pure and unstained.

Our temptation, when we have sinned, is to say, "I am human. I cannot help it." God says something different.

Just for today, be holy.

For the Poor
Leviticus 23:22

For the second time (the first was in Leviticus 19), we see the clear instruction from God to remember the less fortunate when picking the crops and to leave some of the grain in the field "for the poor."

It is interesting that God does not offer any real explanation for this duty. It is a singular part of the process: "Do not reap to the edges of your field or gather the gleanings of your harvest. Leave them for the poor and the foreigner." There is no word about why this is to be done, why the poor deserve the help, or how to measure the amount to be left. It is a simple instruction: don't take it all; leave some for the poor.

We can and do regularly overcomplicate the problem of caring for the poor. Indeed, in modern societies and economies, there are a variety of methods to address poverty, from mandatory tax-supported government programs to entirely voluntary private charitable activities.

This scripture is primarily interested neither with politics nor with economics. It is not concerned with providing a prescription for how to enforce the rule; it simply tells Israel not to pick up every scrap, to allow the poor to pick up around the edges.

Ask yourself why God does not have to explain the need for or the value in such provision. Then ask yourself how often, as you provide and gather for yourself, you are conscious of providing and leaving something for the poor.

Jubilee
Leviticus 25:8-13

Jubilee is the call for liberty. Debts are canceled. Captives return home. Redemption is declared.

Jubilee is the declaration of freedom. The Hebrew word Jubilee is the same as and is related to the word for a ram's horn used as a trumpet—Jubilee is the trumpet blast of freedom.

God mandates Jubilee for Israel.

We all seek for and celebrate Jubilee. Part of verse 10, "Proclaim liberty throughout all the land unto the inhabitants thereof," is inscribed on the American Liberty Bell in Philadelphia. African Americans have found special meaning in the concept of Jubilee. For example, the Jubilee Theater in Fort Worth, Texas and the Jubilee Singers of Fisk University in Nashville, Tennessee focus on artistic expression unique to the African American experience. The word jubilee is related to the Latin jubilo, meaning "shout for joy." Classical church choirs sing works based on the concept of "jubilate"—be joyful.

The cry for liberty is a calling from our souls. Israel has been set free from Egypt. We have been set free from sin. The first public sermon Jesus ever gives occurs after He reads in the synagogue from the prophet Isaiah: "The Spirit of the Lord is on me, because he has anointed me to preach good news to the poor. He has sent me to proclaim freedom for the prisoners..." After reading this passage, Jesus announces that "today, this scripture is fulfilled in your hearing." (Luke 4:17-21)

Proclaim liberty throughout all the land. Jubilee has been declared.

Day 40 / February 9 – Leviticus 27-Numbers 1

Hearing the Lord Speak
Numbers 1:1

G od speaks in many ways.

The book of Numbers begins with a familiar phrase: "The Lord spoke to Moses…" We have read of God speaking directly to Adam in the garden, to Cain before his tragic choice, and to Noah amidst the world's evil. We have also read of God speaking in the form of three men, speaking out of dreams, and speaking from a burning bush. Soon, in this same book of Numbers, we will see the word of God delivered to Balaam through a talking donkey.

Sometimes, we twenty-first century followers allow ourselves to get frustrated when we search for a word from God. Why, we sometimes think, isn't God conjuring up some burning bushes for us? Why isn't the word of God announced to us in the same kind of clear and unmistakable voice that Abraham and Jacob and Moses heard? Some figure that if we don't have burning bushes and talking donkeys today, then perhaps these Old Testament stories are just made up tales.

We may not get a talking donkey, but we hear God speak in other ways.

Unlike Moses, we have scripture to record the words of God. Unlike Balaam, we have the indwelling Holy Spirit of God to speak to us constantly, showing us what God wants and what God is like. Unlike Abraham, we have centuries of church history through which God's will has been made known.

We have Jesus, who shows us exactly what God is like and what He wants.

Day 41 / February 10 – Numbers 2-3

Camped around the Tent
Numbers 2:2

What role does the place of worship play in your life? Israel is instructed by God to set up camp around the tent of meeting, the tabernacle. The tribes are arranged in all directions from the place where God descends to meet Moses and the priests. The place of the Ark of the Covenant is the center of their society.

The role of the church building has certainly changed from what it was only a few decades ago. The sanctuary was once a center, not only of worship, but also of fellowship for believers, and a place held in respect by others in society. Now, even many "active" church members may not darken a church door more than once or twice a month. Excuses about busy schedules and family obligations, complaints about how churches conduct their business, and promises to worship on a beach or a golf course seem to push the "tent of meeting" further and further from the center of society, even for Christians.

God's plan for Israel is different. God places the campsites of the tribes around the tent of meeting. In Numbers 3 we learn more about the specific duties of the Levites in caring for and maintaining the tabernacle.

The lesson here is not to worship a tent or a building. A location cannot save anyone and must not become an idol. Still, there is great value in that place where we most readily meet God. Perhaps we have ventured too far from the tabernacle.

Day 42/February 11 – Numbers 4-5

A Holy Calling
Numbers 4:1-33

The Kohathites, Gershonites, and Merarites have holy callings. These clans of Israelites have God-given responsibilities to care for the "holy things" of the tabernacle. Some care for the materials in the most holy place; some carry holy things from place to place; and some tear down, carry, and then set up anew the framework of the tent of meeting itself at the next settling place.

The call to holy work still exists. Some Christians are called to professional ministry as pastors, ministers, evangelists, musicians, writers, or missionaries. Others are called to religious organizations, seminaries, universities, hospitals, or charities. Still others have apparently "secular" jobs—physicians, farmers, teachers, bankers, mechanics, counselors, nurses, factory workers, nannies, drivers, or cooks—that they use for a holy purpose, dedicating themselves and their work to the Lord, finding a way to share an "Alleluia" and a helping hand.

Your call may be as specific as that of a Gershonite, to a specific place with a specific item in hand. Or, God's call on your life may be like that of a Merarite, to be ready to move whenever God is ready and to assist God's people to prepare for their next step. Your call may be to do whatever your hand finds to do with all your might so you have food on the table and strength for the day to carry out God's will when you are not at your occupation.

Find the holy things that God has for you. God is certainly calling.

Day 43/February 12 – Numbers 6-7

Shalom
Numbers 6:26

The Lord give you peace.
Among the tedious rules for Nazirites and the seemingly endless list of dedication offerings for the temple, Aaron's priestly blessing is a beautiful oasis in scripture. It is a benediction—a well-wishing for those who have worshiped—that remains as meaningful now as it was then.

The Lord bless and keep you. As you leave the place of meeting God, know that God goes before you and with you to bestow His gifts and His presence. Know that God keeps you. Nothing and no one can snatch you from His hand. You are His. You are precious in His sight.

The Lord make His face shine upon you and be gracious to you. You will see God everywhere—in a cloud, a pillar of fire, three visiting men… and in a tender buttercup's petal, a baby's face, the first evening star. His grace, which has been carefully on display since the Garden of Eden itself, is offered to you personally. You do not earn grace or even ask for it, but grace always comes. The Lord will be gracious to you.

The Lord lift up the light of His countenance on you and give you peace. The Lord will make your paths straight. He is the way and the truth and the life. His word is a lamp for your feet.

And He gives you peace. Israel's word for this blessing is "Shalom." Peace. Greeting. Welfare. Prosperity.

The Lord bless and keep you. *Shalom.*

Day 44 / February 13 – Numbers 8-9

Moving when God Moves
Numbers 9:17

A great temptation for Christians is to anticipate what God wants and then conclude that God agrees. We follow our own direction and timing with sincerity and intentionality. The problem, of course, is that we are deciding what God wants instead of listening to God tell us when to move and what to do.

Israel learns to watch the cloud over the tabernacle, the representation of the presence of God, and only to move when the cloud moves. Numbers 9:22 tells us that the Israelites remain in the same place for a full year if the cloud stays put.

We do not always do well with waiting and appreciating the place God has us now. Rest and standing still are foreign to many of us.

Conversely, others of us find a place to set up a tabernacle and feel secure there, and we want to stay where God used to be. If the cloud travels, we can have trouble picking up and moving.

Several years ago, a popular Christian study focused on finding where God is at work and then joining Him there. Israel would say it this way: find the cloud and pitch a tent there. If the cloud moves, follow it.

If Israel's story is our story, then we should look for the cloud in our own lives. Find the evidence of where God is working and go there. Set up your tabernacle and worship, work, and live right there, where God is. Move only when God moves.

Day 45/February 14 – Numbers 10-12

Is God's Arm Too Short?
Numbers 11:23

D o not confuse "God does not" for "God cannot."
Nothing is impossible for God.

Moses does not understand where enough meat for all the people can come from, but God is more than able to solve that problem. The prophet tells us that "surely the arm of the Lord is not too short to save." (Isaiah 59:1) God will put cedars in the desert and pines in the wasteland to show that His power is sufficient for whatever confronts us. (Isaiah 41:20) What is unattainable for us is child's play for God, who specializes in the impossible. (Luke 1:37; Matthew 19:26)

What about the dying cancer patient, the hopeless abused child, the worker subject to the cruel boss, or the poverty-stricken family facing foreclosure? If God can do the impossible… if God's arm is not too short… then why does illness come and cruelty continue? Why are the poor still poor?

That God can does not always mean that He will. How and when God moves are questions beyond our mere mortal minds. Faith does not know the "when" and "why" and "where." But faith knows the "who."

For I know whom I have believed and am persuaded that He is able to keep what I have committed to Him. (2 Timothy 1:12)

Faith may not understand when or where God will choose to act, but faith knows that God's arm is plenty long. And faith trusts that God is good. And then faith leaves the rest to God.

Giants in the Land
Numbers 13:32-33

Israel has followed God to the border of the Promised Land. Now, rather than entering immediately into what God has promised, Israel deploys twelve spies. The report is that the area is "a land flowing with milk and honey." Ten of the scouts, however, are unwilling to accept the gift because of an undeniable fact: there are giants in the land.

The people have followed only to the edge. They have chosen to test the promise of God. Convinced the obstacles in their way are too great, Israel refuses to accept God's offer.

Israel's story is our story.

God presents us bounty and beauty beyond our understanding. Our descriptions of what we allow ourselves to see are as metaphorical and as incomplete as "milk and honey." We know the treasure is there, for we have seen at least a glimpse of it. We have followed God thus far, and He has always been worthy of our trust.

But we are over-cautious. Instead of trusting, we decide to spy things out, and sure enough, we see giants in the land. We know, beyond doubt, that the world that inhabits our Promised Land is frightening and wants to devour us. We see monsters and evils around every corner. We stop short.

Honest faith knows that God has never promised that our way will be without problems. We left our Garden of Eden long ago. Faith follows God anyway and trusts Him to deal with the giants. Faith enters the Promised Land.

Day 47 / February 16 – Numbers 15-16

Defiant Sin
Numbers 15:30-31

These two death penalty chapters are hard to read. In isolation, they can create, for some, a picture of a ruthless, spiteful God. How can we reconcile the God of these chapters with the New Testament God of love?

God is consistent. God who sent an ark to carry Noah, a mark to protect Cain, and His only son to die for all of us is the God of Numbers. We cannot read any one chapter without remembering the whole picture, telling us that God is neither ruthless nor spiteful.

To God's immature people who have the nerve to say out loud that God should have left them in Egypt, the elementary message here is submission. God is God and they are not. God means for His law to be followed. The punishment for apparently insignificant sins is, in context, an exclamation point on the importance of following God's laws. Israel will learn this lesson even as grace follows on its heels.

As we have already seen, holiness is the primary aspect of the character of God. We simply must acknowledge that while God is love, God is first holy.

Defiant, intentional sin that flaunts the Word of God is deathly serious. God calls it blasphemy, and the wages of sin is death. Even the love of God will not change that. Fortunately, the love of God makes a way for us not to die—Jesus comes to show us a new way.

Go your way and sin no more.

Day 48/February 17 – Numbers 17-20

Speak to the Rock
Numbers 20:8

It is the same place: Meribah. It is the same complaint: thirst. It is the same people: Israel. It is the same God.

Surely, God will do the same thing the same way, right? We understand why Moses reasons it must be time to strike the rock again.

In Exodus 17, at this desert place, God instructs Moses to strike the rock, and water comes out to satisfy the thirsty Israelites. This time, God changes plans, telling Moses simply to speak to the rock.

Moses does it the old way. Whether he misses the different message, or stubbornly refuses to change from what worked before, or is simply so angry with the people's quarreling that he loses his bearings ultimately does not matter. God gives a command, and Moses disobeys. And there is a price to pay, even for Moses.

The profound lesson in this passage is that even the mighty Moses misses the mark. This great prophet and leader, who regularly speaks face to face with God… who has seen the burning bush and received the stone tablets… who has delivered God's message directly to Pharaoh… is, like the rest of Israel, prone to wander. Moses himself sins in the face of a direct word from God.

We are in good company. Even Moses sins. Immediately after hearing God's voice, even Moses chooses his own way.

And, of course, in the aftermath of the sin of Moses, water pours from the rock. Even now, grace flows.

Day 49/February 18 – Numbers 21-23

Lifted Up
Numbers 21:8-9

God establishes a curious cure for the infestation of poisonous snakes. Moses is to lift up a bronze snake on a pole, and those who look up will be saved.

God continually supplies their need and leads their journey; yet stubborn Israel is not satisfied. Manna is no longer seen as the miraculous provision in the barren desert but instead is "this miserable food." Israel is spurning the very grace of God.

How familiar that sounds to us today. In our faithful spiritual moments, we see the blessings of the Father, given to us new each morning. In our overly rational and human moment, controlled by our selfish wants and petty irritants, we lash out. We wonder aloud if there even is a God, much less if He has done anything for us lately.

While sin has consequences, as it always does, God is ready with grace, as He always is. Lift up the bronze snake. Look on it. Be saved.

This story is given new meaning in the gospel. Jesus, foreshadowing His crucifixion, says, "Just as Moses lifted up the snake in the desert, so the Son of Man must be lifted up, that everyone who believes in Him may have eternal life." (John 3:14-15) Later, Jesus completes the picture: "But I, when I am lifted up from the earth, will draw all men to myself." (John 12:31)

Lifting up the snake is but a precursor. Jesus will be lifted up, and we will be saved. Grace always comes.

Day 50/February 19 – Numbers 24-26

I Must Say Only What the Lord Says
Numbers 24:13

The story of Balaam is famous for the talking donkey, but Balaam's courageous stand before the king of Moab is perhaps the more important lesson.

There is no confusion about what Balak wants Balaam to do: curse the Israelites. There is money in this for Balaam, not to mention the important place in Balak's government that surely awaits him if he pleases the king. Certain power and fortune present Balaam with a tempting alternative to his call from God.

Early in the story, Balaam is conflicted. God does not want him to go but relents when Balaam is asked again. The talking donkey interrupts the journey to make sure that Balaam knows the power of God and the seriousness of obeying the Lord. Then, Balaam continues to Moab, to the castle of Balak.

In some ways, the story plays out from here as almost a farce. Balak tells Balaam what he wants him to say, and Balaam sends the king's servants scurrying hither and yon to build multiple altars and gather animals for sacrifices. When that does not get Balak the prophecy he wants, they hustle to a different place and try again.

When the king complains to Balaam about the results of this sideshow, Balaam is consistent in his response: "Must I not speak what the Lord puts in my mouth?" (Numbers 23:12, 23:26, 24:13)

Fame, power, and fortune are on one side. The message of God is on the other. Balaam repeatedly makes the right choice. Would we?

Day 51 / February 20 – Numbers 27-28

The Daughters' Inheritance
Numbers 27:7

Ancient Middle Eastern cultures, including the Israelites, can never be mistaken for enlightened egalitarians when it comes to gender rights. Women of this time are—to put it charitably—something less than second-class citizens. Their law does not permit them to inherit, so the very fact that these females dare even approach Moses with their concern is unprecedented.

To be sure, the rest of Numbers spells out multiple differences between the treatment of men and the treatment of women. Still, this passage is an early indication of the beginning of Israel's understanding of the equality of all human beings before God. An exception to the strict inheritance laws is made in favor of the daughters of a man who died without a son. The right of these women to inherit is confirmed.

In contrast with the following verses, where no exception is made for Moses himself to enter the Promised Land, God's response to the prayer on behalf of the women is truly exceptional.

That the Old Testament writers fail to come to a quick and obvious understanding of the equality of men and women before God is not surprising in light of their society and history. In the New Testament, clearer glimpses into the mind of God on this issue are seen in Jesus' treatment of women, and in Paul's assurance that "there is neither Jew nor Greek, slave nor free, male nor female, for you are all one in Christ Jesus." (Galatians 3:28)

God offers grace to all.

Day 52/February 21 – Numbers 29-31

Extravagant Offerings
Numbers 31:50

Why does God look with approval on—indeed, why does God accept at all—offerings of gold jewelry and trinkets from the spoils of Israel's military victories? Why does God command the people to bring firstborn animals without defect to the house of worship?

Paul, preaching in Athens, announces that God "is not served by human hands, as if He needed anything." (Acts 17:25) God created everything and has the power without even a moment's notice to make for Himself whatever He might possibly desire.

If God does not need anything, why does He expect and accept our praise, our worship, and our songs? If God cannot be served by human hands, why then are we called to serve Him? Why should we offer a "sacrifice of praise?" (Hebrews 13:15)

When we give what most would say we cannot afford, we declare the glory and worthiness of God. Our extravagant offering declares that what we have is better in His hands than in our own. When we give sacrificially, we bear witness to God's gracious provision.

Struggling congregations and loyal patrons did not build mighty cathedrals in the Middle Ages to satisfy some selfish need of God's but rather to show faith in one much greater than the builders. Jesus Himself commended the sacrificial and extravagant given personally to Him instead of to the poor, noting the eternal significance of such a gift.

The widow's mite (Luke 21:3) was extravagant in no one's eyes but her own… and Jesus'.

Day 53/February 22 – Numbers 32-34

A Clean Sweep
Numbers 33:52, 55

Reading this passage literally, as a tactical playbook for a military campaign, shows how the Israelites approached war, seeking to conquer and destroy, accepting nothing less than unconditional surrender. Ancient Israel's generals seem not much different than military strategists of much more "civilized" times.

This passage must be read, however, as more than a ruthless battle plan. Remember, the Old Testament is primarily the story of how God deals with God's people. Israel's story is our story.

As we grow into a deeper relationship with God, we are led to our own Promised Lands. Along the way, we all face enemies that would derail us and distractions that would tempt us. Hindrances and roadblocks take many forms. There are always established folk who are committed to the way things have always been, and when we want to come in and do what God wants, these supporters of tradition and the status quo can be a rigid impediment.

God tells us to get rid of all of it. Do not assimilate with it. God's commands not to intermarry, not to put up with foreign gods, and not to sow our fields with more than one crop are symbolic reminders that following God requires single-minded determination. Those things we do not clear out become "barbs in our eyes and thorns in our sides." God knows that we are easily enticed by what we once knew, by what the world around us thinks is "right." God tells us to drive it all out.

When God Is With You, Fight On
Deuteronomy 1:30

Moses reminds the people of Israel that had they entered the Promised Land as God planned, God would have fought for them, and they would have been successful. When the people refused to follow God, however, God changed the plan and told them to head back to the desert. Then, Israel decided—too late—to enter the land and fight, and Moses reminds them now of God's words then: "Do not go up and fight, because I will not be with you. You will be defeated by your enemies." (Deuteronomy 1:42)

Deciding when to act or not act, we often forget to seek—or openly defy—the Lord's guidance. Sometimes, like Israel, we finally see the error of our ways and try to follow God's old commands without acknowledging that God has moved on. The result is wandering to find what God wanted all along.

When we adhere to the plan of God, we cannot be defeated, for God Himself leads us. Whether we encounter giants in the land, the Red Sea, roving bands of tribes in the desert, or the army of Pharaoh himself, God's leadership overcomes what is before us.

When we do not follow where God is directing, however, we risk grave danger. We rush impetuously into enemies we can neither understand nor conquer. The problem is not in our efforts. The problem is in our self-reliance.

Follow God. When we hear and follow His call, we know that victory awaits, because He fights for us.

Day 55/February 24 – Deuteronomy 2-3

Grace in the Wilderness
Deuteronomy 2:7

These early chapters of Deuteronomy are a pause in the laws of the Torah to review the history of Israel after the Exodus. For forty years, the people have wandered in the wilderness because of their unwillingness to enter the Promised Land as God had intended. It would be easy for Israel to look on this desert experience as a punishment, and indeed in some ways it clearly is.

Still, even while wandering under the chastisement of God, the people must recognize and remember that the protective hand of God has been with them the whole way. The pillar of fire by night and the cloud by day have never left them. Manna and quail have fed them. Water has come from the rock. Enemies have been defeated. Friendlier peoples have let them pass through. Even their clothes have not worn out and their feet have not become swollen. (Nehemiah 9:21)

How often we focus on the reprimand without seeing the continuation of the provision. We harp on the penalty without noticing the grace. Sin has its consequence, and we pay that price; but God makes sure that what we suffer is limited.

Take a look around. Your life undoubtedly is marked by the bad decisions you have made, and God may well have disciplined you. Still, can you trace the blessings of God that continue to rain down? Do you see God's hand of grace in your wilderness?

Where our sin abounds, grace abounds all the more. (Romans 5:20)

Drinking from Wells We Did Not Dig
Deuteronomy 6:11

The Bible is about God.

To be sure, scripture contains stories about all sorts of people, from Adam to Paul, from Sarah to Mary. It contains history and poetry and drama. It references science and philosophy.

While scripture includes all of these things, the Bible is the story of God. And thus the emphasis of scripture is not on what we do but on what God does, often through the work of His people.

Deuteronomy 6 contains the *Shema*: "Hear, O Israel, the Lord our God is one... These commandments that I give you today are to be upon your hearts..." (Deuteronomy 6:4-9) That great passage continues with the directive not to forget the Lord and what He has done, because His people live in houses they have not built and eat from vineyards they have not planted. God has a plan, and God has carried it out. They are entering a Promised Land, prepared for them by God.

The same is true for us. We stand on the shoulders of those who have gone before; they in turn stood on shoulders of pioneers before them. But supporting all we have is the Lord our God. We too are served by wells we have not dug. Blessings come new to us every morning, and we have done nothing—indeed we cannot do anything—to cause them or deserve them.

Do not forget what God has done through those saints who have come before. Remember, and be thankful.

Day 57/February 26 – Deuteronomy 7-9

The Old Testament Covenant, Part I
Deuteronomy 7:12

It is the heart of the initial covenant between God and Israel: "Keep My commandments, and I will be your God." Reading through the commands, directions, laws, and instructions, the overwhelming message is plain; keep God's commands and be blessed by God in response.

We have seen this covenant repeatedly broken by Israel. Abraham receives the covenant, and his grandson Jacob the Deceiver takes advantage of his own brother. The covenant is renewed as Jacob's name is changed to Israel, then ten of his sons sell the eleventh into slavery. God leads the children of Israel out of slavery; soon, they build a golden calf idol. Each time, God is willing to look past the sins of the people and renew the covenant. The people grumble and wish they were still in Egypt; God looks forward to when they will finally enter the Promised Land.

Now, the covenant is laid out once again. The instructions and laws meant to keep Israel separate from all other peoples and holy to God are cataloged, and the promise is once again made clear: "If you pay attention to these laws and are careful to follow them, then the LORD your God will keep his covenant of love with you, as he swore to your forefathers."

The way is laid out for Israel, and the people do not follow. God's covenant promise is offered; the people refuse. The same is true of us, for we continue to choose disobedience. Israel's story is our story.

Day 58/February 27 – Deuteronomy 10-12

The Old Testament Covenant, Part II
Deuteronomy 10:12-13

The old covenant, the heart of God's promise to Israel's people as they leave Egypt and head toward the Promised Land, is God's expression of eternal care for His children. But it is more than that. It is also God's plan to take care of His children in the moment. To our twenty-first century minds, some of the laws and rules seem simplistic, out-of-date, and downright nonsensical. In the primitive world in which they wander, however, Israel's absolute best interests are served by keeping the covenant.

Observe the commands, and have the strength you need to live a long life in the land flowing with milk and honey. (Deuteronomy 11:8-9) Faithfully obey and find yourself satisfied. (Deuteronomy 11:13-15) Learn the laws and make them the center of your life, and your days will be many. (Deuteronomy 11:18-21) Walk in His ways, and nothing can stand against you. (Deuteronomy 11:22-25) Obey and be blessed. (Deuteronomy 11:27)

Following God is always the best choice, even if God's way leads into a desert.

The Bible makes sense and falls together clearly when we remember one fact above all others: Because God loves us, God is good to us all the time. When God lays out a plan for us, it is for our best. When God directs us, the way He points out is the best possible way we can go. Even when we do not understand, we can know this: He has laid before us a blessing. Grace always comes.

Day 59/February 28 – Deuteronomy 13-16

Pierce My Ear
Deuteronomy 15:16-7

The search for freedom is an important theme of the Old Testament, highlighted by the Exodus out of Egypt. God redeems His people from the yoke of slavery, from the harrowing taskmasters who have ruled over them for hundreds of years.

Yet, no matter how important it is that we are freed from those who would lord over us, an even deeper theme of the Old Testament is our own voluntary submission to the Lord of lords. The symbolism of this passage in Deuteronomy, and its parallel in Exodus 21, is vitally important. The servant who could be free but instead chooses to remain with the master permanently has his ear pierced by an awl. The Bible explains this as an act of love that tells the world the servant belongs to the family of the master forever.

We all face the moment when we realize that we cannot achieve enough, or know enough, or earn enough to satisfy ourselves. We cannot find our Fountain of Youth or El Dorado. No matter how much we strive for freedom, for individual choice, for self-sufficiency, and for political self-rule, we all come to the place where we declare allegiance to someone or something.

Scripture has a ready answer for us when we reach that point. Jesus stands ready to save us. We escape slavery and choose obedience to a new, better Master.

As Bob Dylan sang, "you're gonna have to serve somebody." Are you ready to ask God to pierce your ear?

Day 60/February 29 – Matthew 5-7

We Are All Blessed in the Kingdom of God – Matthew 5:3-11

On this Leap Day, we break from our consecutive Old Testament readings to hear these words of Jesus.

The Lord looks out at the variety of people who have come to listen to Him. He notices those who have little and tells them that they are blessed, for theirs is the kingdom of heaven. He sees those who are sad and promises them comfort. Then He turns and spots a gentle, mild-mannered woman, and He assures her that she will inherit the earth.

Ready to preach, Jesus sees those faithful in the crowd—the merciful, the pure in heart, and the peacemakers; He assures them that they are blessed as they see God and find their place in His family. He then looks to those barely hanging onto the edges of the crowd: the downtrodden, those who are persecuted and insulted and made to pay for their Christian devotion. Jesus smiles and tells them that they too are blessed, and are a crucial part of the kingdom of God.

Do not mistake these Beatitudes as promises of blessings only if we do certain things. Jesus' kingdom is not based on our actions.

You are blessed. You… and you… and you. Jesus looks at all of us and tells us that the Kingdom is for us, no matter our current circumstances. Whether you are a prosperous and faithful follower or one who is suffering greatly, Jesus says, "Blessed are you."

Accept the offer. Grace has come. The Kingdom is yours.

March

Day 61/March 1 – Deuteronomy 17-19

Who Is Your Model?
Deuteronomy 18:9

"When you enter the land that the Lord gives you, do not learn to imitate the detestable ways of the nations there." This simple direction from God is of immense importance. Because God has directed us to a place does not mean that we are to blend in with what we find.

Of course we seek out fellowship with those of many faiths and traditions. Still, finding friends from all sorts of communities should not mean that our lives reflect the practices, ways, and actions of those people around us.

The fact that we consider many points of view and keep an open mind to the words and thoughts of others so that we can consider their ideas and communicate with them does not equate to the idea that we must agree with what non-believers and immature believers around us say. Aristotle was right when he said that the mark of an educated mind is to be able to entertain a thought without accepting it.

We are salt and light. We do the flavoring and the illuminating. We are to do the influencing. God has placed us in this world and sent us into our Promised Lands not so we will do as they do but rather so we can show them what God is like.

Toleration is not the same thing as imitation. Loving someone does not require us to mimic them. We live in this world, but we are not of this world. Our only model is Jesus.

Day 62/March 2 – Deuteronomy 20-23

Adultery
Deuteronomy 22:22

Fewer truths are clearer in scripture than this: Adultery is evil. It is always wrong. It is the essence of sin.

There is no question that this Old Testament prohibition survives into the New Testament, not to mention the mores and religions of every civilized people known to human history.

Adultery is selfish, sexual sin. Adultery is theft. Adultery springs from covetousness and requires deceit and dishonesty. Adultery attacks. Adultery takes what is another's. Adultery strikes at the foundations of society and civilization.

Not only is adultery wicked in and of itself, but it also becomes the symbol for how Israel rejects God. The prophet Ezekiel will refer to Israel as an "adulterous" people, because Israel will leave God and join with another. Jeremiah will accuse Israel of committing adultery with stone and wood idols. Jesus saves His strongest rebukes for those who will not accept Him, calling them an "adulterous generation."

Why use adultery to be the image of Israel's failure? Because Israel continues to be selfish and indulge shortsighted wants. Israel sees the lifestyles of others and deceitfully chooses to follow the ways of the heathen neighbors. Rather than staying close to God, Israel joins itself with others who put claims on its love.

In Deuteronomy, adultery carries a capital sentence. In the New Testament, turning your back on God to join yourself to another is spiritually disastrous. Our first love is where we belong. Use scripture's model of marriage to learn how to cling to your God.

Different Weights and Measures
Deuteronomy 25:13-16

This short lesson on honesty in the middle of the Deutero-nomic code is not surprising. Be consistent. Do not cheat. Treat everyone the same. Use the same weights and measures in all your dealings. God hates dishonesty.

Ironically, and despite what we would claim, we have trouble following this obvious rule. While we quickly declare our belief in fair and honest practices, it does not take long to see where we use different weights and measures.

How do you react to the slight inconvenience caused by the driver on the road next to you whom you do not know, as opposed to your reaction to the same action by a friend? Do you respond to a word of greeting from the dirty street person with the same measure of hospitality that you would use to respond to a celebrity? How do you measure the distance between yourself and the next person on the pew at church when that person is a foreigner?

With what weight do you dole out your generosity to the people God has created? Is it the same whether you are dealing with a Methodist or a Baptist? How about a Democrat as well as a Republican? What about a Jew, a Muslim, or an atheist?

Is your measure of forgiveness the same to your spouse as it is to your neighbor? Is your welcome of the sinner the same as your welcome of the saint?

How many sets of weights and measures do you really have?

Day 64/March 4 – Deuteronomy 27-28

Blessings and Curses
Deuteronomy 28:1, 15

The Old Testament covenant is often described in exceptionally black and white terms. Using extreme examples intermingled with everyday events, writing in hyperbole and metaphor interspersed with direct and clear language, the lawgiver in this passage sets out the covenant in the simplest of language. You have a choice: Obey and be blessed; disobey and be cursed.

This is the old covenant. This is the original way God lays out the path for life.

Because God is the creator of time and knows our thoughts before we think them, God knows that His people will not walk the simple path, always choosing instead the curse, as Eve chose in the garden. Seeing His people reject this most plain of covenant promises over and over, God knows the curse must somehow be broken, for His people are determined to wander headlong into it.

C.S. Lewis calls this curse a land where it is always winter and never Christmas, presided over by a White Witch who delights in dangling worthless candies to entice children into her control forever. And we always choose the candy.

Blessings lie before us, and we, no matter how clear the warning, choose the curse.

God will not rely on this old covenant. Even as the people prepare to cross the Jordan, God plans a new Promised Land. The White Witch will not prevail. In the words of Lewis, there is a Deeper Magic. God will find a way to bless us, even though we choose the curse.

Choose Life
Deuteronomy 30:19

This verse is more than a political slogan, more than a T-shirt design, more than a statement on a critical moral issue of the day.

This verse is the heart of Israel's relationship with God. And because Israel's story is our story, this verse becomes the watchword for our everyday decision-making.

Placed before us are choices. Nothing is forced. We have free will. God begs us to choose life.

You can choose death. You can set your sights on ways that lead to war and destruction if you want. Choose life.

You can choose chaos. You can head out on a path of indifference to order and beauty and patterns. Choose life.

You can choose manipulation. You can beat down, belittle, and manhandle all those around you until there is no will to live left in them. Choose life.

You can choose cheap imitations. You can indulge in temporary so-called pleasures. You can spend all your time and resources on lifeless trinkets and the people who offer them, focusing on thrills and titillations. Choose life.

You can choose mere survival. You can invest yourself totally in finances and return, security and supply, endowment and assets. You can make these otherwise good things into gods, your total *raisons d'être*. Choose life.

You can choose self. You can focus everything on achievement, power, pleasure, sufficiency, aggrandizement, and reward. But all of those things will die. Choose life.

God has laid the choice before you. Choose life.

Day 66/March 6 – Deuteronomy 32-34

Song
Deuteronomy 32:3

Here, we find a song to God. If you have read parts of the Bible before, you know that songs of praise like this are found throughout the Psalms, Samuel, Isaiah, the letters of Paul, and elsewhere. Moses' song after the parting of the Red Sea in Exodus 15 is similar in form, and this song at the end of Deuteronomy is intended to be used for generations to come as a vehicle to praise God.

The superiority and vastness of God call for responses like "His works are perfect" and "A faithful God who does no wrong, upright and just is He." The song is used to tell the story of God's work with the people, of His reaction to their bad choices, of His judgments and forgiveness.

Outside an old opera house are these words: "Bach gave us God's word. Mozart gave us God's laughter. Beethoven gave us God's fire. God gave us music that we might pray without words."

Paul writes that we should let the word of Christ dwell in us richly, teaching and instructing one another in psalms and hymns and spiritual songs. (Colossians 3:16)

It is Fred Pratt Green who writes: "How often, making music, we have found a new dimension in the world of sound as worship moves us to a more profound 'Hallelujah!'"

Thomas Troeger writes it this way: "The wonders of God to whom we belong… too splendid for speech, but ripe for a song."

Sing your praise to the Lord.

God versus the River
Joshua 4:7

J oshua's leadership career begins with encouragement from God to "be strong and courageous, for the Lord your God will be with you wherever you go." (Joshua 1:6-9) Under Joshua's leadership, the people are finally ready to enter the Promised Land.

God knows that Israel, with a new leader and not so fresh off of forty years' wandering in the wilderness, needs more than encouraging words to find strength and courage. So, God reprises the parting of the Red Sea, this time leading the Hebrews through the Jordan River on dry ground.

After the people have crossed, Joshua leads them to build an altar, with the express purpose of teaching future generations: When their children ask what the altar stones mean, Joshua says that they will be told that "the flow of the Jordan was cut off before the ark of the covenant of the Lord." We remember that God conquers rivers and seas.

What a tremendous event from which Israel can embark on a new life of being strong and courageous.

We are not strong and courageous just because God tells us to be. No, we have seen the power of God, and we know that He can be relied upon. You have known disaster averted, disease healed, discouragement melted, sin forgiven, and unimaginable joys. God is good all the time. Think of the times in your life when the current rushing at you was cut off by the power of God, and you too will be strong and courageous.

Day 68/March 8 – Joshua 5-8

Get Off Your Face
Joshua 7:10

The famous victory over Jericho is in their rear-view mirror, and the Israelites are setting their sights on the next target, the city of Ai. Buoyed by conquest and feeling invulnerable, they expect another triumph. But when they begin to attack, they are overwhelmed and humiliated.

Joshua cannot understand why Israel has lost the battle, so he and the elders fall on their face before the Lord. God's response is immediate: "What are you doing down on your face? Stand up!" There is work to be done, for Israel has a traitor within it. In contrast to the prostitute Rahab, whose courage and faithfulness belie what might otherwise be expected, Achan appears to be a loyal follower of God but is in fact a selfish thief and a liar.

Before Ai can be taken, Israel must be purified. The false follower must be eliminated. Before we can achieve all that God has for us, we have to excise the deceit and unfaithfulness from ourselves.

Joshua and the people learn this lesson of holiness yet again, but there is a deeper teaching here. God is not impressed with their collective sackcloth-and-ashes routine down in the dirt. Falling on their faces before God is doing nothing to solve the problem.

There is a time to prostrate ourselves before God, but that time is not when there is work to be done. God needs Joshua to lead, not to complain. God needs us to get about His business.

Stand up. Get to it.

Day 69/March 9 – Joshua 9-11

The Sun Stands Still
Joshua 10:13

The Bible is God's truth for us, telling us the story of how God deals with people and teaching us what God is like. Everything in it is true, but it is not a textbook of science, history, or mathematics.

Something happens at Gibeon. It is doubtlessly divine intervention. Somehow, the number of hours of daylight is extended. To the primitive writer, the best explanation for this supernatural act is "the sun stood still." Of course, basic astronomy now teaches us that a delay in sunset would be the result of the earth's (not the sun's) standing still, temporarily stopping its rotation.

Is the Bible wrong? Is this poetic explanation a holy error?

Viewing this statement—"the sun stood still"—as a mistake in scripture begs the question. The point is God's miraculous help to Israel, irrespective of any attempt at a precise scientific explanation for it.

The Bible was written by human beings, and many things in scripture are told as best the inspired human authors can tell them, given their understanding and backgrounds. Thus, we are given the perspective that God sends hailstones to destroy enemies and that relatively minor offenses are considered capital crimes.

That the writer misunderstands the physics does nothing to change the miraculous intervention of God. God's revelation of Himself will continue to progress, and we will get the full picture in Jesus. In the meantime, find the truths of scripture that are there, and do not get caught up in what is not.

The Inheritance of the Priests
Joshua 13:33

While all the other tribes are receiving their inheritance of land, the Levites are assigned no real estate, money, or even trinkets. The writer of Joshua tells us that God Himself is their inheritance.

We will learn in subsequent chapters that each of the other tribes contributes out of their own largesse to the Levites, so it is not as if the priestly tribe winds up with nothing. What is important, though, is the process. If you are from Naphtali or Simeon or Issachar, your tribe gets towns and lands in which to settle and flourish, distributed by Joshua as God's manager of the Promised Land. If you are from Levi, however, you have "God for your inheritance," and you must depend on the generosity of the other tribes for a place to live.

Serving as a priest then is not all that different from serving as a minister now. Pastors have "God for their inheritance," and that is no small blessing, but they still are reliant on the other people of God to support and provide for their daily living.

Why is it set up this way? Undoubtedly, serving as a Levite then —or as clergy today—provides unique personal benefit from a relationship with God that grows out of unique sacrifice and dedication. No doubt, also, the need for the rest of us to support and care for ministers and elders is a reminder of our continuing need to support God's work by supporting God's workers.

Once a Slave, Now a Taskmaster
Joshua 16:10

These chapters are long lists. We can easily gloss over the details, our eyes glazing as foreign names and unfamiliar locations follow one another.

So don't miss it. The unthinkable is there in black and white: Israel takes the conquered Canaanites as slaves. Noah had cursed his grandson Canaan with a future of slavery (Genesis 9:18-25), and now the Israelites fulfill that threat for Canaan's descendants.

The focus of this part of the Old Testament on chosen Israel leaves questions about the other peoples God has created, whether they be the plagued Egyptians or the unwitting citizens of the lands promised by God to Israel. While it is hard to understand God, we accept that God has a bigger purpose than we can fathom.

It is harder to comprehend the actions of Israel. How can God's people, released from the horrors of slavery, take slaves of their own?

Even now, in the act of receiving the promise of their faithful God, the Hebrews do not understand what God is really like. They do know the tables have turned, and given the chance to see how the other half lives, they take up the whip.

Are we any different? Can Israel's story still be our story? Do we, even as we experience the blessing of God, fail to see how we are taking advantage of others? Are we guilty of doing to others exactly what we desperately prayed would not be done to us? Once freed, do we become the enslaver?

Day 72/March 12 — Joshua 18-21

Promise Fulfilled
Joshua 21:45

The story of Israel and the Promised Land, starting with Abram and progressing through the Exodus and the wandering of the Israelites in the desert, is only a good story if God keeps His promise in the end. If Israel does not get the land, then the "promise" part of Promised Land is empty. The whole story would then be nothing but a joke.

God does not work that way. God does not play tricks on us. God keeps His promises.

That theme will be repeated throughout scripture… and throughout history. To be sure, Israel's rebellion—like our rebellion—interferes with the directness of fulfillment, for human beings continue to do our best to play havoc with the plans of God. Still, prophecy (a fancy Biblical word for God's promise) is fulfilled again and again: mighty Babylon falls, tiny Bethlehem is the place of the Messiah's birth, Jesus is born of a virgin, the Son of Man ministers on earth, Jesus rides into Jerusalem on a donkey, He is wounded for our transgressions and buried in a rich man's tomb, and on and on.

God is the original promise keeper. God has made promises to you, and you can rely on them. He has promised you His love. He has promised you that a place in His eternal kingdom is yours for the asking. He has promised that He has a plan of hope just for you.

Grace always comes. Israel makes it to the Promised Land. Count on it.

A Stone of Witness
Joshua 22:27

The tribes of Reuben and Gad and the half-tribe of Manasseh cross the Jordan and build an altar as a statement to all who will ask, including their own children and grandchildren, whether and why they worship the God of Israel. In Chapter 24, Joshua sets up a stone as a memento to all the people that they have chosen to serve the Lord.

Have you built, bought, or collected a solid reminder of your faith? What prompts your holy memory? It is one thing to say a silent prayer of commitment or to rely on some long-ago walk down an aisle. Private discipleship can be terribly important, but it can also seem far away in times of crisis or temptation or depression.

Do you have a concrete token of your commitment to God? Is it a piece of jewelry around your neck, a bracelet with initials on it, a certain song in your iPod, or a bumper sticker? Do you use certain words and practice certain routines as a way of reminding you of your aim toward God? Is your worship liturgy a weekly marker of why you are a follower?

Or do you find that these routines are no more than empty talismans? Are you going through motions with plenty of religious things, words, art, and music around you without a regular acknowledgment of their meaning?

Today, look at your stone of remembrance, and say once again, "As for me and my house, we will serve the Lord."

Day 74/March 14 – Judges 1-2

One Generation Away
Judges 2:10

After all God has done, from leading the Hebrews out of Egyptian slavery to parting the sea, from daily manna for forty years to victories over heathen enemies in the Promised Land, it seems inconceivable that Israel could turn its back on God.

The Israelites' rebellion is not merely a possibility... it is an historical fact. In a single generation after the death of Joshua, the chosen people do not know God, have forgotten all that God did for their predecessors, and have forsaken His laws and His worship in favor of Baal and other so-called gods of the pagans who surround them.

God's people abandon Him, and they receive the fruit of their tragic choices; defeat follows defeat. Yet God is still the loving and forgiving covenant-maker. This Book of Judges tells of God's repeatedly raising up leaders from among the people to try to persuade them back to His way.

Once again, we see ourselves in Israel. Our parents and grandparents knew and worshiped God. It was not so long ago that the decadence and self-reliance of this generation would have been unthinkable, and yet here we are. We continually stumble into disaster and heartbreak, and it never occurs to most of us that such adversity follows our desertion of God's ways as predictably and as routinely as winter follows autumn.

Then, as now, God does not leave us without help. God raises up anointed men and women, begging us to hear Him once again. Will we listen?

Israel among the Hittites
Judges 3:5

Disobedience of God abounds. The Israelites have not driven out all the other peoples from the Promised Land. They have not followed the rules against intermarriage. Worse, they have not kept their solemn pledge to serve God alone and to steer clear of all other gods.

God finds it challenging to work with these who will not follow His commands. Individual judges are placed in command by God, and some victories continue, but God has relinquished control. Living in an intensely violent time, Israel has become as violent as any other people. The story of Jael and the tent peg she puts through the temple of Sisera is matched by the violence of Ehud's treacherous stabbing of Eglon. The tactics and choices of God's people are indistinguishable from those of the Hittites, Amorites, and other heathen nations among whom they live.

How fortunate that God does not let Israel stay that way. How blessed are God's chosen people that God continues to reach out to teach them a better way.

It will be through Israel that God will teach love, forgiveness, and compassion. It will be through this nation of brutality and force that the Prince of Peace will be given to the world. These butchers will birth the church.

Israel's story is like our own. How can God reach into your aggression and create reconciliation? God is willing to change you, as God changes Israel. Are you willing to be changed into one who reflects the face of Christ?

Day 76/March 16 — Judges 6-7

Go in the Strength You Have
Judges 6:14

We all see ourselves in the Gideon we meet in early Judges 6. Shocked to be noticed, much less chosen by God, and called to a task he does not believe he can do, he is quick to point out that he is nobody from a nothing family in a nondescript clan. Gideon is certain he is the last person God would want to lead this mighty victory.

Besides that, things have not been going so well. Gideon asks in verse 13: If God is really with us, why are bad things happening?

This entire dialog between Gideon and God is still repeated daily. God calls people like you and me to tasks big and small, and we are quick to tell God how unqualified we are and why He has made a mistake. We make a point to remind God how poorly things are going, and we blame God for our problems: "If you really cared about me, God, here is a list of things that would not be happening..."

God, who acts intentionally, is not interested in our inexperience, excuses, or circumstances. God wants us to trust Him with who and what we are. He does not ask Gideon to begin a training program and return in a year ready to lead an army. Instead, His message to Gideon is the same as He delivers to us today: Go in the strength you have.

God will not call you to anything that you and He together cannot handle.

Day 77/March 17 – Judges 8-9

God Is King over Israel
Judges 8:23

Gideon may not do everything right, but he understands the order of things. He knows Israel is not to be a monarchy, ruled over by a human king. Israel is a theocracy, to be ruled by God alone.

Abimelech does not understand this truth, and his attempt to be king in place of God results in his ruin in Judges 9.

What is the lesson for us?

If the Old Testament stories tell us how God treats us, then what we learn from these violent parts of Judges is this: God will be king over Israel, and God will be sovereign in our lives. We cannot and will not succeed in knocking God off His throne. No matter how we try to replace God with ourselves, or with idols we fashion out of man-made things, or with celebrity, or with power, or with money, or with sex… God will be in control. Getting from here to there may be costly to us, but we will get the message.

Like Gideon, we have opportunities to place ourselves on the throne of our lives. We can decide that our own appetites, yearnings, whims, and pleasures of the moment should be the driving factors. Others may tell us, as they told Gideon, that who we are and what we want should matter most.

God tells us differently. God is king, and our satisfaction comes when we submit to His rule. We say with Gideon, "I will not rule… The Lord will rule."

Day 78/March 18 — Judges 10-13

Shibboleth
Judges 12:6

C alling yourself a follower of God is one thing. Demonstrating it is something else. Since only true Hebrews can correctly pronounce shibboleth, Israelites use the word as a test to weed out spies. Those who only pretend to be from one of the twelve tribes can be detected by their mispronunciation.

Today, *shibboleth* has come to be used as a code word or proof of sincere allegiance. President Bartlet refers to it in an episode of "The West Wing" in which he has to determine if a group of Asians seeking asylum are truly persecuted Christians or are pretenders hoping to avoid immigration laws. The *shibboleth* he uses is to ask their spokesman, "Who is the leader of your church?" The reply is that while different people hold different roles in their congregation, "Jesus is the leader of our church." That is the right answer, and the president is satisfied.

Shibboleths can be appropriate tests of sincerity, but they can also be tools of discord and destruction. More than one church—indeed more than one denomination—has chosen to exclude members and remove persons from position because of their "incorrect" responses to questions of doctrine, interpretation, and policy. Shibboleths established with good intention have become divisive weapons.

Testing faith by any measure other than Jesus is doomed to fail.

Faith in Christ is a shibboleth on which we all can agree; any other basis for determining whether one is a follower is inherently suspect.

Be careful what shibboleth you champion.

Day 79/March 19 – Judges 14-16

Your Hair Grows Back
Judges 16:22

Dedicated to God before his birth, Samson is blessed with uncommon strength and given a place of leadership as a judge of Israel for twenty years. He is a violent, vengeful, promiscuous man who takes pleasure in killing. He is not, however, particularly clever, misunderstanding Delilah's schemes and falling for her ploy even after she has tried and failed three times to ambush him.

Samson is captured and blinded because he allows his hair, which he has promised God would never be shaved, to be cut. If the story of Samson ended there, it would be a lesson in foolishness.

Of course, the story does not end there. It becomes a lesson in redemption, for Samson's hair grows back, and with it returns his strength. Made to perform for the hedonist enjoyment of the enemies of God, Samson finds his strength once more.

Far too often, we allow our dedicated hair to be cut. Whatever our particular calling is, we fall short, allowing the adversaries of God in the world to interfere, to separate us from what gives us our strength, to divide us from God. When that happens to us, we pay a steep price. God is displeased.

But God is also the loving, forgiving giver of grace. Our hair grows back. God makes a way to reach us, even when we have been foolish, violent, and promiscuous. Even when we have allowed the enemy a way to blind us and bind us, God finds us.

Grace always comes.

Day 80/March 20 – Judges 17-20

Such a Thing Has Never Been Done in Israel – Judges 19:30

Israel descends further into the depths. With no king, the people devote themselves to local gods and steal priests from one another. Their violence and blood lust seem boundless.

Now, in a story reminiscent of the despicable people of Sodom and Gomorrah, Israelites seek to abuse a visitor to their town. They ultimately rape and kill in their debauchery.

Israel's story is our story. When we abandon our king, forsake any true social order, and live to satisfy our basest instincts, we find ourselves repeating the worst of our own history and challenging the basic tenets of the God who has led us so far.

For some in Israel, at least, this has gone far enough. The rape and murder lead to a reaction of disgust, and the people seek to expunge the offending tribe from Israel. Looking around at what has happened, they proclaim that their kinsmen have sunk to a new low.

We all are due for self-examination, but be ready for the results. Honest introspection will reveal your worst tendencies, habits, desires, and actions. You will sometimes look at your life in horror and wonder how you have ended up where you are. Your thought will be that "such a thing has never been done."

You are not alone. No temptation has come to you that is not common to all of us. God is ready to lead you out of it. Grace always comes.

Will you turn around? Will you change your ways and follow God?

Day 81/March 21 – Judges 21–Ruth 1

Where You Go, I Will Go
Ruth 1:16

Ruth's famous statement to Naomi reflects three of the Ancient Greek terms for love (all but *eros*—erotic love).

Ruth's loyalty to her widowed mother-in-law certainly indicates *storge*—the almost automatic affection among family members.

Ruth's declaration further is a prototype of what Aristotle calls *philia*—"brotherly love" or "friendship for the good." As we examine our own horizontal relationships with each other, it is in only the highest forms of friendship we see our own desire to be where the other person is, to join with her people, and to live where she lives.

The Greeks also have a word for love found in the New Testament: *agape*. It is the love of God for us, described by the Apostle Paul in 1 Corinthians 13. Surely Paul has his Hebrew school lessons of Ruth in mind when he thinks about the love of God demonstrated by her and mirrored in our best days. He writes that *agape* is patient and kind, not envying, not boasting, bearing all things, believing all things, hoping all things, and enduring all things. Ruth's oath to Naomi is an early Old Testament revelation of the love of God, which goes where we go and stays where we stay.

When Ruth finishes by saying "May the Lord deal with me, be it ever so severely, if anything but death separates you and me," she foreshadows another key element that Paul will lay out for us: Nothing can separate us from the love of God.

Day 82/March 22 –Ruth 2-4

Cover Me, Kinsman-Redeemer
Ruth 3:9

This little book has a lot to say. Love in all its facets, redemption, prophecy, and providence are its story.

Yesterday's key verse is not about *eros* (erotic love), but today's passage certainly is. Do not miss the tender love story and fierce romantic attraction between Ruth and Boaz that culminate when she comes to his bedroom.

The writer of Ruth makes one local custom – the role of the kinsman-redeemer – abundantly clear. The closest relative has a right and a duty to buy Elimilech's property and, in the process, to become the husband of Ruth. When that relative declines, Boaz, who loves Ruth, steps up and fulfills the role.

We are children of God. Jesus, the Son of God, is our kinsman-redeemer. When we are lost, orphaned, worthless, and homeless, Jesus rises to our need and pays the price necessary to reclaim our place, our value, and our home with God. Jesus does this because He loves us and because He knows that without Him, we have no option. Ruth's story is thus our story.

And there is more. Ruth, the foreigner, comes to Bethlehem with Naomi, marries Boaz, and has a child who has a child who has a child who is anointed king. Ruth is the great-grandmother of King David, and she is therefore a direct ancestor of Jesus. God's plan in leading Ruth, the Moabite, to stay with Naomi, the Israelite, is fulfilled.

Kinsman-redeemer Boaz covers Naomi with his bedspread. Kinsman-redeemer Jesus covers us with His love.

Day 83/March 23 – 1 Samuel 1-4

Speak... Your Servant Listens
1 Samuel 3:10

The story of the boy Samuel's hearing the voice of God is poignant in the way it is set up by its context: "In those days, the word of the Lord was rare;" (1 Samuel 3:1) and "Samuel did not yet know the Lord." (1 Samuel 3:7) It is no wonder then that Samuel does not recognize the voice of God.

It is hard for those who are not expecting something to perceive it. Studies show that automobile drivers who have a motorcycle license are much more likely to notice motorcycles on the road than those drivers who do not have a motorcycle license. When you are aware of a possibility, you are far more likely to notice it.

Trick plays in sports rarely work more than once against the same team. Once a defense knows that the opposing football or basketball team has a certain play in its arsenal, that play will probably not be successful. When you are aware of a possibility, you are far more likely to be ready for it.

Samuel does not know God, and he has never heard that God speaks to people, so when God calls, Samuel does not recognize Him.

We do not have Samuel's excuse. Do not miss God's call. Scripture, the witness of many millions of Christians, and experience teach that His voice will come to you. Be aware. Be ready. God is persistent with Samuel, and He will be persistent with you. When you are aware, you will notice.

Day 84/March 24 – 1 Samuel 5-8

Ebenezer
1 Samuel 7:12

The great hymn *Come Thou Fount of Every Blessing* contains these words: "Here I raise my Ebenezer. Hither by thy help I'm come."

Israel has defeated the Philistines. Samuel, who hears the rumblings in the camp and is sensitive to the political winds that are blowing, marks the time and the place. The people are rejecting the idea of following God alone (1 Samuel 8:7-8) and demanding that a king be anointed for them. Samuel tries to head them off by placing a monument called an Ebenezer, which means "stone of help," to remind the people that it is by God's hand—and God's alone—that their successes have come.

You have Philistines in your life. Enemies surround and attack. These enemies may be human—abusive family members, uncaring neighbors, or threatening bosses. These enemies may be physical—disease, addiction, pain. These enemies may be financial or environmental or emotional. Perhaps nature itself has become an enemy of storms. These enemies may be inside your head. Whatever the source, your Philistines have tried, and sometimes temporarily succeeded, to destroy your goals and erode your joy.

You have beaten back Philistines only through the hand of God. You know this is true, for you are unable to do it on your own. Build an Ebenezer. Mark the time and place in your life when God has trampled your enemies for you, and acknowledge, "hither by thy help I'm come." He is the source of your every blessing. Acknowledge and remember.

God Chooses Saul
1 Samuel 9:16

As we read through First Samuel, we will see that the reign of Saul, stained by bloodlust and his jealousy of David, ends up a failure.

Since we know that is what is coming, it is important for us to see at the beginning that indeed Saul is God's choice. Responding to the people's demand for a king, God tells Samuel to anoint Saul. God sends His Spirit on Saul as he leads the Israelites to more defeats of the Philistines.

How can this be? If God is doing the choosing and His Spirit is with Saul, how can Saul turn out to be anything but an extraordinary king?

The answer is a terribly important lesson for us. God can and does bless us, set our feet on high places, and lay a path of success and victory before us; but then He leaves it to us to carry out these plans and live our own lives. God, the author of freedom, never forces us down a road, nor does He ever remove our ability to choose to follow our own way. Even the sovereignty of God does not intervene when we choose the wrong path.

Celebrate the gifts God has given, but do not forget that you and I are able—indeed prone—to wander. Our faithlessness does not mean that God has not been with us all along, planning and blessing. Our faithlessness means that we have failed. Like Israel, we go our own way.

Don't blame God.

Day 86/March 26 – 1 Samuel 12-14

A Picture of Faith
1 Samuel 14:6

How can only two men enter the camp of the mighty Philistines and successfully start the attack that will end up sending the Philistines on the run? Jonathan explains: "Nothing can hinder the Lord from saving, whether by many or by few." Jonathan understands that God does not need our help, our raw materials, or our manpower. Jonathan is fully willing to enter into what is, by any reasonable military thought, a suicide mission because he understands the power of His God.

Faith is not mere intellectual acknowledgment of the existence, power, and love of God. Such head knowledge is important, and it accompanies faith, but it is not faith. Faith is not even the addition of a promise of trust to that head knowledge. Such heart commitment is also critical and goes with faith, but it is not faith.

Faith involves the head and the heart, but faith also requires actual experience. Knowing and promising are not faith; they are the precursors to faith. Faith says, "Because I know and because I trust, therefore I will live. Therefore I will walk as God's. I know God and I trust God, thus I will be what I know God intends for me to be."

Jonathan's faith manifests as definite and profound action. With an insight beyond his age and position, Jonathan walks into the Philistine camp with full confidence in his God.

The confidence in Jonathon's mind is not his faith. Walking into the camp of the enemy is faith.

Day 87/March 27 – 1 Samuel 15-16

God Judges the Heart
1 Samuel 16:7

As we learn more and more about God, we continually discern new ways in which He is unique, unlike us or anything we know. In yesterday's reading, we learn that God's timing is not like our planning—much to Saul's chagrin in 1 Samuel 13. In today's reading, we understand that God's demand of obedience is absolute, even when obedience means that we choose not to perform an expected religious ritual. Simply put, "to obey is better than to sacrifice." (1 Samuel 15:22)

Now, as we come to the anointing of David, we learn again that God does not think or distinguish as we humans do. Outward appearance is no more important to God than pedigree, social status, income, ethnicity, gender, reputation, or history when it comes to the person whom God chooses and calls. If this were not true, God would not have called poor Mary and Joseph, prostitute Rahab, Jewish Esther, Gentile Luke, or Pharisee Saul, who meets Jesus on the way to try to destroy the church and ends up the Apostle Paul.

David may be strong and handsome, but he is young and immature. There is nothing remotely royal about him… and God cannot care less. God is not looking at these outward, human indications of ability. God judges the heart, and He calls one whose heart is after His own. Tall and popular, Saul is not such a man. (1 Samuel 13:14) Young, gangly, and unknown, David is. (Acts 13:22)

God knows the difference.

The Lord Who Rescued Me Then Will Deliver Me Now – 1 Samuel 17:37

An entire army cowers feebly and hapless before Goliath. This man, albeit stronger and fiercer than any faced before, threatens. The king himself has no organized plan to overcome this enemy beyond offering a reward to anyone who will take the chance. Along comes David.

We all have enemies in our lives. And we all have bears and lions —the events of life, often caused naturally, that threaten our health and our livelihood and our well-being. God leads us against the enemy Philistines and the attacking wild animals, and we live to see what God has for us next.

Sometimes—thankfully not very often—we have to face our Goliath: the biggest and worst and most challenging of the Philistines, who haunts us, bigger than anything we could have imagined, taunting with insults and looking down with disdain. Our reaction is disgust mixed with fear. We cannot see a way even to survive Goliath, much less to escape victorious. When Goliath threatens, we often feel like a lowly, armorless shepherd boy. We see that nobody else can or will face the giant, and we are all that is left.

And that is when we remember the bear and the lion. Yes! God has been with us before. We have faced difficult adversaries, and God helped us through. Yes! The God who rescued before will deliver now. The battle is His. We have no armor or military training, but we have five smooth stones and God almighty. Yes!

100   *Grace Always Comes*

Day 89/March 29 – 1 Samuel 20-22

A Tale of Father and Son
1 Samuel 20:17

Jonathan and Saul, son and father, both have intense personal relationships with David. Jonathan is David's friend, one who loves David as only a true friend can, and one whom David loves in return. Saul is David's mentor and king, one who professes to love David as a son but who in fact is driven by jealousy and something akin to madness to hunt David down and repeatedly attempt to murder him in cold blood.

The story of David's escape from Saul and Saul's pursuit of David is interesting theatre, but its Biblical importance rests in the juxtaposition of Jonathan and Saul. Saul hates David without reason; Jonathan loves David beyond reason. Saul pursues David with a vengeance; Jonathan sends David off with a blessing.

How do you treat those whom you claim to love? Do your actions mirror your words? Are you swayed by how you think others see you?

Are you willing, like Jonathan and David, to understand and treasure the relationships that God has given you, making promises that you will keep beyond the death of the other, and taking strides to protect the other even at personal risk to yourself?

Learn from Saul's folly and from Jonathan's loyalty. Guard your heart against jealousy and pride. Seek out those who love you, and whom you can respect and love in return. Relationships are among God's most treasured gifts to us.

Take a lesson from father and son. With the Davids in your life, be Jonathan, not Saul.

Day 90/March 30 – 1 Samuel 23-25

Mercy
1 Samuel 24:4

David is a complicated and often contradictory individual. He is a man of war, conquering with a record that is historically unmatched. He is capable of killing Philistines by the hundreds, helping himself to others' livestock, and ordering the extermination of entire villages; yet he is also a man of tender poetry and music who seeks God's favor.

Now, his character traits come crashing together. In the cave, he has the chance to kill Saul, an easily justifiable act of self-defense that would have cleared the way for David to the throne. Yet David does not see in Saul his foe so much as he sees God's chosen anointed king. David refuses to kill him.

David instead creates evidence for Saul to see how close David has been, hoping Saul will be persuaded once and for all that David is not his enemy. Saul seems to agree. Whether Saul is intentionally lying or is temporarily persuaded is anyone's guess.

Why would David show mercy to Saul? Why does anyone ever show mercy? By definition, an act of mercy is shown to one who is worthy of something much worse. When we extend mercy, we are choosing not to respond in a way that all would agree is justified.

Mercy does not honor the formula. The merciful do not do what is earned. Showing mercy highlights only the good of another, irrespective of what has gone before. David's mercy is a precursor of what we all need—the mercy of God.

Find Me a Witch
1 Samuel 28:7

The story of the disguised Saul's visit to the illegal fortune teller in 1 Samuel 28 is an odd chapter. Its meaning is debated, and potential explanations are endless. One end of the analytical spectrum takes the story literally and concludes that the medium somehow calls the ghost of Samuel to appear and speak to Saul. The other sees this story as a parable demonstrating Saul's desperation and his imminent death. In the middle are ideas of demons masquerading as Samuel and explanations of the woman as a ventriloquist.

Whatever this ghost story means, what comes before it is more important. Impulsive and frantic with fear when faced with a Philistine army that now has David fighting with it, Saul—who has earlier banned spiritists and mediums—makes a curious demand: "Find me a witch."

By now we know that the story of Saul is tragic and heartbreaking. This man who was deemed worthy of royal anointing by God has been reduced by his own breakdowns to a quivering mass of indecision, contradiction, and pitiful spiritual emptiness. God's anointed is lost.

What about us? Do we let our sin, our failures, and our enemies force us to turn to what we know is not right, what we have earlier expelled from our own lives, what we know cannot be of God? In our lostness, do we grasp for emptiness and evil?

Take heed. Learn from Saul before it is too late. This tale is a warning to God's people.

April

April 1 – 1 Samuel 31 – 2 Samuel 2

How the Mighty Have Fallen
2 Samuel 1:19

Saul may be described as disturbed, megalomaniacal, un-aware, and envious. He tries to kill his most trusted deputy and curses his very son. He repeatedly disobeys God and revels in moments of self-aggrandizement. He is not the poster child for obedient servants of God.

Still, David mourns the demise of Saul. David, who has refused easy opportunities to kill Saul, is genuinely distressed over the king's death. David sees neither demagogue, self-important abuser of power, nor lunatic murderer Saul has become; instead, David sees God's anointed, a mighty king brought low by circumstance, enemies, and personal imperfection. He sees Saul as "swifter than eagles… stronger than lions." (2 Samuel 1:23) He weeps over the loss of Saul.

Loving one's enemies is a very New Testament concept. Jesus teaches of turning the other cheek to the person who has struck you and going a second mile with one who forces you to march. (Matthew 5:39-41)

Some may say that David is shortsighted, or even silly, but there is something admirable in his view. David chooses the high road. The defeat of God's chosen one is not to be celebrated. David makes the conscious choice, throughout Saul's life as well as at his death, to see Saul not as an enemy but rather as his king.

The high road is not easy, and it will not be honored by those around you. Loving your enemies is counter-cultural and irrational. Still, God smiles as we remember friends at their best, not their worst.

Day 93/April 2 – 2 Samuel 3-6

Foreshadowing
2 Samuel 3:14-16

Among David's many wives, the first is Michal, daughter of Saul. (1 Samuel 18:27) Saul takes Michal away from David and gives her to another man, and David never forgets her. Now that Saul is dead and David is king in Jerusalem, he demands that Michal be returned to him.

David's wanting his first wife back is understandable, and his claim is valid, but his methods are not befitting of a man after God's own heart. Michal is now the wife of another, yet David is unconcerned about this man, an innocent in all the palace intrigue between David and Saul. This man's name is Paltiel, and the story of his following Michal back to David, "weeping all the way," is terribly sad. (2 Samuel 3:16)

David is just warming up, setting a tragic pattern for abuse of his power. David gets what he wants—another wife to add to his collection, albeit one who has grown to hate him and who will not bear him children—and shows a calloused heart with no concern for the abandoned husband. We will soon see David do this again, although then it will not be to retrieve a woman for whom he has any valid claim. The next time, the woman will be Bathsheba, and her grieving husband will end up dead.

How often our sins are simply paving the way for what is to come. When we do not guard our heart, we foreshadow an even more painful and rebellious future.

Day 94 / April 3 – 2 Samuel 7-10

The One Who Will Build the House of God – 2 Samuel 7:13

David wants to build the temple, but he is not the one to do it. David, accustomed to getting what he wants, begs God to let him begin construction, but God answers David's prayer with a "no."

Behind this "no," however, lies a better promise that David cannot yet imagine.

God's answer is that David's offspring will build a "house for [God's] name." God will establish the throne of his kingdom forever.

You may well understand this promise of God to mean that Solomon, David's son, will build the temple… and indeed you are right. Solomon does build the temple that will stand in Jerusalem for centuries and become the symbol of the religion of God's people.

God's promise is more nuanced and more far-reaching than simply a promise about Solomon, however. Do not view the temple, the "house for God's name," as nothing more than a building. Do not view the throne of David's kingdom as nothing more than a royal line.

From David's family line will come the One who will be the Temple, the one who is God and in whom God will dwell, the one who is King and whose unshakeable kingdom will never end.

The One, of course, is Jesus Christ, who will be born in the city of David and into a family of the house and lineage of David. Of His kingdom there shall be no end, and He shall reign forever.

God's promise is sure. His plan is complete in Jesus.

Day 95 / April 4 – 2 Samuel 11-13

You Are the Man
2 Samuel 12:7

In this famous story, David's serial failures progress assuredly one into the next.

First, David shirks his responsibility as king, staying home at "the time when kings go off to war." His corruptions then involve, in turn, invasion of privacy, lust, and adultery. But David is now bolder, and his sin with Bathsheba, leading to the conception of an illegitimate child, does not conclude with mere adultery.

Indeed, David's sins snowball. He plunges headfirst into an elaborate deception, one in which the innocent Uriah refuses to cooperate. As a result, David orders the murder of numerous innocent Israelite soldiers, including Uriah. The cover-up continues, and David's sin plays havoc with him and his family for the rest of his life.

David's son Amnon rapes his half-sister, David's daughter Tamar, and then despises her and leaves her to a life of shame. In turn, David's son Absalom vengefully murders Amnon. In the end, David's family is torn apart, and David is estranged from his son Absalom.

How ironic, then, that David, when confronted by the prophet Nathan, does not recognize his own sin until Nathan points the finger directly in the king's face and says, "You are the man."

Recognizing your need… your failure… your sin… is the first step to recovery. Do you see your wrongdoing? Are you willing to accept the word of God to you that the sinner is you, that when you look around and see the evil and destruction around you, you are the responsible person?

Conspiracy and Betrayal – 2 Samuel 15:12

The plot thickens. David and Absalom meet and temporarily silence their quarrel, but the apparent peace does not last long.

The results of David's breakdowns will never end. Young Absalom sees the chance to take advantage of a weakened king, and he begins to plan a coup d'état. Leaving Jerusalem under false pretenses and establishing a shadow kingdom in Hebron, Absalom steals advisers from David and usurps the loyalty of David's would-be supporters throughout Israel. Before long, David cannot trust even Mephibosheth, the son of his best friend Jonathan.

How has your sin found you out? What consequences are demonstrated in your life right now? Oh, your specific sinful acts may stay forever secret; you have made sure of that. The corollaries of your choices, however, are everywhere. It seems that you cannot turn around without fearing that someone knows, that someone is striking back, that machinery you have unknowingly set in motion is even now gaining momentum to create a disastrous trap for you.

Even though God has forgiven us, the natural outcomes of our decisions are built into this fallen world in which we live. It is crucial to remember that David is "a man after God's own heart" and God has forgiven David's sin. (2 Samuel 12:13) Nonetheless, that sin has real world effects that cannot be wished away. Clean before God, David nevertheless must live with the upshot of his deeds.

How much easier life is when we make the right choices on the front end!

Day 97 / April 6 – 2 Samuel 17-19

O My Son Absalom!
2 Samuel 18:22

And so the story reaches its tragic denouement. David's collapse reaches its completion in the death of his son Absalom.

Greed. Laziness. Lust. Deceit. Murder. Mayhem. More death.

Review: David takes Michal without sympathy for Paltiel, stays behind and ignores his royal duties, spies on the bathing Bathsheba, lusts after her, commits adultery, lies about it, tries to deceive Uriah, orders the death of Uriah, causes the death of multiple additional blameless soldiers, sees one son rape and disgrace his daughter, sees that son murdered by a second son, is forced to defend himself from the revolt led by that second son, and then has his right-hand man kill that second son.

It is no wonder that David is reduced to abject weeping. Of course the death of his son Absalom is the immediate cause of his grief, but what we really see is the collective weight of this series of sins and consequences crashing down on the king. We understand David's cry, "If only I had died instead of you!"

This extended heartbreaking catastrophe is given to us in scripture for a reason. If someone of David's stature, abilities, and devotion to God can fall so far, then none of us is safe in our own strength. We all stand precipitously close to the threshold of disaster. We remember God's words to Cain, that "sin is crouching at your door; it desires to have you." (Genesis 4:7)

We do not have to make the wrong choice. Learn from David.

Day 98 / April 7 – 2 Samuel 20-22

So Shall I Be Saved
2 Samuel 22:4

I will call upon the Lord, who is worthy to be praised. So shall I be saved from my enemies. The Lord lives! Praise be to the Rock of my salvation! (2 Samuel 22:4, 47)

Despite all the tragedy that has happened to David and the evil that has been caused by David, and irrespective of whatever will happen, he never loses sight of the source of victory, of his forgiveness, and of his place as king. David knows that without God he is nothing. David knows that his conquests have stemmed from the power and provision of God. David knows that he lives only because God lives.

How shall we be saved? It is certainly not through our own abilities, strength, steadfastness, and devotion—that is the lesson of David to us all.

How shall we be saved? It is not through our being good, for we cannot be good enough—that too is the lesson of David, whose righteousness is neither good enough nor long lasting enough to save him before he gives in to multiple temptations.

How shall we be saved? It is not through what anyone else can do for us—that is the lesson of David, as the good wishes and efforts of great men like Samuel and Jonathan are not enough.

How shall we be saved? It is through the Lord God, the Rock of our salvation. We call upon the Lord, who is worthy to be praised. So shall we be saved.

Day 99/April 8 — 2 Samuel 23-24

The King We See
2 Samuel 23:4

As this book ends, the author adopts a decidedly poetic tone to make his most crucial point.

David is not the king Israel needs, but David knows how to describe that king. That king, ruling in true righteousness, ruling based on his relationship with God, will be like the morning. He will be like brightness after rain, bringing flowers from the earth.

David knows… the true king is light. The true king will mirror the brightest, purest, holiest light. The true king will be light that brings forth beauty and growth. The true king will be refreshing life itself.

In Him is life, and that life is the light of men, the true light that gives light to all. (John 1:4, 9) When Jesus declares, "I am the light of the world" (John 8:12), He hearkens back to these last words of David. Jesus' hearers know He remembers what King David has set forth as the ideal.

Light illuminates, heats, nourishes, and chases away darkness. Light becomes a rallying point for those who wander. Light brightens the discouraged soul and leads the lost.

The tragedies of David's life are not the end of his story. While he cannot escape the outcomes of what he has set in motion, he remains the man after God's own heart. At the end, David sees who is to come, and he rejoices.

We too see Him. He is like the light of the morning, when the sun rises, even a morning without clouds.

Show Your Love by Your Walk
1 Kings 3:3

How do we know Solomon loves God? The writer of Kings tells us is that Solomon shows his love for God by following the statutes that God has laid down through David.

In other words, Solomon walks the talk. He practices what is preached.

Words can be cheap. People can promise many different things. True love for God is revealed not by mere declarations of loyalty, statements of profound devotion, or recitations of creeds. Rather, like Solomon, we display our love for God by obeying the commands of the Lord set down before us.

Solomon demonstrates his relationship with God by following God. He shows obedience and models faith.

We must be careful in how we interpret these types of verses, for our actions and good works do not save us. We are saved by the grace of God, for which we cannot work and which we cannot earn, but which we can accept through our faith. (Ephesians 2:8-9) That actions and good works do not save us, however, does not mean obedience is unimportant. To the contrary, God has created and saved us so that we can do good, showing our love for God by keeping His commands. (Ephesians 2:10)

In the Broadway and Hollywood musical "My Fair Lady," Eliza sings to a would-be suitor, "Don't talk of love … show me." While our love for God is exceedingly more important than the crush of silly Freddy, the way others recognize that love is the same. We show it.

Day 101 / April 10 – 1 Kings 3:4 - 4

Solomon's Choice
1 Kings 3:9

Solomon's choice is not wealth, health, longevity, fame, or honor. Given the opportunity to request whatever he wants from God, Solomon chooses a discerning heart to help him understand how to lead God's people.

God is pleased with Solomon's choice. We should learn from that.

Discernment is not a virtue that receives much publicity. Discernment is a complex admixture of the aptitude to know what God would have you do, the knack to see a problem as God sees it and understand how it is to be addressed, the capability to know the difference between right and wrong, and the facility to tell the difference between those who are telling you the truth and those who whisper lies. Discernment is the heart of wisdom. It is a gift. It is the most important gift God can give Solomon, and God is thrilled when it is the gift Solomon seeks.

Do you ask God for a discerning heart? There are Christians who have the spiritual gift of discernment, the special ability given by the Holy Spirit to distinguish evil even when it is masked and hiding. We do not have to have that supernatural gift, however, to receive a more discerning heart from God, who loves to help us see into His mind's eye so we can better comprehend how to address the obstacles of life.

Instead of asking for all your problems to go away, consider asking God to help you solve them.

God, give your servant a discerning heart.

Temple and Palace
1 Kings 6:38–7:2

Solomon does not arrive on the scene as a fully formed paragon of faith. Like us, he has growing to do. We can trace Solomon's maturation through the Old Testament. In Kings, we see him as the newly-appointed king, recipient of wisdom and discernment from God, and builder of the temple. He is a recognized hero of Israel. We can then trace his spiritual development from his prayers in Kings through his many Proverbs and ultimately to his writings in Ecclesiastes when he is older and even wiser.

So, young Solomon is a champion, but he has not yet arrived at all he will be. Notice that, as great a project as the temple is and as impressive a structure it is, it pales in comparison to the palace Solomon builds for himself. Solomon takes almost twice as long on the palace and builds for himself a structure much grander and more impressive than the temple he has built for God.

We are no different. Like Solomon, we have a ways to go. Your mortgage or rent payment is very likely significantly more than your offering. Most of us set aside at least a quarter of our income for housing, so Solomon's expenditures are nothing at which we can point an accusing finger.

Our gifts to God seem extravagant... until we compare them with what we spend on ourselves. God accepts our gifts anyway, just as He accepts and blesses the temple.

How does your palace compare to God's temple?

Day 103/April 12 – 1 Kings 8-9

No Temple Can Hold God
1 Kings 8:27

The temple is valuable, but such a construction does not approach what God requires.

God does not dwell in buildings—temples or otherwise—built by human hands. (Acts 17:24) This important idea, recognized by Solomon in his dedicatory prayer, is crucial for three reasons.

First, God cannot be nailed down. Omnipresent God, the creator of the world, is not limited to a location. His is a kingdom of spirit, and His dwelling place is everywhere. Poets writing in scripture speak of His rising with the wings of the dawn (Psalm 139:9) and living in the abode of light. (Job 38:19) Thinking that God "lives" in a certain temple, church building, tabernacle, or house is a misunderstanding of the nature and eternity of God. Our God is greater than we can imagine. He cannot be caged. He chooses to visit us, but He is not subject to our walls.

Second, God is not bound to any certain people. Having built the temple in Jerusalem, the people of Israel begin to think they own God, that God is unconcerned about anyone else, that they have God on a leash. They cannot be more wrong.

Third, God is seeking His people, not the works of their hands. God wants to dwell within us. He stands at the door of our hearts and knocks, and He waits to come in. (Revelation 3:20)

Do not simply build him a place; open up your life to Him. He waits to live with you and in you.

However
1 Kings 11:1

Wise and Discerning… Builder of the Temple… Hero of the People… all of these titles for King Solomon are true. Like the tragic protagonists throughout literature, though, Solomon is flawed. The writer of Kings signals through the word "however" that the end of the story is not what the beginning has promised.

For Solomon, the snare is his attraction to too many women and to the foreign gods they bring with them. Even at the beginning, when Solomon is described as following the decrees of his father David, we are told that his obedience is true "except that he offered sacrifices and burned incense in the high places." (1 Kings 3:3) Now, we see Solomon's hundreds of foreign wives lead him astray, so that he is not completely devoted to the Lord. (1 Kings 11:3-4)

This tragic blemish is not minor. As the king of chosen Israel, Solomon owes everything to God, and failing to show God the full measure of devotion is fatal. God's covenant with the house of David is premised on faithfulness, and Solomon's decision to wander in his devotion is "evil in the eyes of the Lord." (1 Kings 11:6) The results for Israel will be catastrophic: the kingdom will be divided, and civil war will ensue.

Watch out for the "however" in your own life. Calling yourself a follower is not enough, so you follow through with intense and meaningful moments of obedience. Your intentions are good, your gifts are many; however…

What Share Do We Have in David?
1 Kings 12:16

David and Solomon are gone. Rehoboam is a disaster, ignoring the wise counsel of the elders in favor of frat-boy machismo. Civil war is in the air, and the kingdom is split.

For the moment, Rehoboam is able to maintain a semblance of a reign in Judah where Jerusalem is located. The rest of the people, however, split away and take the name "Israel" with them. They have no need for Jerusalem or Solomon's son. The city of David, and the line of David, hold no fascination for them when the king is evil and their needs are unmet.

David's charisma and military brilliance kept him in power, and Solomon's wisdom and accomplishments allowed him to stay king of God's people; but both of them sinned, repeatedly and continuously, throughout their reign. Now, their heir continues the sin without the achievement or discernment, and the allure is suddenly gone from the dynasty. God's covenant, dependent on obedience, cannot prop up the house, and the people declare, "What share do we have in David?"

It is time for us to examine ourselves. Are we relying on the accomplishments of generations gone before us? Do we assume that our way of life and our values will continue because of what our forefathers and parents did?

It is not difficult to see how it can all slip away, how God withdraws in the face of sin and self-importance to allow even the Promised Land to descend into disarray.

Are we repeating history today?

Day 106/April 15 – 1 Kings 14-17

Demand and Promise
1 Kings 17:13-14

This is an odd story.

Elijah goes to the house of a poor widow who is ready to die. Strangely (to us), Elijah, instead of looking somewhere else, demands that she provide him the last of the food that she has for herself and her son.

Elijah is not asking on his own accord, however. Elijah is a prophet of the living God, and he does not demand the food without also promising—correctly—that the flour will not be used up and the jug of oil will never run out.

God makes demands of us that seem, at times, strange and even extreme. What we see in scripture, however, is that God's covenant demands are always accompanied by His covenant promise. When God demands the last cake of bread in our pantry, He has already made His plan to provide us with everlasting flour and oil.

What does God demand of you? The answer is "everything that you have and everything that you are." Jesus tells us that if we want to follow Him, we have to be willing to take up our cross daily. (Mark 8:34) God asks for the last cake of bread, the last ounce of what we have. Even as He makes that demand, He offers us Himself and His kingdom. Jesus tells us that kingdom is the pearl of great price, worth selling everything we have in order to gain it. (Matthew 13:46)

The demand is always matched with the promise. Grace always comes.

Day 107/April 16 – 1 Kings 18-20

God's Response to Desperation
1 Kings 19:11

Elijah has talked to the creator of the universe. He has seen the soaking bull set ablaze by the power of God before the amazed prophets of Baal. He has been fed by ravens sent by the hand of God, and he has been touched by an angel.

Yet Elijah is tired and depressed. His preaching is not producing converts, and the queen wants to kill him. His many experiences with God—recent and incredible though they are—do not outweigh his desperation. It is as if Elijah tells God that all of His work has come to nothing.

God's response is not what we expect. God neither comforts Elijah with assurances of success nor pats him on the back with recognition for his good work. Instead, God tells Elijah to go outside and experience the presence of God.

That presence does not come in the fire, the storm, or the earthquake. Instead, God famously comes to Elijah in the still, small voice. While that form is important—we must learn to find God in the quiet and not demand the dramatic—what is more crucial is that God's antidote for anxiety and hopelessness is not an overwhelming demonstration of powerful healing. It is simply His presence. Elijah prays the prayer of the despondent, and God responds, "Go stand on the mountain, for the Lord is passing by."

You do not need recognition, success, or material gifts. What you need is what you always get—the presence of the Lord.

First, Seek the Counsel of the Lord
1 Kings 21:5

Evil King Ahab and good King Jehoshaphat make unlikely allies, but time and circumstance, and perhaps Almighty God, conspire to throw them together. Ahab seeks Jehoshaphat's advice about military strategy, and Jehoshaphat's answer is that, whatever else they do, they should first seek the counsel of the Lord.

The answer is this: Let's pray about it first.

Too often, this wise counsel, as expressed by the good king, is taken for granted or, worse, discounted as old-fashioned pabulum for the weak. Praying through a tough situation, or seeking God's direction, seem out-of-date and juvenile to far too many people.

Dismissal as cheesy and out-of-date is not the only reason that praying for guidance is not done nearly enough. Many, many people do not pray because they are afraid God might actually answer. Whether they do not want to admit God exists and do not want people to think they are "hearing voices," many today show no interest in praying for God's counsel.

What about you? When faced with a decision, do you, first, seek the Lord's counsel? Do you pray, consult your Bible, engage in worship, and perhaps talk about the decision with trusted Christian friends and advisors? Are you willing to let a choice be left unmade until God has spoken to you? Are you willing to let God guide you?

True faith does not simply say prayers. True faith seeks the counsel of the Lord, waits for it, and then acts on it.

Pray. Listen. Follow.

Day 109/April 18 – 2 Kings 1-4

Chariots of Fire, Part One
2 Kings 2:11

Grief and uncertainty are ordinary in the face of death. Elijah's last event, riding a chariot of fire away from his watchful servant, teaches about how God's people leave the earth.

"I looked over Jordan and what did I see? A band of angels coming after me, coming for to carry me home. If you get there before I do, tell all my friends I'm coming too. Swing low, sweet chariot, coming for to carry me home."[1]

Death produces grief, for those we love are no longer here with us, and that naturally hurts us. Death produces uncertainty (and, for some, abject fear) because to die is to enter the unknown, to step into the dark from which there is no obvious return.

Elijah knows his time on earth is through, and with his dogged assistant Elisha at his side, he makes ready for the end. When the time comes, a chariot and horses of fire appear, and Elijah is taken "up to heaven in a whirlwind." He is with Elisha, then he is not.

What a glorious description of how we leave this earth! For the children of God, there is no end to life. We are simply passing from this world to the next, swept away by the power of God so that those on earth "see us no more."

Jesuit Pierre Teilhard de Chardin famously said, "We are spiritual beings having a human experience. We've got to realize that we are only here temporarily." Elijah would agree.

---

1   American Negro Spiritual

Chariots of Fire, Part Two
2 Kings 6:17

It is perhaps the most hopeful and sustaining promise of scripture: There are more who stand on our side than those who stand against us.

Elisha has seen angels driving chariots of fire before, and he remembers them.

Those chariots of fire exist not only to carry our souls to heaven but also to encircle and support us in our times of deepest need.

Elisha's servant is afraid for good reason. The king of the enemy Arameans has placed a bounty on Elisha's head, and it now appears that the end has come. Elisha and his servant are surrounded. There is no way out.

Elisha sees things differently. With spirit eyes and faithful heart, Elisha knows the true odds. He knows that those "surrounding" him are in fact both contained and heavily outnumbered by the army of God, pictured again as arriving in chariots of fire pulled by horses of fire.

We do not always see those chariots. The fire of God is not always visible to us. We cannot always feel the heat. We often feel alone and defeated. We do not see a way out. We are like Elisha's servant.

Stories like this one in scripture are the antidote for hopelessness and defeatism. Elisha's faith in the unseen God and his ability to demonstrate the presence of the power of God teaches us that faith is greater than what we see. When we understand this truth, we can truly walk by faith, not by sight. (2 Corinthians 5:7)

Day 11 / April 20 – 2 Kings 8-10

The Beginning of the End
2 Kings 10:31

One historical purpose for the writing and preservation of Second Kings is to explain why God allows the coming destruction of Judah and Israel and the exile of God's people from the Promised Land. God has repeatedly promised, starting in Leviticus and in every book afterwards, that His hand of protection will withdraw from His people if they are not faithful to Him.

Jehu is perhaps the last chance. Anointed by God's prophet, Jehu quickly becomes a man of violence and destruction, condemned by the prophet for the massacre at Jezreel. (Hosea 1:4) Even this chosen king of Israel with a zeal for reversing many of the sins of his forerunners does not understand the way of God.

God has one-way covenants, like His promise to Noah never again to flood the earth, but God's covenant of salvation and obedience ("Walk before me and be blameless. I will confirm my covenant between me and you… As for you, you must keep my covenant.") is a two-way street. God blesses the people and gives them their Promised Land; in turn the people are to keep God's laws and obey His commands.

Over and over again we have seen the people fail. Over and over again we have seen God renew His covenant. This system is not working. There must be a new consequence to try to teach His people. Exile awaits.

Thank God that we live under a new and better covenant. Thank God that we are saved by grace through faith.

The High Places, However, Are Not Removed – 2 Kings 14:4

Even the good kings who otherwise try to follow God are strongly criticized for not removing the "high places." (Solomon, 1 Kings 3:3; Asa, 1 Kings 15:14; Jehoshaphat, 1 Kings 22:43; Joash, 2 Kings 12:3; Amaziah, 2 Kings 14:4; Azariah, 2 Kings 15:4; and Jotham, 2 Kings 15:35)

Why are these high places so repugnant to God?

The high places are pagan worship spots. The Canaanites and others whom God has helped the Israelites drive out of the Promised Land have worshiped in these places built in the hills. God has been clear that these high places are to be destroyed. (Deuteronomy 12:2) God wants His worship to be unique, defined by Him, in the manner and place of His choosing.

The kings of Israel and Judah seem incapable of getting rid of the high places. It is not clear if they simply do not look hard enough to find them, or if the people refuse to destroy them, or if the kings themselves like having them around. It does not matter.

The point is that Israel has drifted far away from God, and even those leaders who make an effort to do good and follow God are so distant from His heart that they do not understand what God really wants. God desires a lifestyle relationship of holy worship, and these kings are more interested in isolated actions. The people need a wholesale return to God, and that is unforeseeable. Exile is coming, and Israel is not stopping it.

Day 113 / April 22 – 2 Kings 15-17

Exile
2 Kings 17:22-23

And so, as warned and predicted, exile comes. The king of Assyria enters the Northern Kingdom of Israel and carries thousands upon thousands of God's chosen people away to a foreign land.

In case we do not yet understand, the writer of Kings lays out the theological and historical explanation for exile in verses 7-23 of chapter 17, ending with this pronouncement: "The Israelites persisted in all the sins of Jeroboam and did not turn away from them until the Lord removed them from His presence, as He had warned through all His servants the prophets." (2 Kings 17:22-23)

Sin, continuing and unrepented, leads to exile. There cannot be a clearer statement written anywhere than this plain truth of scripture.

Adam and Eve's sin leads to exile from the garden. The sin of the people of Noah's time leads to a flood that exiles them all from God and His creation. The sin of Egypt leads to plagues and death. Now, the sin of Israel leads to literal exile in the land of Assyria. It will not be the last time.

It is no different for us. When we sin, we repel ourselves from God's holiness. We separate ourselves from God. We are in exile. Paul says, in our sin we are separated from Christ, in exile from God's people just as the Gentiles were separate from Israel. (Ephesians 2:11-13)

Exiled people need a savior to lead them out of exile. We need the grace of God. We need Jesus.

Remnant
2 Kings 19:31

Even now there is hope, for exile is not complete. The Southern Kingdom of Judah is spared. Jerusalem is not entered by Assyria. Despite attack and ridicule, the remnant of God's people begins to rise.

How wonderfully hopeful it is that exile and derision do not have the final word.

The taunting words of the Assyrian king in 2 Kings 18 are familiar to us. We hear versions all the time, whether aloud or in our spirits: "On what are you basing this confidence of yours?... On whom are you depending?... Come now; make a bargain with my master... Do not let Hezekiah persuade you to trust in the Lord... Make peace with me and come out to me... Choose life and not death! Do not listen to Hezekiah, for he is misleading you when he says, 'The Lord will deliver us.' Has the god of any nation ever delivered his land from the hand of the king of Assyria?... How then can the Lord deliver Jerusalem from my hand?" (2 Kings 18:19-35)

This is the clever language of the enemy, whether from the mouth of the attacking king or from Satan himself. Isaiah, however, knows the truth. He tells good king Hezekiah not to be afraid of these mere words, for the Spirit of God is mighty. Hezekiah prays, and God's incredible promise of 2 Kings 19 provides hope to His people forever: "I will defend this city and save it."

Grace always comes.

Day 115 / April 24 – 2 Kings 20-22

I Have Found the Book of the Law
2 Kings 22:8

Can you imagine? Israel no longer has a copy of the Law. What Moses, and no doubt others, have so carefully gathered—the Pentateuch, the Torah, the first five books of the Old Testament—has been lost.

Picture the scene. During a major remodel of the temple, a priest walking a dusty hallway or sitting in a dank chamber stumbles upon a copy of the Book of the Law. He reads it, recognizes its importance, and passes it to the king's secretary, who in turn reads it to the king.

Josiah, an honorable king, understands the depths of the failures of Judah when measured against the commandments of scripture.

What is truly striking in this passage is the power of a copy of scripture.

Israel is in exile. Judah is tiny and remote. God's word has been largely forgotten, even by those kings who try to follow what they can understand of the will of the Lord. The way that God chooses to speak to these people under these circumstances is through a book. Suddenly, apparently randomly, a lone priest finds a long lost and forgotten copy of the Book of the Law.

Never underestimate the power of scripture. A Bible in a hotel room, on a library shelf, in a glove compartment, or on a dormitory desk can be—we know this because it repeatedly has been—the way God speaks to lost souls time and again. There is great joy when someone says "I have found the book!"

Day 116/April 25 – 2 Kings 23-25

Too Little Too Late
2 Kings 23:27

King Josiah desperately tries to reverse generations of wrong, but he simply cannot. God's judgment is postponed, but the word of the Lord has been spoken and will not be rescinded.

Exile comes even to Judah, not in Assyria this time as the exile of the people of the Northern Kingdom of Israel 136 years earlier have experienced, but now in Babylon. The sin of the people has finally and fully reached the end result laid out by God and warned by the prophets.

Too often, one person tries to reverse the paths established by many. Too often, the current of history sweeps away the efforts of brave and good individuals. Josiah is truly brave and good, but king though he is, he cannot withstand the onslaught. He is too little, too late.

God is not through with His chosen people. He has already promised that the remnant left will arise and that the promises made through the house of David will be fulfilled. Humanity's refusal to follow God has many consequences, and God lets us suffer the fallout from our choices, but God's will is always done.

What Josiah cannot do… what other brave and good individuals cannot do… Jesus can and does do. Jesus is the single person, God in man's flesh, who can and does withstand the incredible destruction that our sin creates. When our efforts are too little, too late, Jesus is the only who can and does bridge the gap of exile we have created.

Day 117/April 26 – 1 Chronicles 1-3

Genealogy Part One: Religious Identity
1 Chronicles 1-3

The books of Chronicles cover much of the same events as the books of Samuel and Kings, but their purpose is different. The writer of Samuel lays out the history and background of the house of David, and Kings provides the theological explanation for the people's entry into exile.

Chronicles is written later, for a people coming out of exile into the restored Promised Land. They need to be reminded of much of their history and their purpose. The goal of the Chronicler, then, will not be to focus nearly so much on the failures and sins of the kings of the past as it will be to highlight their accomplishments and to focus on the plan of God.

As the people of God come out of more than a century of exile, they must be asking themselves this question: "Are we still the chosen of God? Is there any remaining connection between the great patriarchs and us ragtag returners from exile?"

The Chronicler begins to answer these questions with the building block of history—the genealogy. He starts with Adam and works his way through Noah, Abraham, Isaac, Jacob (Israel), and Joseph. Through Joseph's brother Judah, the line is recounted all the way to David and Solomon and on to kings present at the time of the writing.

The message is clear: Your line runs through the heroes of the faith. God is continuing to do His work in and through you. You chosen people are connected to God.

Genealogy Part Two: Family Ties
1 Chronicles 4-6

The genealogies continue as the Chronicler makes a second point to the people of Israel: Not only are you connected to God all the way back to the beginning of time, but you are also connected to each other. Your families are critical.

Descendants of Judah are followed by descendants of Simeon, Reuben, Gad, Manasseh, and Levi. There are Asher, Naphtali, and Dan. Each of these, of course is a son (or a grandson, in the case of Manasseh) of Israel himself. Every person and clan described in the pages of these chapters is related to every other by a common bloodline. Cousins galore dot the horizon.

The genealogies are interrupted to discuss particular prayers answered by God. There is the prayer of Jabez (1 Chronicles 4:10) and the prayer of those Israelites fighting the Hagrites (1 Chronicles 5:20).

Otherwise, these chapters are strict genealogies, tedious and repetitive reminders of the order of Israel's society and the importance to each of them of family, their strong connection.

Family means different things to different people. You may think of your kinfolks, your aunts and uncles and grandparents, siblings and parents, spouse and children. You might, however, cringe at the memory of your natural family but embrace a family of friends who have taken you in. You may not even know your family of birth but call those who have adopted you your family.

Whatever your circumstance, God has ordained family to care for us and tie us together. Embrace your family.

Genealogy Part Three: Societal Bonds
1 Chronicles 9:2

The Chronicler has one more point to make with the genealogies to the returning people of God. They are connected to God, and they are connected with their families, but there is more: They are a bonded nation, a special, select people. The refugees who are coming back to the Promised Land are the children of Judah and Israel. They are the chosen people of God.

The Chronicler details the classes and divisions of those coming back, whether they be laity, priests, or office holders. In the nation of God's people, these have roles as gatekeepers, musicians, and temple servants.

Why is this societal connection so important? To the Israelites returning from exile, their identity as a distinct nation is critical. They have been chosen and given a unique role, and the Chronicler makes sure to assure them of it. The Chronicles will remind them of the victories of David, of the exploits of Solomon, and of the ways in which Israel and Judah have distinguished themselves.

The lesson for us may not be so much nationalistic in nature, for the twenty-first century sees scores of nations across the earth, all of whom include God's people. But the understanding that we are bound to those around us, at home and across the globe, who are also doing the word of God is vital—we work together and live together, and we thrive together. The Chronicler reminds us of God's gift of each other to each other. We need one another.

David's Mighty Men
1 Chronicles 11:10-11

Having finished the genealogies, the Chronicler now turns to a different kind of list, a sort of Hall of Fame of David's warriors, trustworthy subjects, and chief supporters. Moving from the theme of connections, the scripture now becomes a remembrance of the greatness that once was Israel… the greatness that perhaps the people can achieve again.

Looking back on history, even a spit-shined recounting that glosses over some of the negatives of the past can be an excellent motivational tool. Whether you are reflecting on the Founding Fathers of America, the leaders of the civil rights movement, or the original administration of your alma mater, it is to their good deeds and grand achievements you look, and you have no problem ignoring for the moment their tragic flaws and their failures. You know they made errors, but for now you are admiring. It is not dishonest; it is examination for a particular purpose.

So David, flawed and human as he was, nonetheless serves as an inspiration and a role model then and now. He was a man who motivated unswerving loyalty from the best and brightest around him. He was a king who brought great growth and success to his people. He was a follower of God whose writings continue to stir our spirits today.

And his "mighty men," his scores of steadfast lieutenants, are also to be admired. They demonstrate devotion, dedication, and accomplishment on scales we can all seek to emulate.

Find your godly leaders and do likewise.

Day 121 / April 30 – 1 Chronicles 13-15

Hearing God
1 Chronicles 14:14

David, like Abraham and Noah and Moses and Samuel before him, and like many prophets after him, speaks to God and hears a distinct answer. We are not told whether David hears an audible voice, but what is plain in this scripture is that David knows what God has said to him.

However God speaks to us today—through scripture, prayer, the indwelling Holy Spirit, a sermon, a sunset, a song—recognition that God has spoken is only a beginning. Knowing that God has spoken inexorably leads to recognizing that He has spoken to you, and in turn that knowledge leads to understanding of what God has said. Admitting that you "hear a voice" is frightening to some.

Are you willing to admit God speaks to you and you have some idea what He is saying? You may not understand everything God wants for you—indeed, none of us is capable of fully understanding the plans of the mind of the unfathomable God of the universe. On the other hand, we all understand part of it. Perhaps your understanding is rudimentary—God wants you to love Him and to love other people. If you are not doing well with what you know—perhaps the Ten Commandments are not being followed in your life—then it is understandable that God may not be telling you more.

But God is definitely telling you something. Simple or complex, His next step for your life is there, spoken clearly for you to hear.

Listen.

May

Great Is the Lord
1 Chronicles 16:25

The David of First Chronicles is the Psalmist David, writing praise in commanding verse that speaks majestically of the exploits and character of God.

David knows the power of history, and so he reminds the people to "remember the wonders He has done, His miracles, and the judgments He has pronounced." (1 Chronicles 16:12)

David knows the awesomeness of eternity and unsearchable vastness, so he instructs the people to watch and listen as "the heavens resound" and "the sea resounds" and "the trees of the forest sing for joy before the Lord." (1 Chronicles 16:31-33)

David knows the throne of God in the world, so he demands that the people "declare His glory among the nations, His marvelous deeds among all peoples, for great is the Lord and most worthy of praise." (1 Chronicles 16:24-25)

David knows the source of all the good in the world, so he tells his people to "give thanks to the Lord, for He is good; His love endures forever." (1 Chronicles 16:34)

If you have been reading through scripture now for four months, for 122 days, then you have seen repeatedly the wonders of God, His miracles and judgments. You have witnessed the hand of the Creator and the heart of the Father. You understand the earth and skies are subject to Him. You know God's place, and you comprehend just how much you, and we all, owe to the goodness of God, for indeed, grace always comes.

Great is the Lord. Give thanks.

Day 123/May 2 – 1 Chronicles 19-22

Devote and Build
1 Chronicles 22:18-19

Is worship our ultimate goal? Is the end game of following God to present constant praise?

Recognition of God's power, mighty works, and gracious gifts leads naturally, as we saw in yesterday's reading, to praise and thanksgiving. Now, we see the next natural step. David says: Is not the Lord your God with you? And has He not granted you rest on every side? For He has handed the inhabitants of the land over to me, and the land is subject to the Lord and to His people. Now devote your heart and soul to seeking the Lord your God. Begin to build the sanctuary of the Lord.

Understanding what God has done demands devotion of heart and soul, and it demands action. Praise and thanksgiving and reveling in our relationship with God are right and good and necessary, but they are not the end game. Praise, thanksgiving, and our bond with God are followed by devotion of heart and soul and obedience to God's word just as summer follows spring.

Loving through doing, practicing what we preach, saved by grace through faith to do His good works—all of these phrases are central to the Biblical message of grace. God gifts us because He loves us, and He gifts the world with us because He loves the world. He inhabits our worship and appreciates our devotion, but He commands more. Our devotion and commitment must translate into service.

So, now, devote your heart and soul, and get to work.

Every Morning and Evening
1 Chronicles 23:30

Levites have wide-ranging duties as assistants to the priests, from room custodians to unleavened bread preparers.

The Levites have another task. They are "to stand every morning to thank and praise the Lord." They do the same every evening.

Think about the regularity of this thanksgiving and praise. Every morning. Every evening. Good days and bad. Whether the Levites feel thankful or not. Even if they cannot think of one thing for which to praise God. Still, they must stand to thank and praise God. Good times and bad. Rain or shine. Like clockwork.

Now, think about having this duty as part of your job description. A Levite does not simply praise and thank God because he wants to; he has to. David, under the influence of God, has required it of them all. Like a sentry who walks a prescribed beat, the Levite takes his place and fulfills his duty.

Perhaps regular thanksgiving and praise—even when we do not feel grateful or think we have much to praise God about—are beneficial. Perhaps understanding praise and thanksgiving as a requirement will occasionally prompt us to our knees.

In the long run, our praise and thanksgiving must come voluntarily in response to the overwhelming gifts of God. Sometimes, however, especially on days when our scripture reading is tedious and our ability to fight temptation is waning, remembering praise and thanksgiving as a duty may be the only way to press on.

Some days, we just need to be Levites.

Day 125/May 4 – 1 Chronicles 27-29

We Cannot Outgive God
1 Chronicles 29:14

Everything we have comes from God. Even when we raise funds and collect our best things to present to God, we realize that everything we are giving Him has come from Him in the first place.

You may not agree. After all, you are a self-made person. You have worked, studied, and earned. You have perhaps inherited from hard-working parents or received support from helpers.

Saying that it all started with God is not to deny your hard work, your family's generosity, or your benefactors' achievements. The temple in Jerusalem includes wood from surrounding Lebanon, gold from as far away as Sheba, and the sweat equity and material gifts from all over the Promised Land. There can be no question of the labor and generosity and pure devotion that will go into its construction.

What does David mean when he says that building this extravagant temple is simply giving back to God? Another way to ask it is this: What has God truly given us?

Life. Ability. Understanding. Opportunity. Creation. Raw materials. Health. Helpers. Desire. A sense of generosity. Energy. Talents. Spiritual Gifts. Friends. Scripture. His abiding presence. God's calling, leading voice.

And on top of these, God has sent people and situations into our path that have resulted in money in our pockets. Education and jobs and gifts have come our way.

Do not deny the gifts of God. You can never match them, earn them, or live up to them. You can only give back and pay forward.

Day 126/May 5 – 2 Chronicles 1-4

The Curtain of God
2 Chronicles 3:14

The most sacred part of Solomon's temple is the Most Holy Place, called the Holy of Holies. This area, where the Ark of the Covenant is to be kept, is guarded by gilded cherubim and separated from the people by a massive curtain.

The curtain is both beautiful and heavy. A cubit is approximately eighteen inches; this curtain is 900 square feet.

This curtain is meant to separate God from the people. The Ark—the presence of God—is on one side. The worshipers are on the other. Only the high priest can cross the threshold of the Holy of Holies once the Ark is placed there, entering before God to make sacrifice and offer the prayers of Israel. The rest of the people must remain on the other side of the curtain.

The curtain becomes more than a piece of cloth. It is a symbol of the Old Testament system of God's working through the priests. Before the coming of the Son of God and the indwelling Holy Spirit, God works at arm's length from most of Israel.

And then, one day, something happens. When Jesus is crucified, the curtain of the temple is "torn from top to bottom." (Mark 15:38) The top of this thirty-foot-high curtain is beyond reach, so the split does not begin with manmade hands. This symbol of the old ways, this separator of God from His people, is ripped in two.

Symbol of all symbols.

God will be separate from His people no more.

Day 127/May 6 – 2 Chronicles 5-7

If My People
2 Chronicles 7:14

Renewal comes about differently from salvation. It is still a product of the grace of God, but God asks something of us first.

In telling what is now the ancient history of Solomon for the people, the Chronicler is writing to and for those descendants of the great king who are returning from exile, wondering what lies ahead of them and whether God still cares about them. The Chronicler chooses this story of Solomon's heartfelt prayer in 2 Chronicles 6 and God's response in 2 Chronicles 7 to teach returning Israel that there can be renewal. God is ready to take you back. Yes, you who are already and forever Israel, you can once again live in harmony with the living God.

But only if you are willing to do so on God's terms. You, who chose exile, must now make another choice. If my people will…

…"Humble themselves." Bow the head and acknowledge that our way does not work, that God is God and we are not. Confess our failures.

…"Pray." Talk and listen to God. Seek His leadership and His will.

…"Seek my face." Follow the God of Abraham and Isaac, Israel and Joseph, Moses and Joshua, Ruth and David and Solomon himself.

…"Turn from their wicked ways." Stop their sins. Obey God's laws. The New Testament word for this is repent.

Then, gracious renewal comes. Exile is over. Gracious healing and the smile of God will wash over His people.

Then… and now.

Choices
2 Chronicles 10:13-14

Rehoboam, like his father before him, has a choice to make. Solomon has chosen wisely, and his choice will be revered forever.

Rehoboam chooses poorly. Rejecting the good advice that will sustain his rule and give him a chance to follow in the footsteps of his father Solomon and his grandfather David, Rehoboam embarks on the path that leads to civil war and the split of the kingdom of Israel.

And so it is with us. God blesses, follows through on his covenants, leads us to Promised Lands flowing with milk and honey, defeats our enemies, and gives us His law. Then God leaves these things in our hands, asking us to follow Him and keep His commandments, but allowing us the freedom to do as we please.

Sometimes, we are Solomon, choosing wisdom and discernment and asking God to show us how best to live.

Too often, we are Rehoboam, following immaturity and violence and throwing away all that God has laid before us. We choose poorly.

God loves us too much to take away that free will. Automatons that obey without option and follow due to programming are neither obeying nor following. They are simply operating according to their maker's design for only as long as they are wound up. God, who inhabits the praise of His people, seeks the fellowship and honor of those who choose Him over the advice of the foolish, the allure of the world, and the quick fix of personal power.

Choose well.

Day 129/May 8 – 2 Chronicles 12-15

Ambushing God
2 Chronicles 13:13-17

Like many Old Testament stories, the story of this battle between the armies of Jeroboam and Abijah, son of Rehoboam, foreshadows its end to those who understand the power of God. This is an internal struggle between two divisions of the chosen people. Abijah stands on the hill, reminding of God's promises to the family of David, and warning the enemy that while they outnumber his army two to one, his is the army of God. Jeroboam's troops have the trappings of success, but they have evicted the priests of God.

While Abijah pleads for peace, Jeroboam's forces sneak up from behind. The ambush is on.

Jeroboam's troops have numbers, high ground, and tactical surprise. Abijah's troops have the priests blowing trumpets and soldiers crying out to God for help. Even Rehoboam has not caused God to abandon His people.

Guess who routs whom?

This story is not a promise of military defeat for every army that does not call on the name of the Lord, for history belies any such interpretation. Rather, read this scripture in the context of growing civil war between factions of the Israelite nation: This story reminds us that for us, the people of God, our ways can never supersede the power and will of the Lord. Among God's people, human insight, strategy, force, and accumulation are nothing in comparison to what God has in mind. When we attack from behind and hope to catch God napping, the end result is loss, flight, and defeat.

The Battle Belongs to the Lord
2 Chronicles 20:15

This is another story that should not be read as a tactical guide for modern warfare. God makes no promise that every military skirmish can be won by laying down weapons and singing.

What this story teaches is this: As we face each conflict of life, we must recognize that God has a way out for us if we choose to follow it, no matter how unlikely His way may appear.

Building an ark mystifies a man who has never seen rain. Throwing your rod on the floor in front of Pharaoh is a foolish idea. Marching around Jericho seven times blowing trumpets hardly seems to Joshua's troops to be the recipe for success. Pouring water on the altars is not Elijah's first choice for getting a fire to start.

Jehoshaphat is given the key when he is told, "Do not be afraid or discouraged…. for the battle is not yours, but God's."

The New Testament amplifies this idea for us. Paul tells us our struggle is not against flesh and blood but against the spiritual forces of evil, so we must be strong in the Lord and put on the armor of God, for then we can stand firm. (Ephesians 6:10-14) John tells us that the One in us is greater than the one in the world. (1 John 4:4)

Jehoshaphat's story teaches us something else: Praise the Lord. Give thanks to the Lord. For His mercy and love endure forever.

Battles will come. Sing your song. Stand firm.

Day 131/May 10 – 2 Chronicles 21-24

The World's Worst Obituary
2 Chronicles 21:20

"He passed away, to no one's regret."

For some, life has left them, in the words of "Les Misérables," at the bottom of the heap. We should weep for those who die alone, and we should do our level best to make sure that nobody else has to live that way.

Jehoram is no Eleanor Rigby, dying alone in a church to be buried along with her name. This death without regret is not because of homelessness, abandonment, or to the lack of caring of those around.

This death without regret, instead, is different. Jehoram dies without regret not because he is unknown or lonely but because he is unlovable. He is a truly terrible, despicable man. The world at large and the nation of Judah are better off without him.

The death of this thirty-two year-old otherwise forgettable king is instructive. How can someone of such position and power manage to lead a short life that alienates everyone around him? How can the memory of the king of Jerusalem be cast aside before his body is cold? How can a life turn literally everyone's affection away?

It is a stark lesson. Not a lesson on the legacy of memory, for once we are gone, there is nothing we can do about that. No, this is a lesson about the responsibility of living, for while we are here, we can shape our place in the world and in the minds of those around us.

Who will care when you are gone?

Day 132/May 11 – 2 Chronicles 25-28

The Gods of the World
2 Chronicles 25:15

Amaziah is given a great victory by God. He should learn the lesson that his God is mighty and is worthy of worship. The last thing he should do is adopt the practices of the losers.

Instead, Amaziah gathers up the idols of the conquered foe and brings them home, bowing to them and burning sacrifices to them. God's angry response is, "Why do you consult this people's gods, which could not save their own people from your hand?"

God's response makes sense to us as we read this history, for we have scripture open and are prepared to hear a word from the Lord. But what about in our daily lives, when the Bible is on the shelf and we live in our busy, mundane worlds?

Do you know churches who have had God work through them to great effect, influencing their communities and growing, only to come to resemble the world around them? Do you know individuals who have had a real experience with God and have heartily followed the Lord's will to meet and work with people who really need God, only to come out of the experience acting just like the people whom once they were committed to help save?

The world is alluring. Its desires are contagious. Its pretty things are appealing. Even when we move out with the strength of God, the temptation to forget whose we are is real.

Remember what makes sense to you now. Why consult those "gods," which cannot save?

Day 133/May 12 – 2 Chronicles 29-31

And So He Prospered
2 Chronicles 31:21

How tempting it is to read a story like Hezekiah's and create what has come to be called the "prosperity gospel." Hezekiah purifies the temple, reinstates the observation of the Passover, organizes tithes and offerings to God, and in all things undertakes service and obedience. And the Chronicler records that Hezekiah prospers.

In fact, the Chronicler says "and so, Hezekiah prosper[s]," and we long to interpret that *so* to mean *therefore* instead of meaning *in that condition* or *in the way or manner indicated*. Our innermost need seeks the promise that obedience will result in endless blessing.

Our humanity wants a formula. Do good so God will bless. We flock to those promising our best lives right now.

There are certainly some Bible verses that can be read out of context as a promise of health and wealth to the faithful.

A full reading of scripture tells us differently. Noah is no sooner off the ark than his sons are ridiculing him. Joseph is sold into slavery and falsely accused of rape. Moses is utterly unsuccessful at convincing Pharaoh. Paul has a thorn in the flesh. John is exiled. Jesus is crucified.

A simple look around the world tells us differently. Billy Graham has Parkinson's. Innocents are killed by drunk drivers, disease, and poverty every day.

Hezekiah follows God, and Hezekiah prospers.

Job follows God, and Job is afflicted.

We follow, serve, and obey because those are the right things to do, irrespective of the results. Do not believe otherwise.

Along Comes Sennacherib
2 Chronicles 32:1

The Chronicler, who has spent three chapters talking about Hezekiah's obedience, tells us as 2 Chronicles 32 opens that after all Hezekiah has faithfully done, Sennacherib king of Assyria comes and attacks anyway.

It is a fact of life: even for faithful Hezekiahs, there is a Sennacherib. Regardless of how good you are, how faithful your service, and how complete your obedience, the world has evil confrontation waiting for you. In fact, experience demonstrates that attack often comes because we are faithful.

Fortunately, Chapter 32 does not end with verse 1. The fact that an assault is coming is not the end of the story; it is almost always only the beginning. Faithful Hezekiah is not thrown off by the idea of attack; instead he faces it with prayer and continued trust in God.

Sennacherib laughs at Hezekiah's reliance on God and attempts intimidation and indignation in the face of faith. Hezekiah and Isaiah, however, cry out to God in prayer, and the Lord sends an angel.

Sennacherib has no answer for this avenging messenger of God. He withdraws.

There are two clear lessons.

First, no matter how faithful we are, we will be ill-treated. Challenges and evil are in this world, and they will find us out. They will mock our faith and bully our friends.

Second, while you cannot escape the onslaught, you can overcome it. God is still on your side, and His angel is ready to overwhelm the enemy. Faith, prayer, and steadfast obedience still win out.

Day 135/May 14 – 2 Chronicles 36-Ezra 3

Perspective
2 Chronicles 36:21

The end of the Chronicles speaks from a celestial perspective. As awful as exile has been, exile is not the end of the story or even the overwhelming landmark of this history. The Chronicler can look back and find blessing even in the worst of times.

The seventy years of exile is a time of "Sabbath rest" for the land. The penalty carried out through Nebuchadnezzar runs its course, for the people's sin has significant consequence. But while they are in exile, the Promised Land waits and reenergizes and is ready for the return of God's people.

Miraculously, Cyrus becomes king. He has some recognition for God, and he is ready to send God's people home.

Examination from an after-the-fact cosmic outlook does not make the bad things good. Exile is horrible, no matter how one looks at it. Perspective does, however, allow us to look beyond the catastrophe of the moment—or even of the decades—to see that what God has put in place stays in place, waiting until we are prepared to return.

This viewpoint does not require us to conclude that God has sadistically sent all the bad things our way as a part of some unknowable "plan." Indeed, Kings and Chronicles have taught us that exile follows our choices.

Perspective tells us that our failures do not derail God. God's promise takes a Sabbath, and when it is time, miracles happen, a Cyrus appears, and we find ourselves once again coming home.

Grace always comes.

Enemies or Neighbors?
Ezra 4:3

The people of God have returned from exile to Jerusalem and have set about to rebuild the temple. This is a time of new beginnings, of recommitment to the work of the Lord.

An offer of help comes from those who are viewed as enemies. The people of Israel reject the offer, claiming that those who are making it "have no part" with them in building the temple. As a result, the enemies are offended and set out to frustrate the work. By the end of Chapter 4, the work has come to a complete stop.

It is tempting for modern readers to commend the reaction of these Israelites for recognizing these "helpers" as wolves in sheep's clothing who seek to infiltrate with detestable worship practices and sinfulness that got the people sent off into exile in the first place.

That may be the right view, but... what if help from neighbors is an opportunity, not only for manpower and materials but also for alliance? What if this is a chance to influence people who need to know the ways of God? What if our perceived enemies are actually potential neighbors?

Ezra does not tell us for sure. Still, it is worth asking: Are we too quick to retreat into pious fortresses and reject those around us who may in fact represent an occasion to help? Do we turn up our noses at those with whom we can share the love of God?

Sometimes, "insight" is really missed opportunity.

Day 137/May 16 – Ezra 8–Nehemiah 1

Shame
Ezra 9:6-8

Do you ever find yourself ashamed?

Ezra knows how undeserving the people are to be back in Jerusalem, seat of Solomon and center of the Promised Land. When Ezra learns how the people are already returning again to the detestable forbidden practices of their ancestors, he is appalled.

Are you ever aghast at your sin? Do you sometimes examine yourself and how you act and find yourself ashamed?

God certainly does not intend for us to live a life of shame. God's love for us is deep and powerful, and He wants good things for us. Getting from here to there, however, sometimes causes us to weep over our own failures.

Or, it should.

It is not fashionable to be ashamed. We live in a world of therapy and recovery, of upbeat recommitment and looking to the future. All of those are good things, but they are not the only worthwhile things.

God has laid out a perfect plan for us, but we too often feel that we know better. We put ourselves on the throne, dictating right and wrong, choosing to follow whims and ambitions, drives and playthings. We make a mess of what God has planned.

We should be ashamed.

The Old Testament practice of pulling hair out of one's beard is a metaphor. We need not stay in sackcloth and ashes. Still, recognizing, and being appalled by, the chaos we have made of things is a healthy way to begin to return to where God would lead.

Wall-Builders and Shield-Bearers
Nehemiah 4:16

The temple work now expands to rebuilding the walls of Jerusalem. Nehemiah comes with an official royal imprimatur from the king and with help from other nations, and the walls of Jerusalem begin to rise again.

Local enemies begin to carry out their own plans to interfere with the work. Rhetoric and annoyance soon give way to outright attack, and God, working through Nehemiah, meets the threats so that the good work will continue.

Nehemiah splits the workers: half continue building the wall, and half protect the work with shields and bows.

There is plenty of work to be done in the name of God, and it is not all the same. Some of us are called to build, to create, to make new what has been torn down, to help the kingdom rise to heights where it belongs. Others of us are protectors, not necessarily having our own "product" to show but rather filling crucial roles so that the builders can continue.

Paul says some of us are evangelists and teachers, while others fulfill roles of prayer and hospitality. There are a few who lead worship and prophesy, and there are many others who administer and support.

You may be a wall-builder. If so, build with all your heart. You will produce a wall that all God's people can glory in. You may, however, be a shield-bearer. Your role is equally important, even if you have no "harvest" to demonstrate. The work of God is done by us all.

Day 139/May 18 – Nehemiah 6-8

Listen, Celebrate, and Serve
Nehemiah 8:12

The scene played out in Chapter 8 is compelling. Many Israelites are discovering the Law of God for the first time. Ezra reads what they have never heard, and then he—along with Nehemiah and the priests—help the people learn what it means.

Sounds a lot like what happens in churches across the world, doesn't it? The scripture is read, the law of God is proclaimed, and teachers and ministers explain and interpret for those who do not understand.

Then what happens? When church is over, when the Sunday School classes and Bible studies and Christian formation small groups have concluded, what is the result?

For Israel, the results are twofold: (1) they celebrate; and (2) they serve. They feast and make merry, and then they look outward. They serve their neighbors who are unprepared or less fortunate by providing them food. They serve God by seeking to obey, down to the details of building and living in booths as they understand the writings of Leviticus.

When we proclaim God's words, teach His commandments, and interpret His scriptures, we may well not always get it right. We may waste time trying to obey rules He never laid out. We are human, and we are fallible.

But God nonetheless takes joy when hearing His law matters to His children. When we listen and try to follow, we show that what God says matters to us. Do not walk away from scripture the same as you were before you heard it.

What We Learn from History
Nehemiah 9:31

Chapter 9 is an incredible synopsis of the Old Testament narrative of God and His people to this point in history. Stories of creation, the covenant with Abram, divine victory over the peoples found in the Promised Land, triumph over Pharaoh, pillars of cloud and fire, and the sin of the people are recounted.

But something is different now. God's revelation is progressing. Now, with the passage of time and the return from exile, the priests layer onto this familiar history a learned, mature view of God.

They recognize God as a God of love. Just as we see grace and mercy in these early Old Testament stories, even when those words are not used, the priests now see it too. In this extended review of God's role in history, we see repeated verses that say things like "You are righteous" (verse 8); "You are a forgiving God, gracious and compassionate, slow to anger and abounding in love" (verse 17); "You are a gracious and merciful God" (verse 31).

These thoughts have appeared sporadically in the early books of scripture, but we find here a real turning point. The children are beginning to grow up. They have enough history behind them—covenant, slavery, rescue, plenty, failure, exile, restoration—that they can recount it and learn from it. And when they do, they recognize the goodness of the Lord.

Take a moment to remember your own history. See that the Lord is compassionate and merciful. Be thankful that grace always comes.

Day 141/May 20 – Nehemiah 12-13

Celebration
Nehemiah 12:43

There is great rejoicing in Jerusalem. The wall has been re-built. The exiles have returned home. The people of God are once again in the Promised Land, in the City of David, at the Temple of Solomon, learning the Word of God.

And the sound of their rejoicing can be heard far away.

What is worth celebrating in your life?

For some, the cause for festivity is plain. Are you where you ought to be? Has God brought you out of the exile that you walked yourself into? Have you accomplished a mighty feat? Are you and your family learning the meaning of scripture together?

Are you celebrating? Are you reveling in these blessings that God has for you?

For others, you know you are not where you ought to be, whether it is your own fault or not. You find yourself left in a pit by illness, or poverty, or divorce, or cruelty. You may have dug your own rut through inattention.

And you wonder what you have to celebrate.

Think again.

God is reaching out to you. Scripture is there for you to learn and understand. There are walls for even you to build – maybe little walls at first, but nonetheless something you can do to help someone else. Your chance for mighty feats awaits.

There is a Promised Land for you too. God has proven over and over that He does not forget His people in exile. The sound of your rejoicing will be heard far away.

Day 142/May 21 – Esther 1-4

Ready
Esther 4:14

Esther 4:14 is both inspiring and challenging: "If you remain silent at this time, relief and deliverance for the Jews will arise from another place, but you and your father's family will perish. And who knows but that you have come to royal position for such a time as this."

Don't miss either of the points here:

First, God will deliver His people, with Esther or without her. God's bidding is going to be accomplished. If you are not willing to answer His call and participate in His acts of grace, the loss will be yours, not God's. God will still do what He is going to do—the question is whether you will choose to be a part of it or choose to go your own way and risk personal oblivion, irrelevance, and destruction.

Second, you never know when you will find yourself exactly where God needs and wants you—indeed, where God has placed you—just so you can be in position for "such a time as this." Esther is in place because of her fetching figure that wins a beauty contest and apparently because of her feminine wiles. Neither Esther nor Mordecai has had a previous revelation from God about what is in store for her. God has sent her no stone tablets.

Esther, nonetheless, makes the right choice. She understands the gravity of the situation, and she somehow senses her opportunity to be the vessel of God.

God's work will be done. Choose to join in.

Day 143/May 22 – Esther 5-10

Courage as God Works through Us
Esther 5:1

Easter 4 ends with Esther's stirring commitment, "If I perish, I perish."

If the story were to end there, we would miss so much. Heartwarming promises are nice, but actually getting up the next morning and carrying out the pledge is real courage.

Think about Esther's situation.

She is one of dozens of women in the palace, valued only for the physical amusement of the king, a man who has had his last queen banished and deposed simply because she refused to come when he called.

She is a Jew, and the king's right-hand man Haman has persuaded the king to order the extermination of her entire race.

The king has not requested her for a conjugal visit in a month.

Irrespective of all that, the law is that no one may approach the king unbidden without risking death.

In this, the only book of scripture that never mentions God, Esther demonstrates a character of courage that reflects how God works through His people. She has no business taking on the task of approaching the king under these circumstances, but she is moved by something greater than just the wishes of her uncle. Something more even than following through on a promise.

Esther is a part of the working of the hand of God. God's name never appears, but His working is everywhere in this book. These events lead to the celebration of Purim—the Jews' recognition of the delivering hand of God protecting His people.

Day 144/May 23 – Job 1-4

Job: Act I
Job 2:6

Theatre is a literary device that often teaches what an essay or a speech cannot.

The Book of Job reads like a play. Act I, often called the prologue, is set in the supernatural realms. Act II is an extended discussion among Job and his visiting friends. Act III is Job's final ultimate dialog with God.

Act I consists primarily of God's discussion with Satan. God affirmatively allows Satan to abuse Job, but God does not give Satan permission to take Job's life.

There are many lessons here, but at least three are crucial.

God is in control of the entire situation. Satan does not sneak behind God's back, nor does Satan overpower God to abuse Job. Instead, Satan clearly has to obtain permission from God to be allowed to do his dirty work. God's permissions stop short of allowing Satan to kill Job.

The hardships and disasters that are about to befall Job will not be deserved and will not come because Job has sinned. To the contrary, Job stands out because of his blamelessness. The troubles come anyway.

God's reasoning is not explained. He allows Satan to work, but He does not say why, nor does this scripture explain God's motive.

There is much more that this book will teach us, but we have to start with these three points.

Learn well. God is in control, but we often do not understand why He allows what He allows. God is God, and we are not.

Day 145/May 24 – Job 5-8

Job's Complaint
Job 6:2-3

Do we offend God when we put voice to our distress? Job complains, bitterly and loudly, with metaphor and poetry and extreme symbolism. He begs for his death and protests about his friends. Job announces that he "will complain in the bitterness of my soul." (Job 7:11)

There are some who teach that we followers of the almighty God should never express our problems, never notice bad things happening to us, never voice aloud the pain that is in our souls. Scripture teaches differently. To be sure, grumbling about our work for God is fruitless (Philippians 2:14), but honest voicing of real suffering is something different.

It is not only blameless Job who cries aloud in his distress:

Jeremiah asks why the wicked prosper. (Jeremiah 12:1-4)

The Psalmist writes of the exiled people who wept in Babylon. (Psalm 137:1)

The prophet Habakkuk complains about the violence and destruction around him. (Habakkuk 1:1-4)

Paul protests the opposition of the Jews. (Acts 18:6)

Jesus asks that the cup of death be taken from Him, and he is dismayed that His closest friends cannot stay awake with Him in His time of need. (Matthew 26:39-40)

In each instance, God has an answer, just as He will ultimately answer Job. Those answers are not always what the sufferers think they need, but they always come. In the meantime, though, God is big enough to handle our distress. Crying out to God is an important part of being His child.

Day 146/May 25 – Job 9-12

False Promise
Job 11:13-17

It is the universal lie: good things always must happen to good
people.

Here, in the (perhaps) well-meaning but nonetheless witless
philosophizing of Zophar, we find the heart of the false message:
"If you devote your heart to God... if you put away the sin that is
in your hand and allow no evil to dwell in your tent, then... you will
surely forget your trouble... Life will be brighter than noonday."

The dangerous—yet somehow compelling—notion in this message is this: If you are good, then only good will happen to you. If
bad things are happening to you, therefore, you must be bad.

The question "Why do bad things happen to good people?" is
built on this same false notion: that being "good" should insulate us
from bad things.

We live in a world where bad things happen. Why shouldn't they
happen to good people? Do we really believe our goodness should
inoculate us?

Remember the dramatic structure of Job. Act I made clear that
the catastrophes that befall Job are in spite of his blamelessness, not
because of any failure. Satan is attacking Job to make a supernatural
point, not because Job in any way "deserves" it.

Job's friends have no idea what is going on here. They repeat
what they have heard, that blessings follow goodness and that afflic-
tion must be a sign of sin.

Do not believe the lie. You cannot, and you will not, guarantee
earthly happiness by the way you live.

Day 147/May 26 – Job 13-16

True Commitment
Job 13:15

Like His friends, Job does not understand what is happening. He knows he has not sinned in a way to deserve the devastation that befalls him, but he believes, as they do, that the bad things are coming from God. Unaware of Satan's machinations God has allowed, Job perceives that God is the source of the disasters in his life.

Job is wrong about that fact, but he is right about something much bigger. Job's great statement of faith and commitment stands out from the seemingly endless back and forth between him and his friends: "Though He slay me, yet will I hope in Him."

It is relatively easy to believe in God when things are going well, especially when you believe that the blessings in your life are flowing from God. Why not jump on the bandwagon of the blessing giver? When you are promised your best life now if you place your faith in God, when the rich and popular promise riches and popularity, it is not hard to sign on to that deal.

What about when things are going badly? When you, like Job, have lost everything and there is no light at the end of the tunnel, are you still willing to place you hope in God?

God is the creator of heaven and earth, the giver of life and law, the sustainer of the universe. For Job, that is enough. Job places his hope in God, regardless of his own personal circumstances.

What about you?

Day 148/May 27 — Job 17-20

I Know That My Redeemer Lives
Job 19:25

It is the seminal statement of faith in the Old Testament, rivaling Peter's Great Confession in the New Testament ("You are the Christ, the Son of the Living God." Matthew 16:16) as the greatest Biblical testimony. That it comes out of Job's horrific circumstances makes this declaration all the more crucial.

Job is no closer to an explanation for what is happening to him than he was before. His friends torment him with accusations of wrongdoing. His wife wants him to curse God. Job does not understand why his life has fallen apart. His sadness is perhaps encapsulated in verse 17: "My breath is offensive to my wife; I am loathsome to my own brothers."

What could be worse? Job has nowhere to turn, no one to love him, no explanation for the cataclysm that his life has become. He is, literally, ruined.

Yet Job knows he has a living redeemer, and he knows that he will see Him in the end. He knows that his redeemer will be the last one standing. He wants to record his words of faith in rock forever.

Job endures because of his faith. The Book of James discusses the perseverance and endurance of Job (James 5:11), and some translations use the word "patience" to discuss that endurance, but it is a mistake to dwell on "the patience of Job." Far brighter than Job's patience, however, shines Job's faith. Job endures and perseveres because he knows what he knows. He will not be shaken.

Day 149/May 28 – Job 21-24

When God Hides
Job 23:8-10

Taking off in a storm, airplanes rise above dark clouds.

God is everywhere. The Psalmist says we cannot flee the presence of God, even if we travel to the far side of the sea. (Psalm 139:7-10)

While we cannot dodge God, sometimes God seems to escape us. Like Job, we are sure that all will be right once we are in the presence of the Almighty, and we look up, down, left, right, east, west, north, and south; yet we cannot seem to find God.

Often, we have built walls through which we cannot see God. Our guilt and our shame blind us to what is right before us. Sometimes, we have purposefully run so far from what is right that we have lost the ability to perceive the living God.

But sometimes, we, like Job, have done nothing to shun God, and yet God chooses not to make His presence obvious. We do not know why. In this drama, God stands back and lets Job withstand Satan's tests. In our lives, we may never understand why God appears to leave us stranded.

Like that plane's pilot who finds the blue skies beyond the menacing rain clouds, we ultimately learn that God has been with us all along. We know that like blue skies above the rain clouds, God has been there all along. Still, during the storm, we struggle for just a glimpse.

Trusting God in the dark is hard. Job struggles for answers, as do we. Keep reading to the end, for God has not left Job, and He has not left you.

Day 150/May 29 – Job 25-28

Admitting We Do Not Understand
Job 28:12-13

When you cannot understand, focus on what you know. Job has lost any sense of the omnipresence of God, and he does not comprehend the justice of God. Still, Job clings to God's authority and God's wisdom.

Job is able to observe the mighty power and sovereignty of God. He sees the horizon across the waters, notes the suspension of the world in space, and scrutinizes the wonders of the world; seeing these, Job identifies the dominance and command of God. Job wishes for unseen justice, but he cannot dismiss the creator and sustainer of everything around him.

Job then turns to the concept of understanding, especially in the face of the lines of debate reasoning continually made by his three friends. Job does not rebut them point for point, for he realizes that he does not have to. None of them—not Job and not his friends—can understand how the world works and why God does what He does because they are all mortal, and such acumen does not lie in the world of humankind. God alone understands His ways.

Job is onto something. In fact, he is beginning to point to the answer to his own questions. Wisdom cannot be found on earth or bought with what we treasure and sell. True perception lies only in the mind of God, for he laid out the ways of the world, and only He views the ends of everything under heaven.

Job clings to the almighty wisdom of God.

Day 151/May 30 – Job 29-32

Job Ends His Defense
Job 31:35

Job's last best statement is, sadly, to announce what he is not. At the end of his discourses and speeches, what Job has to say is this: "I have done nothing wrong."

In chapter 31, he offers a laundry list of sins he has not committed—sexual lust, dishonest business dealings, marital unfaithfulness, unjust treatment of his workers, mistreatment of the poor, greed, worship of false gods, gloating over misfortunes of others, lack of hospitality, cover-up of sin—as his final defense. This list is positive in the sense that it shows Job's loyalty to his understanding of what is right, and it is negative in that Job's best defense of himself lies only in what he has not done.

Even righteous Job has much to learn. Not doing wrong is of course to be commended, but simply avoiding bad actions is not the goal of life. God wants more. God wants what we are, not what we are not. God seeks what we can be, not just what we do not do. God wants our beings, not our mere avoidance of wrong.

Job's defense is true, but it is not enough. Job has walked uprightly and shunned open sin, but as he repeatedly says, he does not know where to find God. He has no relationship with God. Job lives under God's blessings and pays lip service to the creator, but he does not yet know God.

The answer is coming, and Job will be overwhelmed. Keep reading.

Day 152/May 31 – Job 33-36

Far Be It from God to Do Wrong
Job 34:10

Elihu gets some things right. While he, like Job's other friends, does not understand what is happening to Job, he is right that not even Job is completely without sin, for only Jesus has walked the earth sinless.

Perhaps more important than Elihu's comprehension of Job is Elihu's insight into the nature of God—God cannot do evil. God's nature will not permit it. It is not that God will not do evil; God cannot do evil.

This is a critical concept. God may test us, God may challenge us, and God may even allow Satan to abuse us; still, God cannot do evil. God is good all the time. God is love. God is perfect. God knows the plans He has for us, and those are plans for hope and good.

Too often, we blame God for evil. We look at the bad things that happen and decide the only explanation is that God really does not care for His children. In reaching this conclusion, we are wrong. Scripture is clear on this point. Nature cries out that it is not true. God is a creating, redeeming, sustaining, loving God whose nature cannot create evil or commune with sin.

In God's economy, allowing us free will and allowing evil and temptation to exist in order for the free will to have meaning is for our best. That may not always make sense to us, but this fact is always true: God is love, and in Him is no evil.

June

Where Were You?
Job 38:4-7

The drama of the Book of Job concludes with Act III, the soliloquy of God. God has waited patiently through Job's complaints, the three friends' fruitless diatribes, and well-meaning Elihu's explanation of the ways of the world. After Job issues his last words, God finally speaks.

And the answer is not what Job expects.

Job's "Why?" is never answered with a "Because." God does not choose to reveal to Job the workings of His mind, the supernatural exchange that has gone on with Satan, or the secrets to why evil exists.

God's response is not satisfying to some, who simply are not content unless they know the ins and outs of exactly how the world works.

To others, however, God's reply in Act III is poetic explanation at its finest. God does not bring a "Because" but rather offers a "Who?" response. Who are you, Job, to question God? What do you really know? Where were you when the earth was created, when the foundations of the world were laid, when the measurements of the sea were designed? If you are so smart, tell us how all this happened.

Of course, Job cannot, as we cannot, answer these questions, and in that inability to respond lies God's teaching: God is God and we are not. There are things too complex—indeed, too wonderful—for us to know or comprehend. We simply have to trust God. And in trusting God when we do not understand, once again, grace comes to us.

Day 154/June 2 – Job 40-42

Surely I Spoke of What I Do Not Understand – Job 42:3-6

From what do you need to repent? Do not compare yourselves to others; look inside your own soul.

The repentance of Job is a wonderful denouement to this drama. Job no longer needs the answers he sought in Act II. He now understands he has been asking God to unfold celestial secrets not meant for mortal humans.

Repentance comes in many forms. Your sin may not be the sin of Job: seeking to know what God does not want us to know. Your sin may not be the sin of Judas: betraying the work of God. Your sin may not be the sin of Pilate: choosing to turn away when the power to do good is within your grasp.

Your sin may not be that of the drug dealer, the murderer, the thief, the adulterer, or the child abuser. Your sin may not be the sin of the greedy, the lazy, the gluttonous, or the lustful.

You may, like Job, look around you, compare yourself to everyone you see, and think yourself without sin

You, like Job, are wrong. And, like Job's, your comeuppance will come: You will have to answer the "Where were you when I laid the foundations of the world?" question, and you will know you are unworthy. And you will be faced with Job's choice—to recognize your lack of understanding and beg God's grace, or to go on in your fruitless challenge.

Repent, and see God's grace fall on you as it falls on Job.

Lifter of My Head
Psalm 3:3

As we enter a season of reading the Psalms, we will find ourselves in the midst of poetry designed for worship and exaltation mixed with emotional outcries for explanation and sympathy borne out of great crisis. Today's reading gives us glimpses into both, as the praise of Psalm 1 blends into the distress of Psalms 3 and 4.

Where do these two sides of the Psalms meet? Where does the outpouring of praise and worship seen in verses like Psalm 3:8 ("From the Lord comes deliverance. May your blessing be on your people.") find harmony with the suffering of Psalm 3:1 ("Oh Lord, how many are my foes!")?

The answer lies in the Psalmist's understanding of the nature of God. The Psalms repeatedly proclaim different ways of calling out to God, at different times and in assorted circumstances offering various names for God. Psalm 3:3 discusses God as the one who lifts up our head.

We all find ourselves at times in agony, defeated, unable to understand the ways of the world, asking like Job why the sky has fallen on top of us. We are bowed by the weight of catastrophe.

The Psalms teach us to turn that bowing into the posture of prayer, and we learn that we need not remain beaten down by evil and condition. We learn that our mighty God raises us up. He places His hand on us and lifts our heads so that we can look forward, face our challenges, and walk on.

Who Are We, That You Are Mindful of Us? – Psalm 8:5

We puny humans are weak. We fail. We disappoint. We do not come close to living up to our potential.

The Old Testament thus far has made an overwhelming point—humans are sinful beings who consistently fail to do what God has modeled, asked, and deserves. From Adam to Jacob to Rehoboam, from the golden calf to exile, humans have consistently demonstrated themselves to be unworthy of the favor of God. Some shining lights have tried hard to walk in God's ways, but even they have failed.

And yet... and yet... God holds us humans in incredible regard, just a little lower than the angels. We are crowned with glory and honor. Our King has delegated the rule over the fish of the sea and the beasts of the field to us. Creation itself has been given to us by the Creator for our use and dominion.

Why? It is certainly not because we are worthy, so what is it? Is it some heavenly joke? Is it a scheme to entertain God? Are we just the best God can do?

The answer lies in the indescribable—truly incomprehensible to us humans—nature of God. God is love. That is beyond our grasp. We are left without words. We cannot comprehend God, but we, like the Psalmist, can praise Him. We can honor the glory of the name of God, a name that the Psalmist says is full of majesty. God is love. His is the name above all names.

Day 157/June 5 – Psalms 9-10

Eternal God
Psalm 9:10

God will reign forever. When we are gone, God will reign over the earth. Long after our grandchildren's grandchildren are gone, God will reign.

Eternity is another quality of God that is beyond our ability to grasp. God has always been and always will be. God has no beginning and no end. Omnipresent God is also omnitemporal.

What difference does that make?

First, God's eternity speaks to His power. Neither created nor mortal, God lives, has lived, and will always live. Nothing can kill, stop, or hinder God. God will survive whatever the enemy has in store.

Second, God, the creator of time, who is outside of time and not bound by it, knows what is in store because He sees the past and the future together. When the Bible declares that God has plans for us (Jeremiah 29:11) and promises us everlasting life (John 3:16), God is really able to deliver on those guarantees, for He sees and understands our futures.

Third, the eternity of God means that no problem is too big to take to God. He will outlast the problem and indeed is already beyond the crisis. He looks into our timeline to relate to us, but He is not concerned with the issue.

Nothing can happen to you that God has not seen before. Nothing can be planned to hinder you that is not old hat to God. Whatever disaster, storm, dictator, terrorist, disease, or betrayal may strike, God will still be on His throne. Forever.

The Fool Says, "There Is No God."
Psalm 14:1

The one who denies the reality of God is a fool.

Many deny God's existence, of course. Some are thoughtfully atheist. Others are agnostic, throwing up their hands in willful ignorance. Still others are arrogantly antagonist to any thought of the supernatural.

However careful or reckless, they deny God and are called by scripture "fools."

What makes these people fools? Why does the Psalmist use such language?

A fool is one who either lacks good judgment or, more to the point, has been tricked into being weak-minded. Those who say there is no God either have no sense or have been duped—been made to play the fool—by the lure of the world.

Romans 1 tells us that evidence for the creator is all around us. The Psalmist points out that the heavens declare the glory of God. (Psalm 19:1)

Where do you find evidence of God? Is it in a whale song, a flower, a baby's cry? Is it in a hymn, a sermon, a friend's words, a work of art? Do you feel the presence of God within your being or, tragically, do you hurt because of that God-shaped void that aches in your soul?

Faith is not, as Mark Twain famously quipped, "believing what you know ain't so." Faith is placing your life into the hands of the one whom you have met. Believers do not walk aimlessly into the dark but rather recognize and commit to the one they know is with them and all around.

Hear My Prayer
Psalm 17:6

The essence of our relationship with God is our personal bond with Him. We know He hears us when we call.

Acknowledging God as creator, redeemer, sustainer, and judge is important. Praising His mighty works is crucial. Announcing His power and proclaiming His salvation are indispensable.

But in this relationship, we do not simply talk about God; we talk to Him. We do not simply tell others about Him… we tell Him about others, about ourselves, about our problems.

There is no promise in scripture that we will get the answer that our limited minds think we want to every prayer. The promise of scripture is that God will hear us and respond with the very best answer. Often, that answer is "no" or "wait" or "not now." Sometimes, it is "endure."

This Psalm is a prayer of David, who certainly did not always have every prayer answered as he wished. David wanted to build the temple; God said no. David wanted peace in his family; God did not intervene into the disasters of Absalom and Amnon. David endured.

Still, David writes this Psalm, acknowledging not that God will rig the game so that David will win the prize but rather that God will listen to David's plea, hear David's cry, and receive David's prayer.

No other religion makes such a promise. Worshipers of other so-called gods desperately beg and plead to capture the deity's attention, if only for a moment.

David knows that God hears his every prayer.

Day 160/June 8 – Psalms 19-21

The Desire of Your Heart
Psalm 20:4

God does not always answer "Yes," but that is no reason not to ask. Maybe we do not receive because our hearts desire wrongly.

In this prayer, the Psalmist prays not for himself but for another. Perhaps it is for the king, or perhaps it is for his own children —and ours.

May God make your plans succeed.

May God answer you when you are in distress.

May God protect you and send you help.

May God give you the desire of your heart.

God's giving His children the desire of their heart tempts some to proclaim a prosperity gospel not borne out by the whole of scripture. While the Psalmist asks for great things, scripture does not promise that the Psalmist—or anyone else—will get them. Of course, many heroes of scripture pray for things and hear God's resounding "no." That is much of the lesson of the Book of Job.

Perhaps this Psalm does not teach to ask for what the king, or the child, already desires. Perhaps the Psalmist asks for God literally to give the king, or the child, a new desire.

What if your desires were only those things placed in your heart by God? What if your greed and want for earthly material things vanished and were replaced by holy desires to serve, for peace, to help others, for the will of God to be done?

What is the desire of your heart? Do you pray for God to give you new desires?

Day 161 / June 9 – Psalms 22-23

Shepherd
Psalm 23:1

I f the Lord is my shepherd, that makes me a sheep. That means I am incapable of survival on my own, so self-reliance is suicidal. It means that I am a crowd-follower, so I am in desperate need of guidance. It means I am really not very smart, so pursuing my own inclinations is a terrible idea.

If the Lord is my shepherd, that makes Him a provider. It means that He is the one who decides what is best for me and where I should go. It makes Him the one who leads me to where the still waters are. It means that His green pastures are sufficient. It means that I will not want.

If the Lord is my shepherd, that makes Him a protector. The job of the shepherd is to look after the sheep and to take whatever steps are necessary to ward off attacking wild animals. The job of the shepherd is to find a place of shelter before the storm becomes unbearable. It means that even when I walk through the valley of the shadow of death – as we all surely will – I am not afraid, for the shepherd walks with me.

If the Lord is my shepherd, that means that He knows the way home. He may have led me out into the pasture lands, and He may even have taken me on a journey that is unfamiliar to me, but He will surely bring me home to dwell in His house forever.

Who Shall Ascend?
Psalm 24:3-4

It is the question we all ask when we look in the mirror and contemplate our place in eternity: Who shall ascend to the hill of the Lord?

Only one with clean hands. That lets me out.

Only one with a pure heart. That lets you out.

Only one who has never sworn falsely, bowed to something other than God, or walked in the way of vanity. That lets us all out.

Nobody deserves to ascend to the hill of the Lord, to stand in God's holy place… unless the rules change.

Fortunately, triumphantly, God has changed the rules. Because there is none righteous (Romans 3:10; Psalm 14:1), God knows that heaven is out of reach for all of us unless something miraculous is done. That miracle is for the sinless one, the very Son of God, to have sacrificed Himself to satisfy the wages of sin. That one thing is the cross. The cross event is both a sacrificial atonement and the supreme example of selfless giving. The impact of the cross is this: we can now ascend to the hill of the Lord.

The language of Psalm 24 is important in light of many other Psalms that discuss standing blameless before God. Like Job, we may see ourselves as righteous when compared to many others. Psalm 24, however, compares us not to others around us but to the standard of God. By that measure, we fail.

Who shall ascend? Those for whom Jesus has changed the world.

Day 163/June 11 – Psalms 27-30

Whom Shall I Fear?
Psalm 27:1

We are guaranteed hardship, but we will not fear.

This life comes with many scary things: disease, bullies, dark places, defeat. We will all be hard pressed, afflicted, persecuted, and struck down. Jesus Himself tells us that following Him means taking up a cross.

Yet the scripture also promises that we are not crushed, not perplexed, not driven to despair, not forsaken, and not destroyed. Why? How do we face all that comes with life in our fallen world?

Because The Lord is on our side... the Lord who is faithful through anything and everything... the Lord who rules the winds and waves themselves and yet deigns to be our friend.

Peter Kuzmic says, "Hope is the ability to hear the music of the future; faith is the courage to dance to it today." To call our hope "confidence" is exactly accurate, for whenever scripture speaks of hope, it describes what we "know." We know the end of the story, the joyful, bright end of the story.

We don't pretend what the world throws at us is easy. We may lose our parent or our child or our best friend tomorrow or next year. Between now and then, and afterward, there will be griefs and disappointments, mysteries and sorrows, change and tears. We will indeed be afflicted. We will be hard pressed on every side.

But we will not be destroyed. Our Lord, our heavenly friend will faithfully guide us. He is the strength of our life. Grace always comes.

Day 164/June 12 – Psalms 31-32

Forgiven
Psalm 32:1-2

How can God see who I really am and still want relationship with me? How can the God of Exodus spend so much time giving detailed instructions for worship to people who have built a golden calf?

How can Deuteronomy's God work with people who repeatedly turn their back on His promises, even while the pillar of cloud stands over them?

How can God inspire David to write Psalms and be a great king after his adultery and murder and haughty rejection of everything he has learned?

How can God restore a people so thoroughly worthy of exile back to the Promised Land?

The answer is that God forgives. When God sees His people, He does not see hands that have built an idol, feet that have retreated from His presence, eyes that have looked with lust, or hearts that have turned from Him. What God sees are His children, miraculously restored to Him through holy and supernatural forgiveness.

The gift of forgiveness is by definition something we can never hope to deserve. Yet God offers forgiveness to His children; all we have to do is accept it. Forgiveness, then, is the high point of grace, the highest unmerited favor.

Being "blessed" is something some church members say often, and the term may lose its meaning in its repetition. Never lose sight of the blessing of forgiveness, of the grace gift of God's looking beyond our sin to our need, seeing not our failures but our possibilities. Grace always comes.

Day 165/June 13 – Psalms 33-35

Praise
Psalm 34:1

Praising God makes sense. God is greater than we. God is better than we. God is higher and stronger and smarter and more powerful than we.

God is eternally deserving of praise. Recognizing His worthiness and offering that praise is proper.

Yet, praise is difficult for us.

Perhaps it is difficult because true praise requires acknowledging the Other, and thus praise means we have to get ourselves out of the way. Perhaps praising God is difficult because we have reduced the concept of "praise" to a pat on the head for a child, an encouraging yell to a seven-year-old at an almost-meaningless baseball game, or even a teaching tool for a pet. We have cheapened the idea of praise and thus find it not worthwhile when we address the Father.

Scripture, of course, is full of praise for God. Not cheap words of affirmation but extravagant and selfless recognition and proclamation of the greatness of the creator, the power of the sustainer, the love of the redeemer, and the faithfulness of the one who walks with us day by day. When the Psalmist speaks of praising God with the music of the harp and with our whole hearts, boasting in our souls in the Lord and glorifying Him, the language is something calling us beyond what we naturally say or feel.

Practice praise. It will not come easily. It will not come at all when you first start. Take your time. Repeat. Work at it. Again. God is worth it.

Salvation Comes from the Lord
Psalm 37:39

The Psalms are distinctly Jewish, Old Testament literature. They are scripture and deserve our study, but we must always remember that they come before the life of Christ, before the teachings of the Sermon on the Mount, before the cross, and before the resurrection. The Psalmist speaks with disdain and even hatred toward his enemies, and reading some of the Psalms without the benefit of the knowledge of the New Testament can leave us confused.

But while the Psalmist's view of the wicked is incomplete, the understanding of God's grace for His children demonstrated in these Psalms is masterful. Even when our deeds are seen in contrast to those of the most wicked, we cannot save ourselves. Our goodness does not lift us from the pit.

David knows this. In his eyes, his egregious missteps overwhelm any righteousness of his. A man after God's own heart, David has done plenty of good, but he feels deeply his own failures and knows that his salvation cannot be created by himself.

No, the salvation of the righteous comes from the Lord. God is our stronghold. It is the Lord who helps us. It is God who delivers us. We take our refuge in Him. We cannot look within ourselves for salvation.

Jesus will bring us a message of turning the other cheek, and that affects how we read the Psalms. But in reading the language about evildoers carefully and critically, do not miss the overall message: grace always comes, for God saves.

Day 167/June 15 – Psalms 38-39

Being "Sin-Sick"
Psalm 38:3

The imagery the Psalmist uses is very real to all of us, sooner or later… when we, like the Prodigal Son, have found ourselves struggling to survive in a pigpen… or when we, like Jonah, have made bad decision after bad decision and found ourselves tossed out into the waves.

We sin to a point that makes us sick to our souls.

Our natures are sinful, but our God is perfect. As we strive to find God, our sinning interrupts our quest. The longer we stay separated from God, the worse we suffer. The farther away from God we wander, the less healthy we feel in our bones.

The Psalmist uses this word picture to remind us of his own failures, but more importantly, he gives us a panorama of emotion with which we can all identify.

God, I feel so bad. I have sinned. I have failed you. I have fallen so far short of what you have laid out before me. My guilt has overwhelmed me like a burden too heavy to bear. I am feeble and utterly crushed. I groan in anguish.

Incredibly, God meets us in this place. When we are at our absolute lowest, having run to the far side of the sea and having made our bed in the lowest hell, God seeks us and finds us. The Great Physician is right by our side. God answers the prayer of the Psalm. He does not forsake us.

And better yet, He makes us well.

Day 168/June 16 – Psalms 40-42

Patient Panting
Psalm 40:1; 42:1

Patient panting: a contradiction in terms.

These two Psalms paint pictures that are apparently paradoxical. Psalm 40 tells of waiting patiently for God to put a new song in our mouths. Psalm 42, on the other hand, depicts us panting for God as the deer pants for water.

Upon deeper reflection, though, these ideas are harmonious. We should wait patiently, and while we wait, we should pant for God like a wild creature greedily seeking the nearest watering hole. How can these conceptions coexist?

We gasp and huff because we are needy creatures. We desire the presence of God because God sustains us with his Holy Spirit. We crave God because God is satisfying. We want more and more of what the Father is and has for us, and we want it now.

We wait patiently because we know God is in control and has a plan that is beyond our comprehension. We wait patiently because we know the stories of Abraham and Job and Moses and a people wandering forty years and a nation in exile who finally gets to return home. We wait patiently because we believe that God will hear our cry and lift us up.

And we do both things together. We wait patiently, but we wait with urgency. We subject ourselves to the sovereignty of God, so we wait… but we know the glory that is God, and we wait on the edge of our seats, panting in expectation.

We are a patiently panting people.

In Trouble … Be Still
Psalm 46:1, 10

Be still and know that God is God even while the mountains shake.

The Psalmist tells us that God is our refuge and strength and that we should not fear. The predicate for our confidence is that God is an ever-present help.

It is worth examining how this Psalm is put together. After assuring us that God is our refuge, the Psalmist draws a word picture of foaming waters and quaking mountains threatening us from every side while nations and kingdoms find themselves in an uproar. Juxtaposed against these disasters is a river flowing through the City of God as God does wondrous works and brings wars themselves to a halt.

How are we supposed to react to this tumult and these miracles? We are to be still.

That goes against our grain. We want to join the fray, to be the lieutenants in God's army as enemies are overthrown and spears are shattered. Or at least we want to be the cheerleaders who spread the word to everyone we know about the greatness of God.

To be sure, there is a time for us to join in the fight, and there are many occasions where spreading the news of the power and greatness of God is entirely appropriate.

But first, we are to be still. God will be exalted whether we are doing the shouting or not. God is our refuge simply through His presence. We should be still and take notice, for The Lord Almighty is with us.

Day 170/June 18 – Psalms 47-49

Great Is the Lord
Psalm 48:1

True greatness is rare. To be sure, we call lots of things "great" —basketball shots, dessert recipes, musical performances, ideas—but even as we use that description, we know deep inside that sightings of true greatness are few and far between.

What makes God great?

It is God's dimension. God is spirit, so He does not have a "body" that takes up space in the way we usually think of size. Still, God is everywhere, higher than the highest mountain and deeper than the ocean, extending farther away than the most distant galaxy.

It is God's power. God has created at will without raw material. God controls the lightning bolts and directs the path of the microbe.

It is God's perfection. God is better than good, better than very good. God is the best thing we have ever experienced, better than we can possibly articulate or imagine.

It is God's wonder. We simply cannot imagine or comprehend everything that God is.

It is God's importance. God is great because everything—literally everything—else in the world pales in comparison. What God does, thinks, and feels dwarfs the grandest plans, actions, and emotions of all humankind.

Recognizing God's greatness is not an end; it is a step. Because the Lord is great, He is therefore most worthy of praise. Praise results not from fear but from recognition of God's bigness, dominance, sensation, and consequence. God is of a magnitude that demands praise.

Great is the Lord.

Day 171 / June 19 – Psalms 50-51

A Clean Heart
Psalm 51:10

David recognizes that he is a sinner—his inescapable iniquity is before his eyes. He does not attempt to explain away his actions or compare himself to others.

David knows that his only hope lies in the unfailing love of God, and so he throws himself on God's mercy. David has more sense than to seek what he deserves.

Note that David recognizes that "sin" is a vertical term, a concept that is between him and God. David has obviously wronged any number of people, and his prayer minimizes none of what he has done. His actions have injured those around him horizontally, on his own level as a human being, and he will need to seek their forgiveness. But when it comes to sin, that is against God and God only, and David must first seek reconciliation with God.

David does not seek merely to be polished. David knows he must be remade. He prays for a new, clean, pure heart. He knows that his actions must be erased. He requires God literally to "blot out" what he has done.

David, the man after God's own heart, knows what he needs—God's presence, the Holy Spirit that empowers him, and the joy of salvation. Assured of those things, David will resume his pattern of teaching others about the wonders of God.

We learn from David: our sin requires the mercy of God. We need to be remade and cleansed. Then we return to shouting the good news of God.

Day 172/June 20 – Psalms 52-54

Looking for Salvation
Psalm 53:6

The Psalms are forward-looking, hopeful writings from faithful people who have not yet experienced Messiah. The people of God who inhabit Israel during David's time have descended from those delivered from Egyptian captivity and led through forty years of wandering. They have seen want and war, escape and miracle, forgiveness and renewal.

These three Psalms in today's reading in many ways could be written today. We all see evildoers boasting as though there were no God. We look around and feel that everyone has turned away from the ways of God. We all feel attacked and surrounded by strangers who do not know God.

Unlike the Psalmist, though, we have the perspective of a people who already know Messiah. We are not looking forward in hope that salvation will come from Zion; we face attack knowing that indeed salvation has come from Zion, that the Christ has walked as one of us to save us.

The faith of these who had not yet seen is important to us. Jesus commends such faith (John 20:29), and we should honor people like the Israelites of old who walked among evildoers and unbelievers expecting the coming of Christ.

Still, we do not have to live as they did, looking to what has not yet come. Let us walk as those who have met the Messiah, as those whose hope is not in what is to come but in what has come, as those who daily experience the help and the presence of God.

Day 173/June 21 – Psalms 55-57

Wings
Psalm 55:6-7; Psalm 57:1

D o not fly from fear. Fly to your God.

There is a poignant moment in the movie "Forrest Gump." Young Jenny, hounded by her abusive father, desperately hides. She prays "Dear God, make me a bird. So I could fly far. Far far away from here."

Psalmist David feels the same way. Hunted by enemies and beset by the terrors of the night, he wishes for "the wings of a dove" so he can "fly away and be at rest."

We have all been there, with Jenny and David. If it has not been a vicious parent or a pursuing enemy, it has been a cruel boss or an unfaithful spouse or a devious bully. Perhaps our fear has not arisen from a person at all but from devastating poverty, unspeakable unfairness, or grievous tragedy. Our fears come, and they come for good reason.

As these three Psalms continue, David begins to see past the darkness to the waiting arms of His father. He writes that he can trust in His Father, who hears when David calls to him morning, noon, and night.

Then, as Psalm 57 opens, David turns back to his earlier cry and realizes he does not need the wings of dove. The wings he needs are those of God, who surrounds and embraces us with wings as a mother hen gathers her chicks. (Matthew 27:32)

Don't fly from God; run to Him. Let His wings gather and protect you. When you are afraid, trust in God.

Day 174/June 22 – Psalms 58-60

I Will Sing in the Morning
Psalm 59:16

G host stories are always set after sundown. Bad things happen at night. Under cover of darkness, evil seems to thrive. We are easily frightened at night, for we do not see well in the dark. Our natural protection of light is gone, and we are subject to scary things that, we feel, may jump out at us at any minute.

David is no different. He writes of his attackers, who "return at evening, snarling like dogs." They prowl about, looking for victims during the evil nighttime hours. David knows they are there at night, and they will return on some future night.

Being scared of the dark and what lies in darkness is universal. We all know how that feels. Poets and novelists have used "night" and "darkness" as symbols for evil, emptiness, distress, and fright for centuries. David himself turns to the symbol repeatedly.

Jesus, however, is the light of the world, and whoever follows Jesus does not stay in darkness. (John 8:12) When Jesus comes to us, He brings light, and that light is the life of men. (John 1:4) When Jesus lives within us, moreover, we become the light of the world. (Matthew 5:14) There is no more night.

To David, and to us, the light comes in the morning, and in the morning we sing. Whatever has happened – or whatever we have been afraid would happen – the night before can frighten us no more, for perpetual, permanent morning has broken. And in the morning, we sing.

In the Desert, Remember the Sanctuary
Psalm 63:2

David is wandering in the desert of Judah, trying to escape the clutches of Saul. (1 Samuel 23:14) Being in the desert in the Middle East is what it sounds like—arid, waterless, hot, miserable, deadly. Unable to go home and hunted by the mad king, David is in a "dry and weary land."

David knows He needs water. He is haunted by the image of cool water and its precious taste, but there is no water to be found. He remembers water, but he cannot find it.

We all have our desert moments. Whether we have been chased to the outlying regions or have run there ourselves in fits of selfishness or rebellion, we know what it is to be far from water, far from home, far from God. We want to worship. We want, we earnestly want, to see God again. The question is how to find God. How can we worship in the desert?

David's solution is to call to mind those days when he has been closest to God. David now writes of what it is to behold God in the sanctuary. For it is there, in the spiritual heights and thrilling moments of worship, that David has known the power and glory of the King, Lord of his life. It is there, in the sanctuary, that David has known beyond doubt that God's love is better than life.

When you find yourself in the desert, follow David's lead. Remember what you learned in the sanctuary.

Day 176/June 24 – Psalms 65-67

Come and See the Awesome Works of God – Psalm 66:5

We can observe ninety-one billion light years of the universe, containing more than one hundred billion galaxies. Our own galaxy holds over three hundred billion stars, and many galaxies are much bigger than ours.

The stuff of the universe is made up of quarks, leptons, and bosons. The atom, ion, and molecule in turn form to make up the tiniest of matter, and as that matter combines with other matter, microscopic specks eventually can be detected.

A square mile of fertile soil contains more insects than there are human beings on the entire earth. One human eye has more than two million working parts. Sea turtles have collapsible lungs that allow them to dive thousands of feet to enormous pressures, living off the oxygen stored in their red blood cells and muscles. Earth is just the right distance from the sun to be habitable and tilted at just the angle necessary for growing seasons. Honeybees flap their wings over two hundred times a second.

Snowflakes. Sequoias. Rain. Butterflies. Waves. Childbirth. Roses. Mountains. A mother's love. Human intelligence.

Here are two other incredible works of God: (1) Human beings are made with the capabilities to love, forgive, and create. (2) God has given the world the saving power of Jesus Christ, the sustaining force of the Holy Spirit, the unstoppable church, and His own never-ending love.

Come and behold the works of the Lord, the awesome acts of God. He is in the midst of His people in all the earth.

God of the Lonely
Psalm 68:5-6

Isolation and loneliness are epidemic. To be sure, it is often good to be alone, especially by choice, when we spend time away from the crowds and the rush of life. Sometimes, we find ourselves situationally lonesome, wishing for someone to share an experience or a moment with us. Neither being alone nor being lonesome is a long-term worrisome condition.

Loneliness, on the other hand, is a terrible, heart-rending malady, one that afflicts the isolated, the defeated, the abandoned, and the permanently alone. Tragically, loneliness also comes to many who are none of those things, who are surrounded by loving friends and family and who appear to be on top of the world, yet who feel empty and lost in their souls. The loneliest at times desperately — and often silently — cry out for someone to recognize and value them, and they do not believe that anyone does. Loneliness becomes depression and discouragement.

Even David has his moments of loneliness, whether in the maddening escape from Saul or the recognition of his own ruinous sin. David does not, however, continue to wallow in that loneliness but instead finds the inspiration to look up and see God, in His holy dwelling, as the answer. God is the father to the fatherless and the defender of widows, and His lovingkindess extends to David... and to you and to me... when we are lonely. God gives us families and leads us in singing.

Loneliness is another of our burdens that God wants to bear.

Day 178 / June 26 – Psalms 69-70

Save Me! Rescue Me! Help Me!
Psalm 69:1,14; Psalm 70:1

It is the cry of our hearts: "Help me, God. Save me. Rescue me from this crisis." There are no atheists in foxholes, and the reality of life is that most of us find ourselves in foxholes more often than we admit. Like the Psalmist, we are up to our necks in water, unable to find a foothold on the miry clay sinking into the depths beneath our feet. We are hated without reason, mocked and scorned by those who seem to surround us. Evil flourishes as the world changes again and again.

Sometimes, God's answer is to show us that we are in fact not in a crisis. The changing world around us has scared us because it is not what we have known, and we do not understand how to comprehend seismic shifts in public attitude, government policy, technology, and cultural commitment. We react in fear. Instead of eliminating what the world has brought us, God masterfully rescues us not from the situation but from our own tunnel vision that has created our fear.

Sometime, God's answer is to solve the crisis. The storm is calmed. The disease is healed. The enemy is silenced. Normalcy returns.

And sometimes, God's answer is to reach into the still-raging storm and calm His child. On those days, the waters do not recede. The cancer does not vanish. A sweepstakes check does not appear in the mail. Nonetheless, God overwhelms our souls with His grace and His peace, and we are rescued.

Day 179/June 27 – Psalms 71-73

The Nearness of God
Psalm 73:28

L eft on our own, our flesh is weak. Our hearts collapse. We need Someone to be near.

God never fails. It is good for us to be near to God.

The nearness of God is good because He catches us when we stumble. We are never out of His reach, never out of His sight. When we fall, as we often do, God is nearby to support us and to snag us before we hurt ourselves too badly.

The nearness of God is good because He hears our heart's cry, even when we are too flummoxed to verbalize a prayer. We need not be loud or demonstrative. Indeed, the cry does not have to be audible at all. God is near enough to hear us.

The nearness of God is good because we are never alone. His rod and staff comfort us. Even when we walk through the shadow's valley, He is with us.

The nearness of God is good because we have Him to lean on when temptation offers its allures. We are not alone with sin's fascinations, even when we have wandered far and find ourselves in a far country. He is there to whisper the right way to go and to encourage.

The nearness of God is good because He is our portion forever. We need nothing else. He sustains us. He provides our hearts with all that it needs to flourish.

God the Lord is the strength of my heart. The nearness of God is good.

Day 180/June 28 – Psalms 74-75

Turn Your Steps toward Us
Psalm 74:3

I t is the natural cry of the human heart: "Look at me!"

There are days we feel that the world mocks God, cares nothing for right and wrong, and laughs at our feeble attempts to stand up for good.

The Psalmists feel the same way. The rhetoric and poetry of the Psalms voice these feelings in terms like "why have you rejected us, God?" This is not literal concern that God has changed sides in the cosmic war but rather an expression of the exasperation we all feel when God is not swooping in to solve all of our problems as soon as we would like Him to.

The prayer of this Psalm is heartfelt. Recognizing that God has a lot on His plate, this prayer asks God to remember His people and turn His steps back in our direction. It is a plea for the notice of God, not because we believe we have somehow dropped off His radar but rather because we are needy children, desiring the attention of our Father when we hurt.

There is nothing wrong with a prayer like this so long as it, like this Psalm, ends with our recognition that it is not we on the throne, that God is the king who brings salvation and is control of the world, and that we thus ask for God but know He is not a tame pet who always comes when we call.

We are needy. We ask God to turn in our direction.

The Power of Memory
Psalm 77:11

S ometimes, memory is all you have.

Sometimes, you have wandered far. You have left those who know and love you. You have fallen into a lifestyle that offers nothing to assist you. The church is far in your rearview mirror. Your parents are gone. That teacher who meant so much to you decades before is long since deceased. Your habits and interests have led you far from home.

Perhaps you are alone, imprisoned, addicted, sick.

For whatever reason, you have nothing to sustain you. In the words of the Psalmist, you are in distress, and when you look around for reassurance, it seems as though God has forgotten to be merciful.

God is not the one who has forgotten.

Search your memory. What has God done? What do you remember about His holy ways, His mighty deeds? What did you learn so long ago about the creation of the world, the intricacy of the systems of life, the delicate balance of nature? What was the example set before you by that friend, that parent? What were the words that teacher implanted deep in your brain. What hymns are buried in your heart?

With the Psalmist, remember. God has led you far. He has loved you with an everlasting love. He has sent His son to save you. He has performed miracles that you have witnessed, even if you would not admit to yourself or others that real miracles happen.

God loves you. You know that deep in your soul.

Remember.

Day 182/June 30 – Psalm 78

Learning the Lessons of the Past
Psalm 78:4

Why do we listen to tales of our past? What is the point of studying exploration, early stabs at government, wars, trade, lists of kings, the rise and fall of the Roman Empire? Why spend hours forcing teenagers to learn the reasons for the American Revolution and the words to the Gettysburg Address?

Why do we read poetry and literature? Why do we listen to the words of songs written more than ten minutes ago? What is there to be learned from what people thought and said and did before we were born?

Experience is a superb teacher. When we learn the decisions that others have made, when we retrace the steps of those who have gone before, and when we read the words written in times past, we learn what works and what does not. We figure out how to avoid the pitfalls that have befallen our predecessors. Those who fail to learn history are often, as the proverb goes, doomed to repeat it.

We have the Old Testament for much the same reason. The history of how God has dealt with His people – and how His people have responded to Him or ignored Him or rebelled against Him – is pregnant with information to help each of us. This Psalm recounts part of that history, hoping that its readers and hearers will learn and do better.

Learn from our history – God has so much good in store for us if we do not repeat the errors of the past.

July

Day 183/July 1 – Psalms 79-82

Satisfaction
Psalm 81:6

What has surely been a key lesson of scripture, that God takes care of us, is amplified by the Psalmist to a new and more powerful teaching—God does not only take care of us; He gives us His absolute best. God does not simply feed us; He provides us the finest His world has to offer.

We are His children. We are the sheep of His pasture. He gives us His presence. He gives us His Promised Land. He takes us back when we have wasted all we have on golden calves and disobeyed ourselves into exile.

Why then do we see His new gifts and turn up our noses? Why do we receive what He has for us and simply throw it away?

The Psalmist writes to a people who are distracted by the offerings of foreign gods. In today's world, "foreign gods" can equate to routine celebrity sightings, addictions, or political values that become our entire reason for being. Foreign gods tantalize us with cheap thrills, passing popularity, false hope, and empty promises.

If we would listen to God, there is another realm of blessing waiting for us. He is waiting to satisfy us with the finest of the wheat and with honey from the rock.

Satisfaction is more than simply nourishment. Satisfaction is enough. Satisfaction is receiving blessings that do not simply keep us going but in fact give us joy and fill us with belonging and purpose. Satisfaction is the gift only God can give.

Day 184/July 2 – Psalms 83-86

Dwelling with God
Psalm 84:1-4

S cripture has no hesitancy discussing death. The Bible teaches that death is a part of life, the natural transition from this earthly existence to our permanent life with God in His heavenly home.

The Promised Land, the tabernacle, and the temple in Jerusalem have all been attempts in Hebrew history to represent where God lives. This Psalm is talking not about these but about God's dwelling in the eternity promised to those who love God.

Jesus tells us His Father's house contains many mansions and that He prepares a place there for each of us so that He can take us there to be with Him. (John 14:2-3) This Heaven is not a geographic location or a physical place. The lovely dwelling place of God is not real estate or a house, not a castle or a palace, not a temple or a tabernacle or a sanctuary.

The dwelling place of the most high is a dimension that is beyond our understanding, but that makes it no less genuine. God is spirit, and His dwelling place is a spiritual realm that we have not experienced – and cannot experience - in our bodily, human forms. Paul tells us that when we are away from the body, we will be at home with the Lord. (2 Corinthians 5:8)

Writing long before Paul and Jesus, the Psalmist understands that being with God forever is a good thing. It is the best thing. We cannot understand it fully now, but it will be lovely.

I Will Sing of Your Love Forever
Psalm 89:1

The feeling of euphoria that comes when we originally know God and the spiritual highs that follow special moments we have with God are human emotions, albeit sparked by divine moments. Like all human emotions, they wax and wane. There are times we do not feel the presence of God and do not have a sense of God's glory and love. Knowing that feelings come and go, we continue to serve and love faithfully, understanding that God has not left us and that our perception of Him will return in time.

Dealing with these emotions is characteristic of our lives in this time and this place.

The Psalmist writes of another time and another place. There will come a day when spiritual burnout is no more, when our experience with God is tangible and continuous. And in that day, we will sing of the love of God forever. We will sing without ceasing and praise God with complete understanding because we will be in His presence.

The heavens praise the holiness of God, for the heavens are full of God's angels and creations that know – beyond feeling – of the God they have seen and experienced. We, on the other hand, must still walk by faith and not by sight. (2 Corinthians 5:7) One day we will no longer see through a glass darkly, for we too will see God face to face. (1 Corinthians 13:12) We will see Him as He is, and we will sing of His love forever.

Day 186/July 4 – Psalms 90-91

Saved from the Snare
Psalm 91:3

Psalm 91 is a beautiful picture of the protective reach of God. This Psalm has inspired poets and hymn writers, who find in its words the lyrical exaltation of God's love for His people.

There is a real danger in words like these. In fact, it is this very Psalm that Satan quotes when tempting Jesus: "If you are the Son of God, throw yourself down. For it is written: He will command his angels concerning you, and they will lift you up in their hands, so that you will not strike your foot against a stone." (Matthew 3:5-6) Charlatans and well-meaning but misguided followers alike have used later verses in this Psalm to challenge churchgoers to walk among poisonous snakes.

This Psalm does not promise that nothing bad will happen; in fact, it assures us that arrows will fly and stones will block our paths. The tempter will want you to see lions and cobras and decide that scripture is a lie and God does not care.

The fact that verses can be misused does not make them wrong. God is truly our refuge. God does save us in the end. God loves us with an everlasting love that protects us from the fowler's snare. This Psalm promises that God will not let the disasters of life defeat us. The promise is that He will in fact deliver us. God covers us with His wings to sooth us through the night terrors that attack us all. God is our refuge.

Music
Psalm 92:1

Many of the Psalms, if not the entire collection, make up an early songbook used in the worship of God. The exhortation to praise and worship with music appears repeatedly throughout the Psalms and elsewhere in scripture.

Why music? Why use the arts to describe and revel in the nature and acts of God?

Music is a representation of what we often cannot verbalize. Wonder and awe are reactions to the majesty of God, and our human vocabularies do not really capture that. Gratitude is a poor word to encapsulate our response to the forgiveness of God. Even praise and worship do not come close to representing completely how we can and should approach the God of the universe.

God has created music, and He wants us to use music as a vital part of worship, as a way of expressing what we cannot otherwise say. Instruments and voices can tune to something closer to perfection than perhaps any other human endeavor. Singing choirs find their hearts beating in unison as the name of Christ is raised high.

Music serves the listener as well as the singer and the player. Those hearing music are transported to an understanding of the greatness of God they may never otherwise imagine through hymns and psalms and spiritual songs.

For some, music is secondary, and that is sad. They rely on the spoken and written word, but they miss out on an incredible medium for expressing our understanding of God.

Sing to the Lord.

Day 188/July 6 – Psalms 95-97

Worship
Psalm 95:6-7

Why do we worship? Why should we worship?

Worship is the creature's appreciation of and submission to the presence of the divine creator. When we worship, we are saying, in word and deed, that God is God and we are not.

We bow and kneel in worship to symbolize our place relative to God's, understanding that we would not be worthy to be in His presence but for His leave.

He is our God. We are His people.

God is worthy of praise. We are worthy of nothing, for we are a hard-hearted and stubborn people.

And so this glaring juxtaposition of the needy, sinful, and unworthy mortal daring to enter the presence of the great, perfect, righteous maker is what we call worship. The Psalmist commands us to do it, and we must do it properly. We bow and tremble before Him because we recognize that we have crossed into the splendor of His holiness. Our message is one of declaration of His glory, of saying to the peoples of the world that God reigns. We recognize that the heavens rejoice, the seas resound, and everything in the fields is jubilant before God.

Worship, then, cannot be something done habitually, half-heartedly, automatically, or impersonally. If any of those adverbs apply, then we are doing something else – just showing up, merely going through motions – than worship.

In His hands are the depths. The mountains belong to Him. Recognize who and what you are and whom you are addressing, and worship.

A Joyful Noise
Psalm 100:1

In the words of the King James Version, make a "joyful noise" to the Lord.

There is great majesty in beautiful music. A choir rehearses hours —and accompanists rehearse extra hours on their own—on a piece that the composer has taken weeks or months to write. Editors carefully take the arranger's work to finalize that piece for the choir and accompanists, or the soloist alone, to bring to worship. The result can be breathtaking and awe inspiring as it brings a congregation to its knees in prayerful worship or to its feet in responsive Hallelujahs.

Not all praise, however, is perfectly performed. Not every song is sung by trained musicians, with a pipe organ or a professional quality band. Sometimes for everyone, and always for some, praise is not practiced, measured, or harmonious. Often, worship is spontaneous and imperfect. Sometimes, exaltation is simply loud and joyful.

Not everyone is cut out for the choir. Only a few have the talent to bring instrumental music to the throne in worship. For many, worship and praise are never sounds worthy of anyone's ear but God's. That is why it is so important that the Psalmist, who writes about how to worship with carefully played harp music, recognizes the importance of the joyful noise. Anyone can utter a joyful noise. All of us can enter the gates of the Lord with thanksgiving and come before Him with whatever song is in our heart and on our lips.

No excuses. Worship!

Day 190/July 8 – Psalms 102-103

As Far as the East Is from the West
Psalm 103:12

The 103rd Psalm is a hymn written in response to the overwhelming compassion of God. When we, like David, come before God, we do so remembering and celebrating His incredible acts of love:

He forgives all our sins.

He heals all our diseases. Not always immediately, and not always in the way we demand, He heals us every time.

He redeems us from the pit in which we have fallen or, so often, flung ourselves.

He crowns us with love and compassion of which we are so profoundly unworthy.

He satisfies our desires with good things.

He renews us so that we rise with figurative eagles' wings, as we did at the height of our strength when we were young and strong and most eager.

He is slow to anger and abounds in mercy.

He does not treat us as we deserve.

He has compassion for us as the best of fathers has for his children.

The enduring image from this Psalm is the idea of forgiven sins separated from us "as far as the east is from the west." Do not get hung up on the geography here, for to the ancient Israelites, there is nothing farther apart than the east and the west. The point is clear, the poetry is inspiring, and the meaning is life-changing: God has acted through the cross of Christ to remove us far from what would kill us.

Praise the Lord, O my soul!

Day 191/July 9 – Psalms 104-105

A Poetic Look at Creation
Psalm 104:5

The Psalmist knows the Old Testament. As you read Psalm 104, you should look back at Genesis 1. Relive the familiar creation story through the poetic language of this Psalm, and be amazed once again. If you reexamine the well known creation narrative through the lens of the music of this Psalm, you will find yourself on your knees in awestruck devotion to the Creator.

The Psalmist takes the truth of Genesis and paints it with brilliant new intensity.

In Genesis 1, God creates out of nothing, and we are not shown behind the curtain. In this Psalm, we see the Creator who is already reigning in glorious splendor, clothed in majesty that He turns into what we call "light." In Genesis, the message is that God creates the heavens and the earth; in this Psalm, that creation is a systematic and brilliantly laid out construction, with beams, foundations, and blueprints of celestial complexity.

God speaks in Genesis, and seas and dry land and vegetation appear. The Psalmist adds the color commentary, and we now see the waters waiting for the Master's command before they surge into rivulets and oceans that He has ordained. We see the newly formed thirsty beasts awaiting the overflow of the springs.

Listen to the story of creation from the lips of the singer. Hear the rhyme of God's mighty works from the poet. Understand anew —maybe for the first time—the wisdom that creation displays.

He reigns in glorious splendor. Let there be light!

Day 192/July 10 – Psalm 106

Confession
Psalm 106:6

Learning what has happened is not always enough. There comes a time to take responsibility. In this Psalm, a step is taken beyond the report of history. The admission that "we have sinned even as our fathers did" is an important development in Israel's relationship with God. Simply being God's chosen people has not insulated them from sin in the past and does not do so now. "We have done wrong and acted wickedly" is a confession that leads the Psalmist to understand the depth of God's love. The end of the Psalm, noting that God has "relented" because He has "remembered His covenant," is far more meaningful in the context of the paragraphs of sins that come before it.

What about you? Are you traveling through life, counting on the love of God and maybe even periodically praising God for that love, without really understanding the cost of it? Do you acknowledge your own failures to God? Do you understand that the compassion that God has poured on you and will continue to bestow because of His own covenant promise comes against the background of your – and my – repeated rebellion?

The purpose of Psalm 106 is not to bring us down, to make us sad, or to remind us of so much failure. The Psalmist assumes we know where and when we have fallen. This Psalm serves to highlight the love of God, for continuing His covenant with a people such as us is something only God can do.

Day 193/July 11 — Psalm 107

A Saga of Four People
Psalm 107:43

O nce upon a time, there were four people.

The first person wandered in the wasteland. She never could find a home, decent food, or a job. To her, the world was cruel; she cried out for help, and she waited to die.

The second person was evil. He lived with the darkness and chains that he had chosen. Rebellion was second nature to him because he despised everything good he had ever been taught.

The third person never gave enough thought to life to be good or evil. Instead, he simply acted like a nitwit, over and over again. Never having time to pay attention to what he ate or put into his body, much less how to survive in the world, his prodigal lifestyle led him into chaos.

The fourth person started out well. She had a real idea of how to succeed in the world, and she even occasionally paid lip service to God. Feeling self-confidence that was fool's gold, she took chances beyond her abilities, and as the waves of life surrounded her, she lost all hope.

And God saved them all. He led the first woman to a home with Him (verse 7). He brought the second evil man out of his self-created gloom and broke his chains (verse 14). He rescued the third man out of his own grave (verse 20). He calmed the storm and led the fourth woman to peace (verse 30).

Find yourself in these stories, and give thanks.

Grace always comes.

Day 194 / July 12 – Psalms 108-109

In Good Times and Bad
Psalm 109:30

Individual verses of scripture should be read in context. Reading the Psalms as a compilation of proof texts or instruction manuals is a mistake. This poetry is a series of emotional responses to the extreme ebb and flow of life, and the very real—and often sinful—humanity displayed in them is powerful. These Psalms are indeed scripture and contain God's words to us as we read through the Psalms as a whole. Individual verses, though, can be troubling.

Asking God for children to be fatherless (Psalm 109:9) is not the intent of scripture, but it is an understandable—albeit regrettable and wrong—human response to evil done to us.

Readings these two Psalms back to back shows the highs and lows. Psalm 108 comes when David is on top of the world, when his authority and kingdom are unquestioned, when all the tribes of Judah bow to him and honor him for his triumphs. Psalm 109, on the other hand, grows out of his anguish when wicked and deceitful enemies are getting the better of him. He lashes out in verses 6-20 with words that are nothing more than desperate, emotional cries from the pit of despair, a place where we have all been.

Do not let your reading of these Psalms dwell in that pit, for the theme of each is where the truth lies. In both Psalms, whether from victory or despondency, David praises God (Psalm 108:1; Psalm 109:30).

In good times and bad, praise the Lord.

Day 195/July 13 – Psalms 110-113

The God Who Stoops
Psalm 113:5-6

"He is our Guide and Friend. To us He'll condescend." [2]
In the final analysis, the most amazing thing about God is not that He is high and lifted up. Picturing the creator of the world enthroned and worshiped by all creation is not difficult.

No, the amazing thing is that the God who is high and lifted up does not stay there but instead condescends to us. He, whose realm is far beyond what we can see or comprehend, stoops down to where we are.

God stoops to us when we pray. We seek His attention with our problems, and the one who holds all the problems of the world in His heart miraculously chooses to listen to each of us.

God stoops to us in creation. He has not simply wound up a world and then let it go, but instead He intervenes from time to time to lift us when we fall, to point the way to us, to catch our attention with a leaf or a shooting star or a babbling brook.

God stoops to us with His healing hand. We lie sick, broken, poor, and defeated. He lowers Himself and places His hand of unfathomable power on us, and we are better.

God stoops to us through Jesus. God took on lowly, limited humanity, walking through our dirt and enduring our nails. God lowered Himself then, and comes to us now, as one of us. God stoops to bear our sins.

Praise God who stoops.

---

2 "Come, Christians, Join to Sing," lyrics by Christian H. Bateman

Day 196/July 14 – Psalms 114-118

This is the Day
Psalm 118:24

Yesterday is gone. We cannot undo what happened then. No matter what we do about the mistakes we made, the scars remain. We can spend our time in regret or trying to cover up our errors, but the mistakes stay on the ledger. We do not fool ourselves, and we do not fool God.

Tomorrow is not here yet. It may promise you hope and fulfillment, or it may offer nothing but threat and sorrow. If it is the former, you can prepare and wait expectantly, but tomorrow will not get here until tomorrow. If the future is one you dread, spending your time now worrying about what may come ignores today's opportunities and does nothing to ward off evil or hardship.

This is the day the Lord has made, and the Psalmist tells us to rejoice and be glad in this day. No matter what happened yesterday, today is a gift from God to you. Even if you are sick, unemployed, in pain, and discouraged, you can do things with this day regardless of what happened yesterday. And no matter what you see – or think you see – coming towards you tomorrow, you can spend today squeezing every gift out of it that God has in it for you. Tomorrow will come when it comes.

There is of course a place for learning from the past and preparing for the future, but doing either at the expense of today wastes God's precious gift to us all. Rejoice and be glad.

Day 197/July 15 – Psalm 119:1-56

Hidden in Your Heart
Psalm 119:11

Bible study should never be used as a punishment, where misbehaving children are required to memorize a certain number of verses the way naughty schoolboys are required to write "I will not pull hair" repeatedly on a blackboard.

Bible study is also not a means of distracting us from sin, as if it could be true that spending all our time memorizing scripture means sin will not occur to us.

We hide God's Word in our hearts.

This verse from Psalm 119 is stating truth: The more God's words are stored in our memories—hidden in our hearts, in the words of the poet—the more likely we are to avoid sin. Protection from sin is not a result of our being able to quote verses as an antidote to wish temptation away, nor is it a promise that learning enough verses somehow magically shields us from the power of sin.

Instead, the Psalmist knows that the better we know and understand what God has to say to us, the more our lives are changed. When God's scripture is hidden in our hearts, our choices are different. We react to situations differently. We walk in the way of love and truth. When the opportunity to sin arises, we see in it instead an opportunity to act as the body of Christ, reaching into the world with forgiveness and compassion.

The idle mind is the devil's workshop. Fill yours with God's words and promises, and see how your life is different.

Day 198/July 16 – Psalm 119:57-120

Lamp and Light
Psalm 119:105

There is nothing so imposing as a darkened path. No matter our physical strength or our mental acuity, when we are forced to walk on a road where we cannot see, we are weak. We wonder whether there is a hole ahead into which we might stumble or a tree across our way. The thought that bandits or predators may be waiting for us cannot be shaken.

Even if we are not overcome with fear of injury or attack, the darkened road creates the obvious problem of not letting us know where we are going. Does the road turn? Does it end? Is there traffic coming against us?

And even if we get past all of that, gaining confidence we can step without turning our ankle or missing the bend in the trail, the unseen road leaves us not knowing how far we have to go before we reach our destination.

God wants to change all of that for us. God's word—spoken to us through scripture, represented to us in creation around us, and ultimately, of course, perfectly embodied in Jesus—conquers the darkness of the road. His word is a lamp for our feet and a light for our path.

We travel on, for we know that even when we see only darkness, God can see the potholes and the low tree limbs, and He knows what is around the bend. Trusting, we walk, safely, in the direction He sets. The light of the world lights our paths.

Day 199/July 17 – Psalm 119:121-176

Wonderful Words of Life
Psalm 119:129

S cripture is a great gift to us, for there we meet God's word. This long Psalm contains many synonyms. It employs *word*, *statutes*, *precepts*, *law*, *commands*, and *decrees* all to mean the same thing—what God has to say to us. This entire Psalm deals with how much God's word means to us when we learn and obey it. It is in many ways a tribute to the word of God.

There is a second set of synonyms in this Psalm: *righteous*, *delightful*, *comforting*, *precious*, *eternal*, *boundless*, *sweet*, *wonderful*, *right*, *tested*, and *true*. In any other context, it might be wrong to call those words "synonyms," for they seem, when not read in this particular passage, to be a list of unrelated adjectives.

In Psalm 119, however, these terms are indeed a variety of ways to describe the same thing. God's word is righteous. God's decrees are more precious that gold. God's statutes bring delight to our hearts. His precepts are tested. God's law is sweet. His promises are boundless. God's commands are comforting.

The Psalmist is facing the trouble with language we all experience. Trying to capture the fullness of what God says, how God leads us, and who God is in human terms is impossible. We turn to poetry and song as our best attempts to describe God, and we come up with lists of nouns and adjectives that, try as we might, only scratch the surface.

We love God's word. It is wonderful… and so much more.

Day 200/July 18 – Psalms 120-124

Sleepless in Heaven
Psalm 121:4

As we have made our way though the Old Testament, we have studied many facets of the eternity of God. He is omnipresent, found wherever we may go. He is omnipotent, with power beyond our comprehension that creates, sustains, and heals. He is omnitemporal, existing outside of the dimension of time and able to move through and around time effortlessly. He is all-loving, with mercy and forgiveness and compassion that will become fully visible to us in the person of Jesus.

This Psalm gives us yet another view of the eternity of God: He never sleeps. God is always awake, always watching. He cannot be surprised, cannot be caught napping, cannot be sneaked up on. He does not get tired. He has no need to catnap. When we are overtaken by grief and exhaustion, He is there to lift and strengthen us. The Psalmist tells us that God is present for every slip of our foot, to catch us and watch over our coming and going forever.

Setting these words in his great oratorio *Elijah*, Mendelssohn knew they are more than poetic descriptions of the greatness of God. This is the nitty-gritty. In your darkest night and your foulest dread… even in your late-night attempts to run away and hide, God is right there with you, always awake, always aware, always loving you.

A God who cannot be exhausted is a wonderful friend to have. Remember, Israel's story is our story, and He watching over Israel slumbers not nor sleeps.

Day 201/July 19 – Psalms 125-131

Building in Vain
Psalm 127:1

One of the great temptations for Christians, especially educated and talented Christians with nice homes and good jobs, is the lure of self-sufficiency. Because we can do things well and we understand how to make life work for us on a routine basis, we tend to rely on our own abilities too often.

At first glance, there is no obvious problem with self-reliance. We may get a better job and a nicer house. Our friends still like us. Disaster does not strike.

Over time, however, our choice to do things in our own strength, setting our own course, and depending on nobody and nothing else, is empty. The Psalmist calls it vanity. Sooner or later, we learn—actually we remember, for we learned this truth easily as children—that God is the source of everything. Our next breath is not guaranteed, much less success or ability. It is God who ordains that the stem grows up and the root grows down, that oxygen enters and carbon dioxide leaves, that the storm does or does not come. And we can do nothing to change that.

Unless the builder lets the Lord build the house, the labor is worthless. Unless God is watching, the work of the watchman is in vain. Self-reliance is tempting because it is deceptive – no one is easier to fool than yourself.

One of the beauties of the Psalms is their reminding us of the elementary things: Rest in God. Rely on God. Get out of the way.

Day 202/July 20 – Psalms 132-134

Unity
Psalm 133:1

David knows crisis can result from disunity. Running from the jealous and mad Saul through the desert, setting up a shadow kingdom in Hebron while Saul still rules in Jerusalem, and later seeking to avoid the coup d'état planned by his own son, David is plagued by separation and infighting throughout his career. There are moments, though, where he experiences the blessings of unity – the unification of the kingdom under his rule in Jerusalem, the blessing of his relationship with Jonathan, the successful military campaigns.

Why is unity so pleasant? What is good about unity?

Pay attention to what David says here. David does not tell us that uniformity, unquestioned subservience to authority, or obsequious obedience is good and pleasant. No, his focus is on unity. Unity exists even where there is not uniformity—indeed, the different parts of the unified body do different things. Unity exists alongside questions, for the mind is a crucial part of the body.

When the questions and the differences become interruption, antagonism, and rancor, then real unity is gone. When the atmosphere of a modern political campaign begins to characterize the people of God, there is no unity.

Jesus, foreshadowing Lincoln, tells us a house divided cannot stand.

Among believers, unity allows the work of God to proceed afoot. We are the body of Christ, and when all the parts of the body are working in unison, walking the same direction without struggling against one another, that body is an unstoppable force for good.

Enduring Love
Psalm 136:1

Psalm 136 is a litany, a repetitive responsive reading to be used in worship. As the leader recites different character-istics and actions of God, the congregation responds "His love endures forever."

Why does the Psalmist use this word *endures*? Why not say "God loves forever" or "God's love is everlasting" or "His love continues forever?"

The word *endures* is intentional. God's love is a life force, a positive, active, spiritual power that works through pain and betrayal and abandonment. Understanding that God is love (1 John 4:8) helps us see the very personal nature of love.

Love endures because God, who is love, endures.

God has not simply given us love. God is love.

When we turn our backs on love, we turn our backs on God. Yet His love endures forever.

When we decline His love and follow our own prodigal paths, He runs down the road to meet us. His love endures forever.

Endurance is a concept that we all understand. When we think of enduring, we immediately picture difficulty, for no one has to "endure" good things. To say that God's love "endures" is to understand the multiple hardships we throw God's way.

What does His love have to endure? It endures God's disappointment, our failures, our sin, our active denials, our choices not to reflect love in our own lives, and our willfully ignoring that love.

This litany repeats to make a point.

His love endures. His love endures. His love endures.

His love endures forever.

Day 204/July 22 – Psalms 138-140

You Have Searched Me, Now Search Me Again – Psalm 139:23

God, you have searched me. You know me. Wherever I am, there you are. You know when I sit and when I rise. If I run to the darkness, it is not dark to you. If I fly high or sink low, you are there before I arrive. If I travel to the other side of the earth, I arrive only to find you waiting. Whatever I do, you see. I cannot hide from you. Indeed, nothing about me is ever hidden from you.

You are there.

You know me. After all, you made me. You planned me in the secret places before the world existed, and you wove me together to be what I am. You know my every characteristic, my whims and my talents. You know me.

So here I am again, wishing ill on people you have created. I hear them curse you, and I feel hatred arise in my soul. My enemies surround me, and I want to cast them away, as though they are worthless.

As though I should not love them.

As though you do not love them.

Once again, you know me better than I know myself. Hatred for those who hate you seems natural, and yet I feel you gently remind me that I am offending.

I need to be shown myself by the One who knows me.

Search me, O God, for you know me. Look into my heart and show me my offensive ways. Lead me in your way everlasting.

Day 205/July 23 – Psalms 141-145

The Eyes of All Look to You
Psalm 145:15

Is it true? Will everyone recognize God, eventually? Do the eyes of all look to God?

The Bible makes this point again and again. God is the creator and sustainer of all, and at the end of the day, every created thing will recognize its creator and return from whence it came. The eyes of all will look to God.

The prophet quotes God: "Before me, every knee will bow; by me every tongue will swear." (Isaiah 45:23) The Apostle Paul notes that we will all stand before God's judgment seat. (Romans 14:10)

God's love and exaltation of Jesus is such that at the name of Jesus, every knee will bow, in heaven and on earth and under the earth, and every tongue will confess that Jesus Christ is Lord. (Philippians 2:9-10)

So what does this truth mean for you and me?

It means it is not a question of "if" but rather of "when." As the master of the universe and the most powerful—by far—being in existence, God's rightful place will be recognized by everyone. We will all have our "due season" before the throne of God.

God offers eternal abundant life beginning now. You need not wait until there is no choice, until you are not serving God as your Lord but rather acknowledging Him in a desperate act when your false gods have melted away.

The heavens declare the glory of God. Every tongue will confess Him as Lord.

The eyes of all see God.

Everything that Has Breath, Praise the Lord! – Psalm 150:6

The Book of Psalms ends with a rush. Praise, and more praise, and more praise. After all is said and done, after the complaints of bitterness, the songs of wonder, and prayers for forgiveness have been uttered and sung and offered, what is left is praise.

We praise with every instrument we have. We praise everywhere we are. Every created being praises God, and the Psalmist ends with praise upon praise upon praise.

Do you move past your honest questions to praising God? Do you weep by the waters of Babylon but then find a tambourine? Do you stand in amazement at the honor God has given you and then move on to the sounding trumpet and the harp?

Praise God from the heavens and the heights. Listen to the praise of the trees and the winds, the moon and the stars, the old men and the maidens and the little children.

The Psalmist does not end with a definition of praise; the Psalms end with a repeated command to praise. Your praise may sound different from that of your neighbors, hence the need for a lyre for one and a set of cymbals for another. One person may praise with dancing while another praises in humble silence.

The method is not the point. The tone of our hearts directed to a single recipient, an audience of one, is the point.

Mercy calls for praise.

Forgiveness calls for praise.

Grace always comes, and it calls for praise.

Praise the Lord.

Day 207/July 25 – Proverbs 1-2

Wisdom, Knowledge, and Understanding
Proverbs 2:6

Wisdom, knowledge, and understanding are three different and distinct things. Yes, they all come from God.
They are all gifts to be used for His work and His glory. But to confuse the three of them is a mistake.

Knowledge is the learning and retention of facts, theories, ideas,
and concepts. Knowledge creates a repository from which we draw
information.

Understanding is deeper than knowledge. Understanding is the
ability to analyze knowledge and figure out what it means and what
to do with it. Many have knowledge but are unable to function well
in the world. Those with understanding have the ability to take information and use it to their own benefit and to the betterment of the
world. Some call it common sense.

But wisdom is something far different from either. When the
Bible speaks of wisdom, it is describing the ability to see the world,
with its situations and problems and crises, as God sees the world.
The wise person sees a problem and hurts as God hurts, comprehends as God comprehends, and grasps the solution that God has
laid out.

None of us on earth will attain perfect wisdom. Only some have
the spiritual gift of wisdom, but all can seek to become wiser. That
is the primary purpose of Proverbs, a book of practicality springing
from the fear of the Lord. (Proverbs 1:7)

As you study Proverbs over the next couple of weeks, look for
the ways God sees the world, and emulate His wise view.

Day 208/July 26 – Proverbs 3-4

Our Own Understanding
Proverbs 3:5

This famous scripture does not tell us to trust God when we do not understand. That would be too easy. No, it commands that we trust God even when we don't think we need to, when we believe that we understand all on our own.

The natural corollary to trusting in God is that we do not trust in anything or anyone else... including ourselves. There is no such thing as partial trust, or trusting sometimes, or trusting for only some issues. You either have given your life to trusting God or you have not.

Trusting God when you do not understand, when you have nowhere else to turn, is the easier side of trust. It is much harder to trust God when you think you already understand, when you "have it under control." Our understanding is human and therefore limited and marred by our own failures. When we lean on our own understanding, we are choosing the wrong road, even when... especially when... we are sure we understand.

God gave us brains, and we are to use them. There is nothing wrong with doing our best to figure out what is going on and how to deal with it. The problem is in deciding that once we understand, we have no further need for God on that issue. Scripture does not teach us to trust God when we do not understand. Scripture says trust God even when we do understand.

Lean not on your own understanding.

The Full View of God
Proverbs 5:21

These chapters are dedicated to warnings against specific sins: they focus primarily on adultery but also list deceit, pride, and dishonesty. In the midst of these cautions is a fundamental truth about God reminiscent of Psalm 139: God sees everything, and nothing we do is hidden from Him. Everything is in the full view of God.

At first glance, the importance of this truth is that punishment follows sin. You cannot get away with it because God always knows what we have done. That is of course true. Sin is a violation of the will of God, and sin separates us from God. There is no way to commit sin without God's knowing about it, and we all have to face consequences when our sin finds us out.

To those who have walked with God for a long time, there is a much more nuanced—and comforting—import to this truth. We always walk and act and speak and relate within the full view of God. It is negative to say that we "cannot hide from God." It is uplifting to realize that God will never let us out of His view. Yesterday, we read about trusting in God. Today, we learn that that trust is well-placed, for God always has us in His sight. It is not a matter of hiding. It is a matter of the greatness of God, who always watches, always knows, and always guides.

You are always within the vision of God. Praise the Lord.

Day 210/July 28 – Proverbs 8-10

Wisdom Leads to Life
Proverbs 8:35

The words of Proverbs can be misused. These relatively simple sayings, if taken out of context as individual proof texts for life, can lead to all sorts of misunderstanding.

Think of famous proverbs in our own culture. We instruct our children that those who work hard will succeed, that the big bad wolf is always defeated in the end, and that slow and steady wins the race. Life teaches us that there are times when these so-called truisms are in fact not true: some of our hardest workers have little to show for their labors; the big bad wolves of the world seem awfully victorious at times; and cheaters and short-cutters seem to be winning all around us. We do not often see many race-winning turtles.

Does our experience mean that our children's proverbs are not true? Of course not. We know this wisdom of life is crucial to teach our children, for the underlying values represented by our stories and homilies will lead them, and us, in the right way.

The Book of Proverbs should be dealt with the same way. Do not get hung up with individual verses, particularly those that seem to indicate that taking a certain action or adopting a particular attitude will guarantee some kind of success. Instead, seek the underlying truth, the wisdom that begins with the fear of the Lord. (Proverbs 9:10) It is this truth, the word of God, that leads to wisdom, and it is this wisdom that leads to life.

Day 211/July 29 – Proverbs 11-13

Detestable Lying Lips
Proverbs 12:22

Some of the Proverbs seem so obvious that we may wonder why they need to be in scripture. The idea that the Lord detests lying lips may be one of those. We are taught the importance of honesty from our earliest days. Taking what was not ours, misrepresenting facts, and failing to admit what we knew to be true were all actions that, for most of us, brought swift consequences as we grew up. Our parents and teachers were unanimous in believing it was paramount that we learn honesty.

Still, somehow, those lying lips find their way onto our own faces. How can we, who have been taught the value of truth and honesty our entire lives, be the ones who need to be reminded how much God's hates lying?

Perhaps it is because we lose sight of what it really is to lie. As long as we are not blatantly making up great swaths of facts, or if we are simply making things "look better," we feel as if we are not liars. So long as our narrative is pretty close to the truth, we do not see ourselves as lying. We do not devise great misstatements; instead, we shade things to avoid hurting someone or to make ourselves appear slightly more heroic.

Lying, like any other sin, get easier with practice. The better at it we are, the more likely we are to conclude that we are not really lying. God knows better.

God detests our lying lips.

Day 212/July 30 – Proverbs 14-16

Pride Goes Before a Fall
Proverbs 16:18

The Proverbs have many ways of saying the same thing. Just in these three chapters, we read the same message again and again:

There is a way that seems right to a man, but in the end it leads to death. (Proverbs 14:12; 16:25)

A fool spurs his father's discipline, but whoever heeds correction shows prudence. (Proverbs 15:5)

The Lord tears down the proud man's house, but He keeps the widow's boundaries intact. (Proverbs 15:25)

The fear of the Lord teaches a man wisdom, and humility comes before honor. (Proverbs 15:33)

These are all ways of saying that when we are wrongly proud, when we rely totally on ourselves, when we trust in our own understanding instead of in the Lord, we are heading for problems. The King James language that we have all heard (actually a paraphrase or at least an abbreviation of Proverbs 16:18) is "pride goeth before a fall," and we all know this to be true. We can see object lessons in despots—Hitler, Saddam Hussein, Stalin—whose overwhelming trust in themselves left them on the ash heaps of history. Today's sports pages are littered with examples of talented and blessed individuals who have forgotten the source of their abilities and ruined themselves.

Pride is another word for undue self-reliance. The proud lean on their own understanding.

What about us? Do we rise up in our own strength, abandoning God, only to fail? The fall waits for those who are proud.

Jesus in the Old Testament
Proverbs 18:24

Finding Jesus present in Old Testament verses is a power-ful exercise. In human form, Jesus was born in Bethlehem, lived and died, and assumed His position at the right hand of God. But as a part of the eternal trinity, in His divine form, Jesus has always been, for He is God.

Where might we have seen Jesus already? Do you see Jesus in the ram sacrificed in place of Isaac? (Genesis 22:13) What about as the Passover lamb (Exodus 12:21-23), the scapegoat (Leviticus 7:10), water from the rock (Numbers 20:11), and the cities of refuge (Deuteronomy 4:41-42)? Perhaps He is the personification of the Promised Land or is the perfect Kinsman-Redeemer? As we read through the Psalms, we saw Jesus as the shepherd. In Genesis, he wrestled with Jacob and came to Joseph in dreams.

Now, amidst these Proverbs that can be seen simply as guides for daily living, we have this odd verse: "There is a friend who sticks closer than a brother." Jesus will teach His disciples about laying down one's life, but Jesus goes beyond the spoken teaching. Jesus actually lays down His life, not just for His friends, but for the entire world.

When we turn our backs on Jesus, He does not turn His back on us. When we despise Him and announce we want nothing to do with Him, He loves us and pursues us. Not even a brother does what Jesus does.

Jesus is the friend who sticks closer than a brother.

August

Day 214/August 1 – Proverbs 21-23

Train up a Child
Proverbs 22:6

We all know adults who were raised in the ways of God and who nonetheless have chosen a different, less righteous path from what was planned by their parents. Seeing such grownups leads some to conclude that, since training a child in the way that child should go is no guarantee that the child will not depart from that way, the Proverbs in specific and perhaps scripture as a whole should be discarded.

In fact, of course, reading the Proverbs not as series of individual proofs but rather as a consistent guide to life with God, leads to a far different conclusion. This Proverb, in the midst of a series of Proverbs that describe the best way to live in general, is of course correct—the best way to help someone live in the way of the Lord is to raise that person in that way when he is still a child. Not everyone raised that way will walk righteously, and not everyone raised badly will be unable to find the ways of God; in general, though, life teaches that this Proverb is true.

How do you participate in the training of children? Whether they are your own children, family members' children, children in your church, or kids on the block, are you taking the step to guide them in the ways of God, modeling the way they should go? Do you remember your own teaching as a child?

Do your part to train up a child. Believe the Proverb.

Day 215/August 2 – Proverbs 24-27

Iron Sharpens Iron
Proverbs 27:17

Who is your sharpener?

It is noteworthy that to sharpen an iron knife, one uses an iron sharpener. Better yet, the chef can take two iron knives and use them to sharpen each other, for as they come into contact in the hands of the master, they each serve to better the other.

The writer of this Proverb uses this easy analogy to make a point: We are all in this together. When you set out on your own, no matter how perfectly honed you are when you begin, you will grow dull. The best of knives, even in the hands of the greatest of cooks, grows dull if used alone. It is only the iron knife in contact with other iron knives that remains sharp.

You need your fellow followers of Christ. If there is no other reason to attend corporate church worship—and in fact there are many other reasons—it should be enough for you to join together with other believers just to have your edges sharpened. The fellowship of church members allows each of us to grow and develop in the ways God has for each of us. We are challenged, encouraged, taught, and ministered to.

If you have a best friend who is a Christian, you already understand this truth. You and your friend constantly work to better one another. You leave that friend's company knowing you are better than you were when you arrived.

You can be sharper. You are iron. Find more iron.

Add Nothing to the Words of God
Proverbs 30:6

D o you rely on God? Is God's word to you sufficient? Scripture is verified by God's words in prayer, through sermons, and by the words of Christian friends. God teaches us through nature and often speaks to us through our own experience. Nevertheless, many are tempted to add to what God has said. Consider:

"The Lord helps those who help themselves."

"God will never allow more than you can handle."

"I am not my brother's keeper."

None of these is in the Bible. Whether consciously or not, too many people have chosen to consider these sentences – and many others – as if they were scripture itself. In fact, all three of those sentences are directly contradicted by scripture.

Sometimes, additions to the words of God are not these easily disproven maxims but instead are subtle temptations to shade the will of God. We can and do add to what He has told us with slight alterations all our own. We add a condition on when we will help the needy, a qualification on which people are worthy of our forgiveness, or a certain circumstance when we do not really need to share the gospel. Suddenly, our lives are governed not by the words of God but by our own convenience and paraphrase. There is a real danger in trusting manmade augmentation to the clear teachings of God.

Do not add to what God has told you. His every word is flawless. What He tells us is always enough.

Day 217/August 4 – Ecclesiastes 1-4

Chasing After the Wind
Ecclesiastes 2:11

The abrupt change in tone and perspective as Proverbs ends and Ecclesiastes opens is jarring. Wisdom, the ideal of Proverbs, now seems tossed into the night. Ecclesiastes seems to be telling us that all those Proverbs are for naught.

This shift in tone is not a contradiction; it is a maturing view. The idealistic purveyor of Proverbs has grown into a Teacher who knows the world well. Just as we do not discount the proverbs of our own traditions because we find exceptions to them, we do not discount the Proverbs of scripture because we learn that our work and our wisdom can seem meaningless. Instead, we understand better.

Take a second look. While there is nothing new under our sun, Ecclesiastes is not taking the position that all is meaningless. The writer asks, "Without God, who can find enjoyment?" (Ecclesiastes 2:24-25) With Chapter 3's discussion of seasons, we begin to understand that the Teacher is pointing us to a designer beyond our understanding. God is not under our sun.

When we pursue wisdom and happiness and wealth on our own program and in our strength, we are chasing after wind. Whatever we think we are pursuing will vanish into thin air. But there is more to life than that. The mature writer knows that the key is to receive the blessing of God. (Ecclesiastes 3:13)

There is nothing new under the sun. Where we find something new is in another world. We must learn to turn our view heavenward.

No One Can Comprehend
Ecclesiastes 8:17

The world loses its meaning when we abandon God's plan. God made us upright, but our choices and scheming have led us to a place where all is meaningless. (Ecclesiastes 7:29) And thus, we who chase the wind cannot comprehend what goes on under the sun, no matter what effort we put into trying to discover the meaning of life. What God has created and how God works are truly inscrutable to us.

That puts a different, and far more mature, spin on the repeated use of the word "meaningless" in the first few chapters. The world is not empty and worthless, but its meaning escapes us. We are so small in the vastness of what God has created, and our human minds— truly puny to begin with and then clouded by sin—simply cannot capture the nuances of life.

Do not read this conclusion as a discouragement. The message is in fact one of hope and joy: there is so much more to the universe than we can see, and God has all of it prepared for us. No eye can see nor can the mind of man imagine what God has in store for us. (Isaiah 64:4; 1 Corinthians 2:9) The writer of Ecclesiastes has glimpsed the mind of God and has seen a phenomenal, loving, exciting panorama of ideas and gifts and pleasures that the rest of us cannot yet comprehend. It is all waiting for us.

No longer are we chasing wind; we are following God.

Day 219/August 6 – Ecclesiastes 9-12

The Whole Duty
Ecclesiastes 12:13

This strange and wonderful book ends with "the conclusion of the matter: Fear God and keep His commandments, for this is the whole duty of man."

We do not know the source of the wind or how the human body is formed in the womb, and we do not comprehend the ways of God. (Ecclesiastes 11:5) Our lives under the sun do not bring us meaning that we can understand. Seeking our own way is vanity.

But there is an alternative, a place to turn, a way to go. It is to fear God—to approach the creator with loving reverence that acknowledges His great power and mysterious ways—and to do His will, to keep His commandments.

Much of the New Testament will be devoted to teaching us what it really means to fear God and keep His commandments. For now, perhaps not even the Teacher knows for sure what the details are, and maybe that is the point. We may well not understand the fine print, but we cannot and must not let that failure to understand keep us from following God anyway.

For there is nothing else. Everything in this world, under our sun and made by our hands, lacks meaning outside of its place in the overwhelming will of God. To love our God, however, is to recognize there is more than what is here, more than what those around us see, more than is simply under the sun.

That is the conclusion of the matter.

Unquenchable Love
Song of Songs 8:7

The Song of Songs is beautiful love poetry, erotic and sensual, and unique in scripture. The eroticism bothers many, who are uncomfortable with such frankness in scripture so they search for an alternative reading, seeing the Song as an allegory for the love between God and God's people. While that reading may be an accurate interpretation, one does not have to read the Song as a complicated extended metaphor in order to garner great meaning from it. Glorying in God's gift of love is meaning enough. Romantic love is one of God's great gifts.

The desire of the lover for his beloved, and in turn her desire for him, arise because they are human and they each find the other overwhelmingly attractive. I am my beloved's and she is mine, says the lover. The beloved responds in kind, that she belongs to the lover and he to her. This love calls for unique bonding that allows for no other, and it is the goal that God has set and made possible in our lives.

The love between the two culminates in the beautiful poetry of chapter 8, verses 6 and 7, where they vow their love: "Set me as a seal on your heart… for love is stronger than death." This is a love that cannot be quenched even by many waters.

What a gift of God! What a standard by which our marriages should be judged! What a goal for each of us!

Unquenchable love is stronger than death.

Day 221 / August 8 – Isaiah 1-4

It Is Going to Be All Right
Isaiah 1:18, 2:4

We shift gears again to the greatest of the writing prophets, Isaiah. His message will include much judgment and condemnation of the actions of the people of Israel as he predicts the oncoming exile. More importantly, he will announce the judgment of God that will ultimately fall on the shoulders of the suffering servant, Jesus.

But Isaiah starts—before diving into the details of judgment, sin, exile, and condemnation—with the conclusion of the story. He begins by making sure everyone knows that, in the end, it is going to be all right. Grace always comes.

There are two facets to this prophecy. The first is on a spiritual level. God is waiting to reason with us, and He offers forgiveness. Though your sins be as scarlet, they shall be white as snow. Though they be red as crimson, they shall be as wool. This poetry, familiar to so many of us raised with the hymns of the church, is shocking and new to Isaiah's readers, who will desperately cling to the hope of forgiveness that transcends the pain of exile and judgment.

The second hopeful message is personal. It is about how we will treat each other. Our weapons of destruction and death will be transformed into implements of growth and development, for we will no longer seek war. There are miles to go between here and there, but our swords will be beaten into plowshares.

Transformation is coming. In the end, it will be all right.

Holy, Holy, Holy
Isaiah 6:3

The Hebrew language uses repetition in the way that English uses comparative and superlative adverbs. If in English we were to say that a fruit tree smells "very, very sweet" or is "the sweetest," the Hebrew version would translate "sweet, sweet, sweet."

The seraphim use the Hebrew superlative to sing the holiness of God. The point is twofold: there is nothing holier than God, and there is nothing more characteristic of God than holiness.

To be holy is to be uniquely pure, set apart, entitled to be worshiped. The point of the song of the seraphim is that the purity of God—sinlessness, utter cleanliness, incapability of consideration of doing wrong—is matched by God's entitlement, alone and apart from anything and anyone else, to be revered and worshiped by all creation.

It is noteworthy that nowhere in the Old Testament is God described as "powerful, powerful, powerful" or "righteous, righteous, righteous" or even "love, love, love." God is, of course, powerful and righteous. God is love. Yet, the overwhelming characteristic that infuses the song of the creatures of heaven is God's holiness. Before we understand God's power or righteousness or love, we first come to grips with God's holiness.

When you think of God, is the first thing that comes to mind holiness? It should be. Your first concept when God comes to your mind should be His absolute purity, His worthiness of your worship, His holiness. We worship the God who stands alone.

God is holy, holy, holy.

Day 223/August 10 – Isaiah 9-13

On the Holy Mountain
Isaiah 11:6-9

In the middle of Isaiah's chastisement of Israel for its failures to follow God and his prediction of the exile to come, he interrupts his forecast of doom to present the Old Testament version of the gospel. A child will be born to us who will become the Wonderful Counselor, Mighty God, Everlasting Father, and Prince of Peace. Just after we have been taught that the bough of the people will be cut off, we learn that from the stump a branch will grow, a rose will bloom that will be the one on whom the Spirit of the Lord will rest.

And this juxtaposition of punishment/promise and exile/salvation comes to a head with the description of unlike creatures lying down together: the wolf and the lamb; the leopard and the goat; the calf and the lion; the infant and the cobra; and the young child and the viper. On the holy mountain of the Lord, all creation will be at peace.

What is the key? What will cause this radical alteration in what otherwise would appear to be the natural order of things?

A little child will lead them.

This child who will rise from the line of Jesse, this son given to us who will take the government on His shoulder, will do more than simply make people be nicer and give a little more to the poor. This coming child will change the way the world works. Exile comes, but Christ conquers.

Even here, grace always comes.

Day 224 / August 11 – Isaiah 14-19

Seeing the Enemy Fall
Isaiah 14:12-15

Exile is coming, but deliverance will follow. Isaiah's prophecy is replete with the bigger picture. These chapters start with the promise that the Lord will have compassion on His people, and these chapters continue with prophecies of doom for enemies from Assyria, Philistia, Moab, Damascus, Cush, and Egypt.

The king of Babylon, the leader of the great army to take some of the people of God into exile, gets unique attention, as Isaiah speaks of his fall to earth as though he were a falling star. Some read this passage as a description of what they believe to be the fall of Satan from a position with the angels.

Kings come and go. Supernatural battles we cannot understand continue. Whether you see this passage as only applicable to the Babylonian king, as a description of a *Paradise Lost*-like battle of the angels, or something else, it is important to see the bigger message here.

God will defeat our enemies. Grace always comes.

We all have figurative Philistines, Moabites, and Egyptians in our lives. They attack, hinder, and enslave us. We find ourselves fighting a personal multi-front war without success.

And that is where the promise of God comes in. Yes, our sins will find us out, and we may have to go through a period of exile. But God will have compassion on His children, and He will defeat our enemies, including our ultimate enemies, Satan and evil. They will fall to the depths in defeat.

The good news continues.

Day 225/August 12 – Isaiah 20-24

Look to the Maker
Isaiah 22:11

A re you a builder of reservoirs?

Most of us are. We open bank accounts, buy extra clothes, store food, and plan ahead for retirement. Good for us. Scripture does not teach us that preparedness and planning for the future are bad.

The problem appears not when we build but when we trust in our reservoirs. Pools hold water. God made us, and God knows we need water. But when we trust in the water and the container, but not in the creator of water, we find ourselves in trouble.

When we put our trust in our homes, our jobs, our economy, our armies, and our merchandise, we are in trouble. God know we need shelter, work, an income, protection, and material, but He too often is left on the outside by us, looking in as we treasure our own creations.

When we put our trust in our arts, our music, our education, and our writing, we are in trouble. God has given us great gifts, talents, and minds, but when they come before Him in importance, we have forgotten the maker.

Too often, our trust is in family, friends, and other people. They are great gifts to us, no doubt, but they too easily replace the Giver in our hearts.

Eventually, we trust ourselves. We look within our own lives and abilities for reservoirs on which we draw, and we once again have forgotten the Maker.

Exile awaits those who forget the Maker. Live your life by trusting in God.

Perfect Peace
Isaiah 26:3

The idea of "perfect peace" seems like a pipedream, and yet… the prophet says God will keep those whose mind is steadfast, those who trust in God, in perfect peace. He has called Jesus the Prince of Peace. What is Isaiah telling us?

It is the same thing Paul means when he teaches about the peace, which passes all understanding, that guards our hearts and minds in Christ Jesus when we choose not to worry anxiously but instead present our needs to the Father in prayer. (Philippians 4:6-7)

It means that trusting in God leaves nothing for us to fret about. It is the complete giving of oneself to the protection of the Father. Think of the infant child in her mother's arms, literally without a care in the world. Think of the new bridegroom, saying "I do" while looking at his new bride with all the love and confidence his heart can create, never once betraying a fear for what will come next. It is the patient giving himself to the surgeon, the student to the teacher, the congregant to the rector.

The relationship between trust and peace is inexorable and inscrutable and divine. And that is why we rarely experience perfect peace… because we rarely really trust. Trusting God requires one to give up control, to believe that someone other than oneself is best-suited to run things. And that goes against our grain.

Do you want perfect peace? Trust God, your Father. Set your mind firmly on Him.

Day 227/August 14 – Isaiah 29-32

Bad Worship
Isaiah 29:13

Many people say religious words and call what they are doing worship.

We can dress events up and call them a "worship service," a "mass," a "celebration," a "retreat," a "festival," "Eucharist," "fellowship," "devotion," "contemporary praise," or any of a thousand other titles; but if they are full of words that mention God but follow manmade rules and do not represent hearts that are near to God, they are a waste of time. God hates them.

"Hate" is not too strong a word. In Amos 5:21 and Isaiah 1:11, scripture tells us that God hates religious festivals of those whose hearts and actions do not reflect Him. In 1 Samuel 15:22, God tells Israel He despises their feasts and solemn assemblies when they do not flow out of a contrite heart.

It is not hard to find examples of so-called worship that are full of song with worship-ish words and rituals that have been carved, sometimes through the centuries and sometimes in the last fifteen minutes, by the human powers that be. You can find some by turning on your television. You can find others by walking to a nearby church building. Faulty worship is epidemic.

Examine your worship. If your personal time of devotion is not built on your relationship with Christ and your heart's search to be closer to Him, change your ways. If your congregation focuses on calling out "Lord, Lord" but does not do His will, challenge your leaders.

Worship is too important to do badly.

Streams in the Desert
Isaiah 33:3-7

This beautiful passage describes not just renewal but transformation. Feeble knees are strengthened. Fearful hearts are made strong. The eyes of the blind open, and the ears of the deaf can hear. The mute shout for joy.

All of these contrasts are clear statements of what God has in store for us. Two of them in particular stand out in their imagery.

The first is the picture of the lame leaping like a deer. The prophet/poet could have simply said "the lame will walk again," but that sentence—true though it may be—does not fully express the transformation awaiting the people of God. Walking is mundane. Those who could not walk before will now be leaping, and they will leap not as happy people do but as does the deer.

The second is the idea of streams in the desert. The Israelite people know about deserts. The Middle East where they live is desert upon desert, and to write of water "gushing" is a sure fire attention-getter. The reminder of water gushing from the rock in Meribah to the wandering Israelites (Exodus 17:7) tells these people of the awesome power of God to create what they need when they need it.

The picture of streams in the desert is renewal to be sure. It is transformation. It is what happens when God comes, bringing His grace that always comes with Him, replacing what was with what could not have even been imagined.

Take a good look. This is heaven.

Day 229 / August 16 – Isaiah 37-40

Fly, Run, Walk
Isaiah 40:31

When grace comes, those of us whose hope is placed in the Lord will fully realize the comfort and the blessing He has for us.

We mount up with wings as eagles. We fly. We are able to do things that were never possible before. Miracles characterize our lives as we are transformed into something new. Our worship is ecstatic as we think about flying, walking on water, and living forever. We will be changed.

And then, at other times, we run and are not weary. We are in a race, and at the end, we will look back and see that we have finished the contest, fought the good fight, and exhausted every energy we have for the work of God. Our worship is exalted, dignified, constant as we know what it is to run the race of God.

And sometimes, when grace comes, we walk without fainting. Life is hard, and many times we are battered by what the world has in store. In those instances, perhaps the greatest gift of grace and hope is simply the ability to get out of bed in the morning, make it through the day, and survive. Grace allows us to walk without fainting. Our worship may consist of daily work in the trenches of the church, handing out another hot meal and pausing for the simplest of payers.

Flying is great, but steady walking is more often what we need.

Grace comes, and God allows us to fly, run, and walk.

When You Walk through the Fire
Isaiah 43:2

The message of the prophet that we should not be afraid must not be confused with a happy but overly simplistic claim that "there is nothing to fear." The prophet says no such thing. Those who preach that faith makes all obstacles and dangers disappear are wrong.

There will be waters that are so high that we cannot float over them but must pass through them. There will be floods that cross our way, threatening to sweep over us. There will be fires on our paths, poised to set us ablaze. God makes no promise that these perils will evaporate in the face of grace.

No, the promise of God is so much greater than a desperate attempt at some sort of magic trick to make the bad things immediately disappear. The promise of God is that we will overcome these hazards. God will be with us, so the floods will not sweep us over and the flames will not burn us.

Paul says the same thing, guaranteeing that in this life we will be hard pressed, perplexed, persecuted, and struck down. But grace always comes, and we will not be crushed. Grace means we will not be in despair. Hope means that we know that we are never abandoned. The presence of God means that we are not destroyed. (2 Corinthians 4:8-9)

Do not be afraid, for God will be with you. He is the holy one. He is your savior. Fear not, for your Redeemer calls your name.

There Is No Other
Isaiah 45:5

God's message crescendos. While there has been discussion of "other gods" in the context of the tendency of the ancient peoples to worship many different things, the prophet now makes one thing perfectly clear: God is unique. There is no other god.

"I am the Lord, and there is no other; apart from me there is no God." (Isaiah 45:5)

"There is none beside me." (Isaiah 45:6)

"And there is no God apart from me, a righteous God and a Savior; there is none but me." (Isaiah 45:21)

"They will say of me, 'in the Lord alone are righteousness and strength.'" (Isaiah 45:24)

"I am God, and there is no other." (Isaiah 46:9)

"I am he; I am the first and I am the last." (Isaiah 48:12)

"Then all mankind will know that I, the Lord, am your Savior, your Redeemer, the Mighty One of Jacob." (Isaiah 49:26)

Clearly, we are intended to notice this repeated message. Young Israel is growing up, and it is time to put away childish things. God is not the best choice; God is the only choice. This is our story; it is time for us to get rid of our immature ideas as well. There is no other god. There are not other different spiritual beings out there with whom we can commune. God is God, and nothing else comes close. If we pay attention to this truth, He gives us peace like a river. (Isaiah 48:18)

Be clear. There is only one God.

The Suffering Servant
Isaiah 53:3-7

That Isaiah writes these words in the past tense as if they depict an event that has already occurred is a masterpiece of visionary description. In the timelessness of God's world as told by this greatest of Old Testament prophets, the saving actions of Jesus are clear. Isaiah sees the prophecy as clearly as history itself.

What does this passage proclaim about Jesus? The prophet tells us that the very Son of God, the picture of love and the Prince of Peace, voluntarily takes upon Himself our failures, our sins, and our sorrows. No wonder we reject and despise Him, for He looks like someone who has been stricken by God. He is pierced by sword and nail and thorn, not for anything He has done, but as a result of our transgressions. He is crushed with the weight of the world's sin on His shoulders as His broken legs cannot hold His own body enough to take another breath on the Roman cross of execution.

We wander like sheep, going astray from the path that the Father has patiently laid out for us.

And how does God handle our failures? He puts them all on the shoulders of His Son, the greatest servant who will ever live. When He is called the "Lamb of God," this is the picture: this most innocent of victims, who walks into sacrificial slaughter without a single peep of protest.

He bears our sins. We are healed as He is wounded.

Grace always comes.

Day 233/August 20 – Isaiah 55-60

Not Our Thoughts; Not Our Ways
Isaiah 55:8

It can become easy to think of God in human terms. He is "the man upstairs." We picture Him as the perfect parent, teacher, friend, and mentor. We read personifications of God in scripture, and we begin to picture His arms, His face, His finger, and His smile.

We in fact seek and find a personal relationship with God.

In all of this, we must be careful to remember that God is not one of us. He is not like us. We relate to Him only because He stoops from His heaven to find us where we are.

God is perfect. God is holy. God is eternal. God is omnipotent, creating everything in our world and giving us our next breath.

God is other. He does not do things the way we do them or even the way we would do them if we could. He does not think as we think, nor does He think the way we wish we could think if we were not so self-centered.

No, God operates on a plane and in a dimension we cannot understand. Isaiah says that God's ways are "higher" than ours. This means many things, among which is that we cannot understand God. He is simply too complex for our comprehension.

This is good news, for our problems are far too great for us to decipher. Evil is too cunning and too powerful for us to defeat. Death is too final for us to conquer.

But God has higher ways.

To Comfort All Who Mourn
Isaiah 61:2

This great book of prophecy ends where it began: It is going to be all right, because grace always comes.

The words of the first two verses of chapter 61 announce the message that the prophet brings—good news, peace for the brokenhearted, freedom for captives, release for prisoners, and comfort for the mourners. Despite sin and rebellion and exile, God has a plan to rescue His people, who will once again see God's favor.

Jesus quotes these very words in His first public sermon, in the synagogue in Nazareth, telling the listeners that the words of Isaiah 61 are fulfilled in Christ Himself. (Luke 4:18-21) Jesus is the good news. Jesus binds up your brokenness, frees you from your captivity, releases you from what would hold you, and comforts you when you grieve.

We are now nearly two-thirds of the way through the year and two-thirds of the way through scripture. What has all of this meant to you? You have read about the power of God. You have seen the love of God played out in the forgiveness of Jacob/Israel, whose story is our story. You have read the message of Job and the poetry of the wisdom literature. God has appeared at every turn.

Now, you have read the great prophet, and you know the plan that God has laid out. You know grace always comes.

Rejoice with Jerusalem and be glad for her, for God satisfies and comforts.

Is this good news speaking to your heart?

Day 235/August 22 – Jeremiah 1-2

Two Sins
Jeremiah 2:13

Jeremiah uses metaphor repeatedly in his prophecy to lay out to a people headed for exile exactly why they will soon be carried forcibly from the Promised Land. He starts his prophecy using the image of water—simple, universally recognized as essential, and life-giving. And where water is concerned, Israel is in trouble.

The failure of Israel that will lead to deportation is twofold, as Jeremiah points out. Not only have the people forsaken God, the source of living water, but they have also sought out and created their own holding tanks, their own cisterns, for their water.

Do not write this off as an ancient word from an irrelevant priest. We too have water problems.

Like Israel, we are in danger of forsaking the spring, the source of or life. We sin, we choose not to follow, and we turn our backs on the giver of life, the source of our living water. Like Israel, we forget who has brought us safe thus far, and who is leading us home. We are distracted by the shiny things of the world.

And like Israel, our breakdown does not stop there. We do not leave the paths of God without a destination: our target, whether we know it or not, is our own self-creation. When we stop following God, we start pursuing our own devices, our own dreams, and our own delusions. We build our own cisterns, and they are broken.

We abandon the source. We create worthless replacements.

Two sins.

Return and Acknowledge Your Guilt
Jeremiah 3:12-13

J eremiah embarks on another metaphor to explain the unfaithfulness of Israel and Judah to God, referring to the
people of God as prostitutes and unfaithful wives. The pain God
has experienced is compared to serial adultery and rampant sexual
wickedness because God has pledged Himself to His people and
accepted their promise to give themselves to Him, only to find them
again and again giving themselves to other gods, heathen traditions,
amoral practices, and foreign peoples.

And yet, this spurned husband yearns to accept His wife again.
God tells Jeremiah that despite their repeated unfaithfulness and
the disgusting spectacle His people have made of themselves, God
stands ready to take them back.

God asks only that the unfaithful own up to their wanderings,
admit their failings, and return to God's ways that have proven themselves for centuries to be the only true source of protection and
salvation for the people.

God pleads with His people to return, to set aside their idols and
their wandering eyes. Despite the continual choices of His people
to ignore Him and to take up with others, God is ready to forgive.

What wondrous love is this! How marvelous is the love of one
who stands ready to accept the return of a people so perverse, so
unfaithful, so unworthy of love.

This is the essence of the unmerited favor of one who stands
with arms open, waiting for you to return.

Forgiving the unforgivable, loving the unlovable, wanting the
unwantable... grace always comes.

Day 237/August 24 – Jeremiah 6-8

Trusting in Deceptive Words
Jeremiah 7:8

There are many charming and attractive leaders in this world who offer worthless maxims and wrong directions. When those people are—or claim to be—Christian leaders, there can be real damage to the work of God.

Greedy for gain—material, social, political, and psychological—that comes with popularity, these false prophets peddle the political, the happy, the feel-good message. They call out "Peace, peace" when there is no peace. (Jeremiah 6:14 and 8:11) They do not bring a message of truth or even of hope: there is no possibility of peace in any foreseeable future for Israel as Jeremiah writes, for an army from the north is coming. But truth and hope are not the goals of these charlatans. Their goal is to scratch the itch of their listeners, to say what they perceive audiences want to hear. Jeremiah knows that what the people need is to get off their high horse, to confess and repent and desperately seek the mercy of God. The prosperity preachers understand that the need to debase oneself is never a message that wins friends, and they go instead for the easy applause.

These false preachers have no shame about claiming sanctuary in the local place of worship. As long as they are behind their pulpits, they claim the protection of "the temple of the Lord" and then say whatever they want. (Jeremiah 7:4)

The warning is clear. These false religious figures, still today, are worthless and dangerous.

Be aware, and stay away.

Ready for the Thickets
Jeremiah 12:5

Jeremiah interrupts his prophecy of doom to teach a great theological lesson. In the first four verses of the twelfth chapter, Jeremiah presents the complaint of the people to God, asking why injustice has stricken the devoted when faithless people seem to live at ease.

The answer is not easy, but it demonstrates with incredible insight the amazing confidence God has in His people, even when they have no faith in Him. God has great things in mind for us, and He knows that we are not naturally ready for them. So God has to get us ready. God always prepares us for what He has prepared for us, but that preparation comes at a price.

God wants us to compete against the strongest and fastest horses, not simply run races against ordinary people. God wants us able to make our way through the densest thickets, not simply to play it safe in easy country.

And the only way we will be able to plunge headlong into and through the jungle undergrowth is to be tested, to be tried, to face and overcome the obstacles of injustice and hatred and disease and storm.

It is a hard lesson. God does not send every—or even most—hardships that come our way, but He certainly uses them to buffet us to a musculature that prepares us for greater things than we can imagine.

Thickets and challenges await, but the reward for making our way through them is staggering. Are you ready?

Day 239/August 26 – Jeremiah 13-16

There Is a Reason for Exile
Jeremiah 13:22

If you wonder why this is happening to you, Jeremiah says, there is a reason. It is because of your many sins.

To be sure, there are many terrible things that happen that we do not cause. Most of the horrible happenings in the world are not a result of sin. The reasons for storms and sickness and crime and war are multiple, and the fact that evil has a foothold in the world is primary among them.

But, just as God does not always intervene, it is true that, from time to time, God at least allows proverbial armies from the north to enter our world and attack. Take note: God does not act in a willy-nilly fashion, and He never punishes us without plenty of notice. But with forewarning, and in a deliberate manner, God has assuredly entered into history. The nature of things is that people's sins find them out.

The point of these verses is not to send us on a witch hunt whenever terrorists attack or famine appears. The point is rather to make us aware when God is speaking, to assure that we will listen to God when He warns us of oncoming disaster that we are bringing upon ourselves. The point is to teach us that turning from God is choosing exile.

Our sins have consequences. Sometimes grace means that mercy intervenes and protects us. Sometimes grace means we have to go through the exile and come out better on the other side.

The Deceitful Heart
Jeremiah 17:9

At the end of her diary, Anne Frank writes, "In spite of everything, I still believe that people are really good at heart."[3]

That famous line, poetic and inspiring though it may be, is wrong. At heart, we are not good. We are deceitful. Our nature is sinful. We are prone to wander. Left to our own devices, we choose wrongly. People are not really good at heart.

This has been the message of the Old Testament over and over again. We eat the forbidden fruit, make an inadequate offering and burn with jealousy towards the one who offers better, build towers to ourselves, deceive, lie, kill, and build golden calves. We refuse to follow the will of God. We covet the wife of our friend, murder faithful patriots, commit adultery, and then work to cover up our failures. We repeatedly violate our covenant with God. We are lost.

What an important lesson. As long as we think we have it within ourselves to do good, we will never see the need for the direction of God. While we think we can find the right way on our own, we will not understand our need for a savior.

Our hearts are deceitful. We are corrupt. We are beyond cure, and we do not understand why.

Jeremiah is leading somewhere. A new covenant is coming. God loves us. God has made a way that we cannot make for ourselves.

Do not rely on your heart. God is greater than your heart.

---

3   Frank, Anne, *The Diary of a Young Girl*, 1947.

What Has God Done for Me Lately?
Jeremiah 23:7-8

Exile approaches. God knows that His people are destined for captivity. The only way to survive now is to submit to the coming invaders.

God already knows that restoration will follow exile. God, who embodies love and mercy, has built into His world the plan that grace will always come.

Jeremiah looks to this future and remarks that a day is drawing close when people will not refer to God as the one who brought His people out of Egypt but rather as the one who brought them out of Babylon to return to the Promised Land.

He is the God who brought His people out of slavery, who restored His people after exile, who sent His son to die for our sins and then conquered death by raising Jesus from the dead, and who built a church against which the gates of hell itself cannot prevail.

But that is not all.

You do not have to rely on ancient history and centuries-old blessings to find a reason to love God. You have experienced God in a worship service, in a song, or in the words of a friend. You still see prayer answered, catastrophe avoided, sickness healed, and peace bestowed.

God is continuing to work. He is the God of your last breath and your next, the God who has brought you safe thus far, and the God who is leading you home. Praise God for the past, but revel in what He is doing for you even now.

At What Risk?
Jeremiah 26:8-9

Jeremiah is a target, facing and enduring great personal turmoil as a preacher of a most unpopular message. Many who hear him are offended, or frightened, or enraged by his message to the point where he is in danger of death.

Fortunately, cooler heads prevail, noting both that other prophets have brought a similar message and lived to tell about it and that Jeremiah is speaking on behalf of God Himself. Jeremiah's life is spared.

Does Jeremiah know at the beginning of Jeremiah 26 that he will live to speak the words of Chapter 27? The answer is no, he doesn't. Still, he preaches anyway, marching into the courts of the leaders of the people who are marking the path toward exile.

Why? What pushes Jeremiah to take such a risk?

Why did the early Christian martyrs stand up to the Roman authorities like Domitian who had no use for them and their Christ? Why did Martin Luther and Martin Luther King speak words they knew would not be tolerated? Why did Stephen and Mother Teresa and a high school girl in Columbine, Colorado continue to bear witness to the Jesus who was anathema to those around them?

Because they must.

The example of the martyrs and the prophets is hard for some to understand. These heroes bear witness to the truth and the power of the Word of God. They knew the Father and heard Him speak, and they had no alternative but to obey, no matter the risk.

Day 243/August 30 – Jeremiah 28-31:20

Healing the Incurable Wound
Jeremiah 30:12, 17

These chapters contain rich language about the promise of restoration to come. When Jeremiah tells Israel to pray for the city of Babylon and to seek its peace because that is where God has carried them (Jeremiah 29:7), he is promising them that, in the short term, they will be living among the enemy. Modern parlance for Jeremiah's message is this: the Israelites should bloom where they are planted. When Jeremiah tells them that God knows the plans for hope and a future that He has for them (Jeremiah 29:11), He is promising that, in the long term, they will be returned to their home, the Promised Land of God.

And when He explains that only God can cure the incurable, that only God can bring health to those injured beyond healing, that only God can touch our grievous wounds and leave us perfectly well… it is then that Jeremiah is reaching beyond even the long term. Jeremiah is now talking about the longest term, the eternal.

The God we serve is the great physician. Our God is the specialist in fixing what cannot be fixed. What is impossible with humans is child's play for God. (Matthew 19:26; Luke 1:37)

We have an incurable malady. Sin, universal among us all, separates us from God, and there is nothing any of us can do about it.

Yet, God will restore. God will rebuild. In the short term, in the long term, and forever.

God brings us near, and we are healed.

The New Covenant
Jeremiah 31:33

It is perhaps the climax of the Old Testament. It is certainly a clear preview of the theology that will develop after the cross. It is the promise of our relationship with God.

It is the New Covenant. It is Grace.

The covenant of the Old Testament, beginning with Abram in Genesis, can be described as this formula, laid out by God for His people: Keep my commandments, and you will be my people. Time and again, the people of Israel have violated this covenant; and, time and again, God has forgiven the people and renewed the covenant.

By the time of Jeremiah, it is clear that people are hapless and hopeless. History, not to mention human nature, teaches that we will not keep the old covenant. We are prone to wander. Our hearts are deceitful. We sin and do not keep the commandments of God.

So, we need a New Covenant. And it is here, in Jeremiah 31, that we get our glimpse of what the covenant will be after Christ has done His work.

The New Covenant will not be based on tablets and written commandments; it will be written on the hearts of God's people. The New Covenant will not be based on humanity's search for God, for God will make Himself known. The New Covenant will not be based on our failings, for God will forgive our wickedness and remember our sins no more.

The New Covenant is coming. That is no surprise; grace always comes.

September

Day 245 / September 1 – Jeremiah 34-36

Perhaps
Jeremiah 36:7

Even in the last moments before the Babylonian armies invade, God and Jeremiah are trying to save the people. God tells Jeremiah to write more scrolls filled with the words of God.

Perhaps Israel will hear God's words and petition God for help.

Perhaps they will hear Jeremiah's prophecy and turn from their wicked ways.

Perhaps they will take the time to think through their errors and radically change course to avoid the coming disaster.

Perhaps the word of God will have the effect of changing their mind. Perhaps the king will not tear the scroll page from page and burn it. Perhaps God will be honored…

Perhaps…

Of course, we who are on the other side of history know that none of these things will happen without decades of exile, multiple prophets, occupation by the Roman empire, a virgin birth, a crucifixion, and a resurrection. It will not happen without a new covenant.

But, just for today, we have to admire God's persistent optimism. God, who knows that His people will continue to wander, nonetheless posits another way, a means of salvation. There is power in the prophecy of Jeremiah. The people of Israel choose not take advantage of that power, but that does not mean God speaks in vain or Jeremiah writes for no purpose. These prophecies live today, for us to read and understand. We still are prone to wander, and God still optimistically points us the right way.

Perhaps we will finally learn to follow Him.

Jerusalem Falls
Jeremiah 38:28

It is a sad day. Jerusalem—the city of David, the headquarters of the Promised Land, and the mighty capitol of God's people—falls. God allows the heathens to invade, to capture, and to destroy. God allows His people to be carried off.

The great plan that dates back to Abram and Moses seems to be over.

The idea of a separate people dedicated to God seems to have failed.

To be sure, the failure is not God's doing. God has provided the people a home, led the way, given leaders, parted seas, laid out the ground rules, miraculously solved problems, and forgiven them again and again.

Still, it appears now that God's faith in these people has been in vain. Despite clear warnings and what, in retrospect, we know to be obviously better choices that could and should have been made, these people—the ones God chose—have run headlong into exile. Their fortress is gone. Their great city has fallen.

It is a sad day.

Where has God led you? What forgiveness has God given you, only to have you turn your back again and again? How are you doing following God's direction?

Have you lived a life worthy of the faith that God has placed in you? As you look back and see how God has provided manna and healed your wounds, are you the person whose choice and direction reflect those gifts?

Are you running straight into exile? Are the invaders at your door?

Don't Go Back to Egypt
Jeremiah 42:17

The irony of these chapters is hard to miss. Long ago, when those escaping slavery ran into hard times in the desert, some of the Israelites began to romanticize what they had left behind and openly suggested that they had been better off in Egypt. (Numbers 11:17) They "in their hearts turned back to Egypt" when they built the golden calf. (Acts 7:39)

Imagine announcing that you were better off in slavery. Imagine desiring in your heart to go back to the place where you were forced to make bricks without straw, where you were whipped, where you desperately wanted to escape.

Now, it happens again. The remnant of Judah, who have seen their city burned, ask Jeremiah to pray for them. Jeremiah assures them of God's protection if they will simply stay put. The only prohibition Jeremiah gives them—the forbidden fruit of their day—is going to Egypt. If they go back to Egypt, the land out of which their ancestors marched during the funerals of the firstborn, they will walk into disaster.

It is unthinkable that we would want to go back to Egypt… isn't it? We would never decide to go back to that place of slavery and despair… would we?

We could never choose to walk into what God promises will be disaster… could we?

Yet, temptation always waggles a finger in our direction. What once bound us lures us again. Addiction never truly gives up.

Do not go back to Egypt. Disaster awaits.

Restoration for Moab
Jeremiah 48:47

The message of restoration is a theme of Jeremiah's prophecy from the beginning. Israel is heading for well-deserved exile, and there will be decades of struggle in a foreign land, but there is a very real light at the end of that tunnel. God will not forget His people, and He will bring them out of exile and back home.

What may be surprising is that this message of restoration is not limited to God's chosen people. The kingdoms of Judah's enemies—Egypt, Philistia, and Moab—all receive messages of condemnation from Jeremiah, for they too have wandered far from God's wishes. They too face imminent invaders who will attack and overcome and bring them their own brand of exile.

Moab, homeland of Ruth founded by descendants of Lot, has long been in conflict with the chosen people, fighting against Jehoshaphat and invading Israel. Moab, despite its beginnings, finds itself on a list with Pharaoh and the Philistines, promised coming ruin.

And yet, God promises restoration for Moab.

The Old Testament—indeed the entire Bible—is not the story of any one nation, even of Israel. It is the story of God. To be sure, it is largely told through the lens of one nation, the chosen people of Israel, but it is the story of God. We often have trouble seeing God's affection for peoples who are different from us. God plays no favorites, and His promises are extended to all whom He loves.

Even the Moabites.

Even us.

God is Greater than Babylon
Jeremiah 50:29-40

Even though the Babylonians are coming, they are not the world's greatest power. Another army from the north, the Persians, will one day march in and conquer Nebuchadnezzar (Jeremiah 50:2-3). But just as the Babylonians do not hold the last word, neither do the Persians.

The holder of the keys is and always has been God. The Babylonians are arrogant, the Persians are powerful, and evil runs amok; but the Redeemer is strong, and the Lord Almighty is His name.

We all, from time to time, find ourselves swimming against the tide with danger all around us. We have chosen the wrong pond, and before we know it, we have swum over the dam and into the current where the big fish are waiting to devour us. It is little comfort that those fish in turn will be eaten by bigger fish; all we know is that we are surrounded with no way of escape.

Disease, disappointment, enemies near and far, want, need, betrayal, and loss nip at our heels. We bypass some and conquer others, only to face divorce, unemployment, humiliation, anger, pain, and selfishness in a never-ending stream that jeopardizes our existence.

We know the end of the story. Babylon loses.

Our God is strong. The biggest fish cannot withstand the Redeemer. Rest easy… though the menaces are real… and while you must walk through the exile… the Lord Almighty will vigorously defend you. He is greater than anything the world can throw at us.

Day 250/September 6 – Jeremiah 51-52

Not Forsaken
Jeremiah 51:5

The last words of Jeremiah are strong, scary, and eerily prophetic. The adversaries are at the gate. The powerful enemy will win this battle. The book ends with the burning of the temple and the routing of everything Judah holds dear.

This finale brings to a close the message of the coming exile that Jeremiah has preached to the kings, priests, and people without being able to affect their behavior. Their sin and rebellion have not waned, and the consequences of their conduct have blossomed.

But exile is not the premise of Jeremiah. As much as Jeremiah warns about coming exile and punishment, they are not the theme of his prophecy. The topic of Jeremiah's prophecy, a subject that is never far from his writings of the heartbreak to come, is God's love for His people. The theme of Jeremiah is chapter 51, verse 5.

When you are in exile, God has not forsaken you.

When your sins find you out, God has not forsaken you.

When your land, your household, and your life are full of evil, God has not forsaken you.

When the enemies surround you and you, like the Psalmist, mistakenly feel that God has forsaken you (Psalm 22:1), God has not forsaken you.

When you are the Son of God, bearing the sins of the world and quoting the anguished Psalmist (Matthew 27:46), God has not forsaken you.

The people of God are always the people of God. God has not forsaken you.

Grace always comes.

Morning by Morning New Mercies I See
Lamentations 3:21-24

The Book of Lamentations is filled with imagery of dread and terror—people wandering the streets looking for food… eyesight failing… destitution… rejection… cannibalism… shriveled skin, hot as an oven.

These laments are the cries of the defeated. This is the chorus of exile.

But scripture never, ever leaves us in hopelessness and despair. In the middle of these poems come some of the clearest and most uplifting verses of scripture:

"My soul is downcast, but I call to mind this hope: Because of the Lord's great love, we are not consumed. His compassions never fail. He brings us new mercies every morning. Great is His faithfulness. Therefore, I will wait on Him."

If you do not recognize it, the writer of Lamentations is reminding the people of a simple truth… Grace always comes.

What have you found new from God today? What new mercy arrived that you did not know or recognize yesterday?

Was it a moment of rest? A late-blooming flower? The first breeze of autumn? Was it a word from a friend, from your spouse, from your child? Did you catch a different tone that tells you that in this one relationship, things are taking a turn for the better?

Was it on the news or in an email? Did you hear a new song?

What will it be tomorrow? Is your heart prepared to hear God's new word for you?

Every morning, new mercies come, for God is always faithful.

Following God's Call
Ezekiel 3:11

We all have a call from God. It may not come to us as clearly as it came to the Old Testament prophets, but it comes to us nonetheless. For some, like Ezekiel and Jeremiah and Isaiah, it is to speak God's words. For some, it is to heal wounds, or plant crops, or teach children. For still others, the call is not to a specific occupation or skill but rather to a time and a place, a call to plant themselves so they will be where God wants them when God needs them there.

If you are not yet sure of God's definitive call for you, think about what calls you have already heard. You know God is calling you to follow the Ten Commandments. You know God is calling you to love your neighbors. You know you are called to be kind. If you are restless for God's ultimate call, start by making sure you are following those calls you already hear.

Ezekiel's call was to speak God's words. Notice, Ezekiel was not called to convince anyone. In fact, God is specific that Ezekiel is to speak whether the people listen or not. Ezekiel is to follow the will of God irrespective of how others react.

No matter how well you understand God's call for your life, learn the lesson taught to Ezekiel. Follow God's will whether others honor you or not, whether they recognize God's call on you or not.

God is calling you. Listen and follow.

They Think the Lord Will Not See
Ezekiel 8:12

The end has come. God's patience with Israel and Judah has ended. The Assyrians and Babylonians are released to impose exile on God's people.

In the midst of this havoc, when those who call themselves priests of God should be seeking the face of God at close range, we find them actually turning further away from God. Idolatry, worship of fertility gods, and prayers to the sun are characterizing the so-called religion of these so-called priests.

Even worse than their detestable actions is their incredible brazenness. They believe they are hiding, and that they can hide, themselves and their violation of the most basic of the commandments from God.

How can this be? How can they have forgotten the power of God? Can those who call themselves the people of God really turn away at the point of crisis?

Whatever the answers are to those questions, the more important question is this: Why do we think we can hide from God today?

We go through all the right motions and make all the right noises. We attend church and give to charity. We coach Little League and attend school concerts. We pay our taxes. We are nice to our co-workers.

But deep inside, we have no use for God. We are polite, we are pleasant, and we do not seek God. Alone, we turn our backs to focus on the sun, our personal possessions, and our own fertility gods. We truly believe God cannot see.

How can this be?

Day 254 / September 10 – Ezekiel 9-12

The Glory Departs
Ezekiel 10:18

These verses are among the saddest passages of scripture. Exile brings destruction. Exile means that the bulk of the people are forcibly taken away, with only a poor remnant left to stay in the Promised Land. Exile will mean burning buildings and scorched earth.

But now, exile means something much worse. God is leaving. The glory of the Lord, led by the cherubim, departs from the temple.

God is of course omnipresent: He will not—indeed He cannot —"leave" any place. Symbolically, however, when God withdraws His glory from the Jerusalem temple, He is finalizing the prologue to Israel's exile.

God has been present in a ram on a mountain, in a pillar of fire and a cloud, in radiance shining from Moses' face, and in a kinsman redeemer's promise. The people have marched confidently behind the Ark of the Covenant. God has shown Himself repeatedly to His people through prophecy, poem, psalm, and proverb. The people have followed detailed instructions to build an extravagant temple solely to be the place where the presence of God may reside.

Israel and Judah have celebrated God's being among them. They have counted on the abiding presence of the Lord.

Now they have turned their back on God, and the price for their choice is severe.

God has withdrawn.

Yes, it is symbolic. No, God will never leave us or forsake us. But when we choose to abandon God, he lets us wander into exile. His glory is left behind. It is sad.

Out of Their Own Imaginations
Ezekiel 13:2

It is not only the faithless priests who draw the ire of God. In today's reading, the false prophets who proclaim words that do not come from God hold a special place of disdain for Ezekiel.

When these people announce ideas and instructions that they are simply making up, they are called those "who prophesy out of their own imagination," and those "who follow their own spirit and have seen nothing." "Their visions are false and their divinations a lie." They claim to quote God; however, "the Lord has not sent them."

This phenomenon—people taking the public stage to claim to speak for God when in truth they have no such authority—if anything is more prevalent now than it was in the time of Ezekiel. Social media, television, "religious" bookshelves, and hallway conversations are rife with individuals all too ready to publicize their agenda and claim that their words have the imprimatur of God. Whether they believe their words are from God or not—indeed, whether they know God at all—is not for anyone else to say. What is subject to discernment is whether their words are from God.

Test what you hear. If a supposed prophecy is inconsistent with God's statements in scripture, you know the source is not God. Be careful.

The motivations of false prophets are many. Some are seeking attention, others financial gain, and still others power. Some may sincerely believe they are the newest mouthpiece for God.

Discern. Test what you hear.

Day 256 / September 12 – Ezekiel 17-19

Your Destiny Is Your Own
Ezekiel 18:20

In the midst of allegory, prophecy, and poetry, Ezekiel chang-es style as his words become very practical. The people have taken the extreme position that every person's destiny is determined by the action of his or her parents, that the father's sin determines destiny and punishment for the son. Ezekiel speaks plainly to debunk their fallacy.

Ezekiel makes what to us seems an obvious point: each of us lives or dies according to our own choices and actions. Ezekiel tells of three generations of men, the first and third of whom are righteous but the second of whom is a scoundrel. Ezekiel explains that the second man has to answer for his sins and is saved by neither his father's nor his son's good behavior; similarly, the first man is not condemned by his son's waywardness, and the third is not predetermined to be stained by his father's lawlessness.

While this may seem to be a self evident focus, today we find manifestations of the attitude against which Ezekiel is warning all around us. There are far too many who believe that because of the family in which they have been raised, they are automatically "Christian," as if God has a roll sheet that only includes surnames. On the other hands, far too many decide that they have no hope in life because their hand has been dealt by those who came before, leaving them no option, as if grace cannot be intended for such as them.

But grace always comes.

The Old Testament History Lesson
Ezekiel 20:13-17

Ezekiel 20 is a review and summary of the highlights (and some lowlights) of the history of God's dealings with His people throughout the Old Testament: God and His people make a covenant that calls for obedience; the people break the covenant; God forgives, offering to renew the covenant if the people will simply agree to follow and obey; the people agree; the people disobey and break the covenant; God again forgives and renews the covenant; the people again disobey. And so on.

Grace has come again and again to the people. Ezekiel says that God has repeatedly refrained from punishment for His own name's sake. Finally, God says that He will let the people go their own way and that they will afterwards once again return to Him. In the shorter term, the way the people choose leads straight into exile.

The blueprint of grace is set. Restoration is planned and promised for God's people before the first Babylonian soldier arrives to take the first Israelite away.

In the longer term, God has designed a new covenant—one that involves a cross—to survive the repeated disobedience of the people, because God knows that we are not going to follow His commands for any length of time. (Jeremiah 31:33)

Just as restoration is promised before exile begins, the death of Jesus on the cross that makes the new covenant possible is a part of God's plan before Eve takes the first bite of forbidden fruit.

Grace always comes.

Day 258 / September 14 – Ezekiel 22-24

In the Gap
Ezekiel 22:30

As Ezekiel catalogs the laundry list of sins of Jerusalem, we are meant to understand that this is not a situation where Jerusalem is on-balance sinful, where the good deeds of some are outweighed by the failings of others. This is not a situation where a majority of the people in the city has failed.

No, this is a unanimous, universal problem. Ezekiel, the priest from Anathoth sent to preach to the City of David, reports there is not a single native of Jerusalem who will heed God's warning and "stand in the gap," who will "build up the wall" to protect the people from the coming punishment of God.

It takes only one person. God says that He will hold back the tide if merely one person dares to repair the damage created by the sins of the people.

Look behind the simple words of Ezekiel. God says He needs someone to stand in the gap on behalf of His chosen ones.

There is such a person. His name is Jesus: one person to stand in the gap, the canyon created by our own sins that separates us from God. None of God's people can be found to stand in that divide, to bridge that gulf, so God Himself has done it, taking the form of a servant and climbing a cross to stand in the gap created by our failures.

God looks for the one and does not find Him, so God becomes the one. Grace comes again.

The First Temptation
Ezekiel 28:2

God speaks to nations other than Judah and Israel, for universal sin is not just a Hebrew problem.

Ezekiel's word to Tyre reflects the sin of their king, who holds himself out as a god. This sin in turn flows from the earliest temptation recorded, the simple lie the serpent offers: we can be like God. Eat the forbidden fruit and be godlike. This temptation—the chance to make more of ourselves than is intended, than is good for us, than we can really be—has always lured us. What makes the difference to Adam and Eve, the lie they believe that draws them in, is the suggestion that they can actually see what God sees. The temptation is to go beyond their limited human view and to become godlike.

That is, always has been, and always will be the first temptation. We do not like natural limitation. We chafe under the idea that there is something out there that is better, stronger, faster, smarter than we are.

To let go of this temptation is to accept that we are what we are. We can achieve, we can grow, and we can learn; still, there is only so far we can go. Accepting that there are things we do not understand and cannot do is difficult for most of us. That acceptance, however, is key to our reliance on God.

Like the king of Tyre, we like to think we can be gods. That is the first great temptation.

Taller Trees Yield More Firewood
Ezekiel 31:10-12

The metaphor of Assyria the tree, the tallest and proudest cedar in the forest, is a warning to Egypt. Just because Egypt is large and powerful does not mean that it will survive.

When God's hand is withdrawn from even the grandest and strongest, they fall. And when the largest tree falls, it can be cut up into many pieces and burned in the ovens of even the poorest stragglers. What is left of it will become a home for stray birds and ravaging beasts. Whatever splendor it once had is quickly forgotten.

The message here is not so much about size, or even pride. The message is about perceived self-sufficiency. The cedar has gained its height solely because God's deep springs have nourished it, because God's sunlight has allowed its branches to grow strong and long. Its majestic beauty is due to roots reaching deep into God's earth for stability and food.

When God withdraws His hand of protection and strength, the enemies come with their axes. That the cedar is so tall only means more firewood for them to take home.

You are not your own. You cannot guarantee your next breath. Stand on a jump rope and hold its ends in each hand, and you will quickly discover that you cannot lift yourself up.

Do not make the mistake of the Assyrian cedar. Stand tall because you are reaching to the heavens, not because you are showing off your own height. The axes are always close by.

Help Wanted: Good Shepherd
Ezekiel 34:10-12

The shepherds of Israel have lost sight of their charges, the sheep given to their care. Like the watchmen—charged with blowing the trumpet to warn of coming danger—who have abandoned their God-given posts (Ezekiel 33:6), the shepherds have let the sheep wander and scatter and have not looked for them.

God realizes He has no choice. Relying on those called as watchmen to warn and those called as shepherds to protect has resulted in disaster. The lion and the bear attack the sheep without consequence. God's people are selfish, distracted, immature failures. They are sinners.

God sees there is only one solution. He Himself must be the shepherd, enter the pasture, and become the one to search after and take care of His sheep. He will bring us out of the darkness into our own land. He will search for the lost, bind up the injured, and save His flock.

He is our shepherd, leading us beside still waters and restoring us. (Psalm 23) He has sent His son Jesus to be the Good Shepherd, laying down His life for the sheep who know Him and who will listen to His voice. (John 10:11-16)

The essence of good shepherding is the willingness to die for the sheep. The essence of our Good Shepherd is that not only does He lay down His life, but He takes it up again to lead us to eternal life, for no one can pluck us from His hand. (John 10:27-29)

Day 262/September 18 – Ezekiel 35-37

The Foot Bone Is Connected to the Ankle Bone – Ezekiel 37:7

God presents Ezekiel with a picture of dry bones covering the floor of a valley. God tells Ezekiel that these bones can and will live, just as Israel can and will be restored from its exile to flourish once again in the Promised Land.

That now-familiar restoration theme is punctuated by what happens to the bones.

First, they connect one to another. Like the remnants of Israel and Judah which must join together under the reign of God (Ezekiel 37:19-24), each of us individually must join with one another to form the restored church of God.

Then, tendons appear. Our connected bones begin to function, for tendons flex and pull so joints can bend and muscles can lift and push.

Next, flesh is added. We get meat on our bones. We are not simply a structure, waiting once again to be broken. There is something to us as God builds us up.

Then, the skin is added. We are covered, protected, ready to face the world.

But one thing is still lacking. We need breath, for we cannot stand up as God's people until He breathes into us His life, His Spirit. The Hebrew word we translate as *Spirit* means "air in motion." It is the same word for "breath." It means "life."

We are connected, functioning, substantial, and protected. But what gives us life is God's Spirit, our air in motion.

Sin and disobedience and exile and the desert sun cannot overcome God's plan of restoration. Grace always comes.

Building a New and Better Temple
Ezekiel 40:4

There is a new temple to be built. God has something greater in mind.

This "new temple" described to Ezekiel is not the tent-and-
poles tabernacle of the wandering Israelites, for it is permanent in
place and structural design. It is different from Solomon's temple,
which has been destroyed by Nebuchadnezzar. It is not the later
temple that will be built after the exile and the return to Jerusalem
by Zerubbabel and those who choose not to stay in Babylon, because that temple will be much smaller and less grand than what is
described here.

Is Ezekiel describing what might be if all the people were to
leave Babylon when they are given the chance? Is he describing what
might have been if God's people had never rebelled against Him in
the first place?

Is Ezekiel describing something yet to be built, at some time in
history, of immense importance?

Is Ezekiel metaphorically describing the New Testament church?

Is Ezekiel talking about each individual Christian, whose bodies
serve as temples for the Holy Spirit? (1 Corinthians 6:19)

Is Ezekiel describing what God will make of each of us?

Do not try to decipher each detail of these verses, for even
scholars do not agree. Some refer to these closing chapters of Ezekiel as the most difficult to understand in the entire Old Testament.
What we know is that God has something new in mind for us. There
is a better temple waiting to be built. God has something greater in
mind.

Day 264 / September 20 – Ezekiel 41-44

Filled with the Glory of God
Ezekiel 44:4

W hat God is building with us and for us is meant to be filled by God.

God's glory—the visible representation of the presence of God —fills the temple that Ezekiel sees. This sight is so majestic that Ezekiel is moved to a facedown posture of worship in the awesome presence of God.

Some of the descriptions of this new temple—its rooms for the priests, its most holy place—are familiar to us who have read Exodus and First Kings, but something is far different. What God is preparing for us now, and that for which He is preparing us, is to be filled by Him. If these chapters about the new temple are metaphorical descriptions of what God will make of each of us, then the key to our "new temple" is that God will be there. God's glory will shine.

Restoration is not simply a return to a place, even the special place known as the Promised Land.

Restoration is not simply the rebuilding of a structure, even one as monumental as Solomon's temple.

Restoration is not simply the replacement of a royal line, even one that can be traced back to David himself.

No, restoration is beyond our vision. We have marched ourselves into exile, across a gap that none of us can span, and God is making a way for our return. This return will far exceed our imagination and our expectation and our experience, because God will be within.

And it will be glorious.

The River of Life
Ezekiel 47:8

E zekiel saves one last picture for the end of his book. Out of the new temple flows a river. It gets progressively deeper as Ezekiel is led through it, and when it reaches the salty Dead Sea, a miracle occurs. The salty water becomes fresh.

When the water that comes from where God is reaches through the desert to the place where no life is, suddenly there is life. Fruit trees grow on the banks; their leaves will not wither, and new fruit will grow monthly. All sorts of fish cavort in the current, providing for fishermen who crowd the shoreline.

How can this be? How can a single stream freshen what was bracken? How can life re-energize death?

The answer lies in the source of the river. It flows from the temple, where God is. The God of restoration is signaling what is to come.

John the Apostle writes of the river of life, flowing from the throne of God, where there is no more night. (Revelation 22:1-5) The Psalmist sings of God's river of delight, quenching the thirst of those who love Him. (Psalm 36:8) Jesus tells us that whoever believes in Him has this river of living water flowing within. (John 7:38)

Amazingly, God is using you and me, whom He is making into His new temple, as the starting place for His life-giving work. His river flows from us. He works through us and in us.

I've got a river of life flowing out of me.

Day 266/September 22 – Daniel 1-2

Revealer of Mysteries
Daniel 2:29

Anyone who tells you that life is simple is either not paying attention or is out to deceive you. Life is complicated. The forces that play out on the supernatural stage as evil and good lock horns operate on a level that we cannot comprehend. How the caterpillar becomes the butterfly or sunshine turns the leaves green or a seed becomes an apple tree instead of a rose bush are questions beyond our ken.

The world is not simple. Mysteries surround us.

Yet, there is much we know.

We do not know inherently. We do not know the keys because we are smart. We do not learn the most important truths through hard work.

We know because we serve the revealer of mysteries.

We continue in His word, and then we are His disciples and we know the truth. (John 8:31-32) The knowledge of the secrets of heaven are given to us. (Matthew 13:11) The Holy Spirit makes known to us what is in the heart of God. (John 16:14) In Jesus, we are enriched in all knowledge. (1 Corinthians 1:5)

We of course see as through a glass darkly, not knowing everything now the way we will one day know it. (1 Corinthians 13:12) Still, we have access to knowledge that anchors our souls securely. (Hebrews 6:17-19)

God is the reveler of mysteries. Dreams and signs and parables and stories mystify many. But behold! He tells us a mystery and unfolds the stories of the universe for His children.

Even If He Does Not
Daniel 3:18

We know that God can. We do not always know that God will. We do not understand all of the factors that influence when God chooses to intervene and when he withholds His hand.

The question becomes how we react when God chooses not to intercede on our behalf.

Shadrach, Meshach, and Abednego are facing the fiery furnace for their refusal to bow to Nebuchadnezzar. The evil king challenges their faith, taunting them as they stand on the threshold of the deadly oven, questioning when God is going to swoop in and save them.

Their response is far more important than simply saying that they believe that God can save them. What they say is that even if Jehovah does not choose to intrude into Nebuchadnezzar's evil plan, they will still not alter their faith in God. Many refer to these men's "nevertheless" brand of faith.

The heart of faith does not put stock in what the world counts as important but instead believes in the One who holds out the promise of eternal life. You may not see in the moment what God has in store, but you always see God. There may not be an answer apparent to your mind, but there is always the Answerer in your heart.

God may not change the circumstance; nevertheless, we believe anyway. Do not allow your faith to be dependent on what happens to you in this instant. Their 'nevertheless' commitment has inspired God's followers for centuries.

Day 268/September 24 – Daniel 5-7

Sometimes, God Shuts the Lions' Mouths
Daniel 6:22

It is doubtless that God does not always intervene into the troubles that beset us, and as we learned yesterday, our faith must be based not on what God has done for us today but rather on who God is and what He will do with eternity.

Still, a rich part of our faith is the recognition and celebration of the times when God does intrude into the world to halt wickedness and malevolence in their tracks. The power and the love of God are on display when he parts the Red Sea, when He sends water from the rock, when he helps the shepherd boy slay the giant, when he fells the walls of Jericho, when He heals the sick, and when He raises the dead.

Yesterday, we saw God keeping three faithful men alive in the furnace. Again, the power and love of God are on display when he shuts the mouths of the lions.

Daniel's story reminds us that, sometimes, the innocent are saved and the godly are exalted.

It happens more often than you may realize:

The car that does not hit you on the interstate…

The nagging cough that goes away and does not turn into a dread disease…

The temptation that misses your spouse because of a channel turned or a website avoided …

The drink your child does not order…

God is still in the business of healing, of restoring, and of shutting the lions' mouths.

Grace still comes.

Deliverance in the End
Daniel 12:1

Daniel, dreamer of dreams and seer of visions, seems to write in code. Many students of scripture have offered detailed accounts of what all these apocalyptic visions and dreams, rife with symbols and portentous words, mean. Those explanations may or may not make sense to you as you read through what is obviously complicated imagery.

Whatever you make of the representations of these chapters, two things are remarkably clear.

First, the future is no riddle to the creator of the world. God knows what is coming and has a plan for each of us.

Second, and probably far more important, the outcome for God's children is secure. There will be distress. There will be warring kingdoms and forces that rise up to take their turns making a run at controlling the world. But when the end comes, God's people— those whose names are written in the book of life—will be delivered. Those who sleep will wake into everlasting life, and those who are still alive will shine in the brightness of the heavens.

Daniel's message here is no different from that of the New Testament, where we are told that the final judgment will be based on whose name is found in the Lamb's book of life. (Revelation 20:12) Thanks be to God, those of us who belong to Christ find our names there. (Luke 10:20)

Behold, I tell you a mystery. We shall not sleep. We shall be changed. Death, where is your victory? (1 Corinthians 15:51, 55)

Day 270/September 26 – Hosea 1-3

Hosea Loves Gomer
Hosea 3:1

What a beautiful, complex, confounding, disturbing, frustrating, and ultimately comforting story!

Hosea is commanded to marry Gomer. She bears three children and then leaves to pursue a life of adultery, prostitution, and wantonness. At the height of her reckless unfaithfulness, God begins to talk of drawing her back to her family and recognizing again the betrothal and commitment shared between husband and wife.

And then, ultimately, God commands Hosea to take Gomer back again and love her as his wife, notwithstanding what she has done and not being afraid of others who may pretend to love her and who may lay claim to her. Could love like this really be?

As we read this book, the parallels between Gomer on one hand and Israel and Judah on the other will be made clear, but already we cannot help but understand that Gomer represents the people of God. Despite God's loving us and taking us to Himself, we are serial violators of the covenant, unfaithfully leaving the Lord and flirting with all manner of suitors, taking up with some and selling ourselves to others.

Still, God takes us back.

The story of Hosea and Gomer is allegory, but maybe it is also true on a historical level. Can it be? Maybe there really was a Gomer, and perhaps a young prophet was ordered by God to disregard her gratuitous and shameless behavior in order to portray a personal immediate picture that, no matter how undeserving we are, yes, grace always comes.

What God Wants
Hosea 6:6

These are a disheartening six chapters, cataloging our flagrant sins. We ramble unfaithfully, flouting the direction
of our master and aching for the affections of what cannot sustain.
We sell ourselves for a pittance, reveling in what lasts but a moment.
We drift from this to that, never finding satisfaction.

It is fortunate that chapters 1-3 came first, that we have already
seen, as it were, the rest of the story: God will take us back. As Hosea retrieves Gomer, so too does God search for us in the pigsties
in which we lie so that He can wrap His arms around us and restore
us as His bride.

But that is for tomorrow and for yesterday. For today, we read
about the failings we all recognize in ourselves. We are convicted by
the Holy Spirit.

What is the essence of our failures? For most of us, it is not
murder or torture. Few of us are tax evaders or car thieves or drug
kingpins. Not many of us are wife beaters. Some are, but not most.

Most of us are church-going doers of admirable deeds, memo-
rizers of pledges and proverbs, and givers to charity. We go through
the motions and make the right noises.

That is not what God wants. He is not interested in our ritualis-
tic sacrifices and offerings. He wants us to show mercy. We have to
have and acknowledge a need for and a relationship with Him.

Know what God desires. Then be what God desires.

Day 272/September 28 – Hosea 10-14; Joel 1-2:17

Rend Your Heart
Joel 2:13

R*end*—to tear into two or more pieces. When something has been rent, it is finished. What was is no more.

Rend is not a word we use often, so it is striking that most of the major English translations of scripture agree to use this word – "rend"—in Joel 2:13. God calls us to rend our hearts in repentance.

Repentance is not simply saying we are sorry, although regretting our actions and our thoughts is certainly part of it. Repentance is not simply stopping the sin, although immediately quitting is part of it. Repentance requires us to end the sin, to destroy it.

Picture yourself running headlong toward the edge of a high cliff. Yelling out "I am sorry that I am running towards my downfall" would do nothing for you, no matter how much true regret you actually felt. Stopping short of the precipice would save you temporarily, but you would still be stuck on the edge of destruction. What the Bible calls "repentance" means that you turn your back to the cliff and run as fast as you can the other way, toward safety.

Rend your heart. Tear it in two. This metaphor is another way of telling you to run the other way. Change your ways dramatically. Turn around. Go the opposite of where your momentum is taking you.

Joel gives us the reason: God is slow to anger and abounding in love. Rend your heart; repent, because God will have pity, because grace will come.

All Who Call on the Name of the Lord
Joel 2:32

It is drama worthy of a Hollywood screen: Smoke, blood, and fire... Sons and daughters prophesying in the streets... The moon turned to blood. The "great and terrible Day of the Lord" commences as the world prepares for judgment.

Peter quotes these words in his great sermon (Acts 2:16-21), then explains that the real significance of the prophecy of the Day of the Lord is its call for acceptance of the salvation offered by Jesus Christ. All who call on the name of the Lord will be saved.

Most of our lives resemble neither Hollywood disaster films nor great apostolic sermons delivered to Jerusalem crowds. Most of the time, our lives are mundane. We get up, we eat, we help our families prepare for the day, we work, we eat, we come home, we bathe, and we sleep. If we are lucky, there is some time to watch TV or do a crossword puzzle. Our lives are not bad, and we are not dissatisfied; still, no one can say that much of what we do or experience is exciting. No one is looking to write a script about our existence.

Be aware. The Day of the Lord is coming for us all, breaking through even our mundane routine.

Do not let the work-a-day nature of your life mask the eternal importance of what scripture, whether it be through Joel or through Peter, says. The Day of the Lord is coming, and Jesus offers you eternal salvation.

Call on His name.

Day 274 / September 30 - Amos 5-9; Obadiah 1

Measured by the Plumb Line
Amos 7:7

God's standards are exacting. God is holy and perfect. God calls on us to be holy and perfect. There is no wiggle room. Whether we are obedient is not graded on a curve. We do not have the safety net of comparing ourselves to someone even worse than we are.

Either we are or we are not.

A plumb line is a cord or string with a weighted plumb on one end used to make sure a wall is exactly vertical. An engineer and a builder require the wall to be built to plumb because nobody wants a house or a building that has even the slightest lean to it.

God speaks through the prophet Amos to let His people know the standard to which He holds us. It is no different from His words to Moses that we are to be holy (Leviticus 19:2), Jesus' command for us to be perfect (Matthew 5:48), or the Psalmist's promise that only those with clean hands a pure heart deserve to ascend to the hill of the Lord (Psalm 24:3-4). God expects us to toe the line, to keep all of His commandments. His standard is that we do not sin. He holds a plumb line and measures us against the exact vertical.

Except, of course, we cannot do it. We do not live to plumb. We desperately wish God did not require perfection.

Exile is inevitable. We must have restoration.

Failing to meet the standard, we require grace.

We need Jesus.

October

After Salvation
Jonah 3:2

The story of Jonah is an amazing tale of salvation. Running away from God, Jonah rocks the boat until his fellow sailors have no choice but to throw him overboard. Jonah's rebellion has caused the wind and waves to rise dangerously, and he soon is flailing among them. Miraculously, and for no good reason that is apparent to Jonah, he is saved. He spends three days in what has to be a dark, smelly, uncomfortable passage through the sea; but he realizes that he is not dying and manages to pray, recognizing that his salvation has come from God. He is then spit out onto the beach, saved from the storm and out of the waves.

What a picture of our own salvation! What a symbol of what has happened to each of us who know Christ. We have wandered (or run headlong) far from God, and the results have been disaster. We find ourselves in deep water, in a rancid place where we could never have imagined ourselves; out of nowhere, Jesus has come to our rescue.

So, now what?

Jonah gets a call from God, and if you compare Jonah 3:2 with Jonah 1:2, you will find that after his salvation, Jonah is called to go back and do what he refused to do the first time. After we are saved, we are called to obey.

You have prayed for salvation, and you have thanked God for it. Are you now ready to follow His call and obey?

Day 276/October 2 – Micah 4-7; Nahum 1-3

Swords into Plowshares
Micah 4:3

Things are going to change. We have learned there is a time for war and a time for peace. (Ecclesiastes 3:8) As a part of that time for war, there will be a time to beat our plowshares into swords and our pruning hooks into spears. (Joel 3:10)

But in the end, when restoration is complete and all peoples of Earth are streaming to the holy mountain of the Lord, there will be a new season. We will walk with God and listen to Him teach us His ways. Then, we will beat our swords back into plowshares and our spears back into the pruning hooks from which they came. Growth and cultivation will replace death and destruction. Weaponry will be ancient history. As the old spiritual says, we will study war no more.

The lame and the exiles and the grieving will be gathered together. And Micah tells us that their leader, Isaiah's "little child," will come from a small town called Bethlehem.

We will find sincere Christians on both sides of the aisle when we debate disarmament, pacifism, just war doctrine, and political theory. We can and will disagree on foreign policy and political questions of war and peace.

But that is for here and now. Whatever the right answers are, there is no question where we are heading in eternity. We are marching to Zion, the house of God, where we will walk in the name of God, in peace, forever. We will study war no more.

The Cry Becomes the Song
Habakkuk 3:17-19

This prophet begins his book with weeping, a cry that sounds very much like our prayers today. How long, God, will violence continue to strike with no intervention from you? Why do you put up with injustice?

Habakkuk is complaining. He is devastated by the evil and the terror and the unspeakable that are a part of his world... and ours.

God responds, and at first His response may not be clear to us. He says that He will raise up the Babylonians. In other words, God responds to the cry by saying something like, "if you think things are bad now, just wait." As the book progresses, the Lord begins to explain to Habakkuk that the plight in which the people find themselves is the result of their many sins, their selfishness, and their shameful choices.

The tide turns with the end of chapter 2. The cries and questions are not answered, but... God is in His holy temple. He has not left us even when we have left Him.

By the end of chapter 3, the prophet is singing the great song of the Old Testament. He does not have answers to his questions, but it does not matter. The fruit tree may not bud. Violence may go on. Yet he will rejoice in God, who has not abandoned His rebellious people. He will be joyful in the savior who is his strength.

God is not put off by your cries. Let Him turn them into songs.

Greater Glory
Haggai 2:9

It is the story of a temple to be rebuilt, but it is much more than that. Like Nehemiah and Ezra before them, Haggai and Zechariah are prophets who return to Jerusalem to reconstruct what has been destroyed: temples, walls, and the souls of God's people.

The promise this time is more far-reaching, for God's plan has advanced to the final restoration of His people. The issue now is not blueprints, cubits in a wall, and how thick a curtain should be. The issue now is the crown jewel in the new covenant, the savior who will come and put a final end to the problem we have created for ourselves and for God.

The new temple, the new Jerusalem, the new place for God's people will be with God Himself. The Way to this new place will be God's Son, the promised Messiah who will be present and who will bridge the gap between us and God.

It is the great promise to an exiled people: the glory of what is to come will be greater than the glory of what has been. What is coming will make Solomon's temple pale in comparison.

Whether you are happy or defeated, what a remarkable promise! If you have struggled through anonymity, betrayal, and loneliness, there is a great glory waiting for you. If your life has been a blessing and you have enjoyed every minute of it, it still does not compare with what is to come.

Greater glory is coming.

Day 279/October 5 – Zechariah 1-7

No Boundaries
Zechariah 2:2-4

When the angel describes the new Jerusalem to the measurer as a "city without walls," the description is not structural or architectural. The limitless nature of God's new creation is a profound statement about God's plan for us all. There is nothing keeping anyone out, nothing delineating the foreigner from the citizen, nothing making one person a resident and another an alien.

If you feel you do not belong, you are wrong.

God's kingdom, His new Jerusalem created for us all through the salvation and restoration of the Messiah, has no circumference. There is nothing to mark off a perimeter.

God's kingdom has no boundaries.

Make no mistake, God Himself is at the center, and the kingdom revolves around Him. And to be sure, God Himself protects those who are within His kingdom by forming a "wall of fire" around them with His glory. (Zechariah 2:5)

God has been in the business of tearing down walls for centuries now. Joshua's troops blow trumpets and the walls of Jericho tumbled. (Joshua 6:20) Paul tells us that Jesus becomes our peace by breaking down every wall of hostility and division among us. (Ephesians 2:14)

It is a basic Biblical principle: Whosoever will may come. Whoever calls on the name of the Lord will be saved. (Joel 2:32; Acts 2:21; Romans 10:13; John 3:16) Jesus says that whosoever chooses to may drink freely of living water. (Revelation 22:17)

There are no boundaries, no walls. This kingdom is for all who want to enter.

Day 280/October 6 – Zechariah 8-14

The King Is Coming
Zechariah 8:9

Zechariah is the prophet who takes the restoration story to the next level.

Zechariah prophesies a king coming to Jerusalem riding on a donkey's colt. In a land of few horses, the donkey is a princely mount (Judges 12:14) yet a decidedly humbler steed than the warhorses of Egypt and Babylon and, ultimately, of Rome. Jesus' triumphal entry into Jerusalem on Palm Sunday takes place on a borrowed donkey, and the gospel writers remember Zechariah's prophecy. (Matthew 21:5; John 12:15)

The specificity of the donkey ride as it plays out in Jesus' life is widely discussed, but often lost in that Palm Sunday story is the more important prophecy that Zechariah is bringing us:

The king is coming.

As we have faithfully wound our way through multiple prophets, from Isaiah and Jeremiah through Micah and Zephaniah, the theme of the promised restoration of God's people has been repeated. Now, through the writing of Zechariah, this theme sharpens—the restoration will be centered around and led by the king, the king who comes to Jerusalem to proclaim peace and to save.

This king comes the first time in a town called Bethlehem, growing to teach and heal and tell parables, ultimately dying for the sins of the world. We are about to launch into His story as we read through the gospels in coming days.

This king will come again, to bring a close to this world and to lead each of us to His eternal kingdom.

The king is coming.

Day 281 / October 7 – Malachi 1-4

Confusing Evil and Good
Malachi 2:17

Good is good and evil is evil. As in the beginning, when we say evil is good and ignore God, we eat forbidden fruit, and we weary God.

When we take what we know, what is clear, and what we have been taught and declare them to be wrong, we weary God.

When we refuse to obey, choosing instead to follow a road made by our own desire, our own convenience, and our own interpretation, we weary God.

When we tell God that we do not care what He has to say, or that we know better than He what is best for us and for the world, we weary God.

When we deny what we know to be truth, we weary God.

Fortunately, Malachi uses "weary" in the sense that we try God's patience, that we again and again require God's forgiveness and mercy.

Fortunately, Malachi does not mean that God gets tired of us. As this great book begins, we are reminded once again that God's relationship with us is based on love.

When we weary God, He looks for new ways to rain His grace down on us. If we need to be judged and washed clean, then He comes as a launderer's soap. If we need to have impurity removed from us, then He comes as a refiner's fire. If we need to see His blessings, then He opens the floodgates of heaven for us.

We end the Old Testament where we started: Grace always comes.

Day 282/ October 8 – Matthew 1-4

Immediately
Matthew 4:18-22

The New Testament opens with an invitation. "Follow."

We are not told if Simon and Andrew have met Jesus before. Matthew does not explain whether or not James and John have heard this carpenter preach on some earlier date. We do not know if any of them has been considering Jesus for a while or whether the words recorded in the gospel are the first time they have ever laid eyes on Him.

What we do know is that when Jesus calls them, they drop what they are doing and follow Him. Simon and Andrew leave their nets "at once." James and John get out of the boat, leaving their father, "immediately."

When Jesus calls, we are to follow. Whether we have had a long time to ponder who Jesus is and what He wants us to do or we have never heard of Him until right now, the time frame for response is the same: right now. We should imitate these first disciples, these apostles, and leave what we are doing at once.

The point is not to set some sort of speed record. The idea is not that Jesus refuses to wait on us or that His call for us will expire quickly.

No, the lesson is that everything else in life pales in comparison to the opportunity to follow Christ. Doing one's job, following what we think are our dreams, and even staying with family must take a back seat when Jesus calls, "Follow me."

Follow.

Immediately.

Day 283/October 9 – Matthew 5-7

Priority
Matthew 6:33

These three chapters constitute the Sermon on the Mount, chock full of crucial statements of Jesus. Its theme is this: Seek first the kingdom of God and His righteousness.

Jesus' premise is not that we should seek God. Everyone seeks God, sooner or later, rightly or wrongly, easily or through some difficult manmade labyrinth. No, the point is not just to seek God, but to seek God first.

The priority of God is as old as scripture itself. The only rule laid out for Adam is to obey God. The first of the Ten Commandments is that nothing comes before God. The Levitical priestly code is a series of rules to recognize the preeminence of God. Ezra rediscovers the law and leads the people once again to worship God alone. Isaiah and Ezekiel and the rest of the prophets have taught over and over again that the Lord is God and must be raised high above all others.

Jesus tells us that we have to be willing even to leave father and mother and spouse and home for the sake of our Father. (Luke 14:26) Yesterday, the initial apostles taught us to drop everything when Jesus calls.

Anyone can—and will—seek God. The mark of Christians is that God is our priority. We seek Him now, first and foremost. Before we hunt for success, happiness, fulfillment, earthly love, or fame, we search out God. Before anything else, we find God.

See first the kingdom of God and His righteousness.

What Do They See in Jesus?
Matthew 8:16

These two chapters reveal stories of people coming, seemingly out of the woodwork, to see Jesus. A man with leprosy comes and kneels before Him. A Roman centurion, friends of a paralytic, a ruler whose daughter has just died, and two blind men come to Him for healing. If it were just these, then we might conclude that word has gotten out that a miracle worker has arrived; we would understand the rush, for everyone wants to be healed.

But it is more than that. Matthew, a tax collector employed by the Roman government with no need for physical healing, gets up and leaves his booth when Jesus asks.

The gospel tells us that the crowds are amazed by Jesus and are filled with awe when they see and hear Him. (Matthew 9:8)

Perhaps most telling is the odd encounter Jesus has with two possessed men. The demons address Jesus from inside these men, recognizing Him as the Son of God. (Matthew 8:29)

That is the key. When you see Jesus, you see the Son of God. Not just a healer. Not just someone asking you to follow Him down the road.

You see divinity. You see the creator of the world. You see the face of your maker. And you are different because of it.

The sick know. The soldiers know. The tax collectors know. Even the demons know.

And now you know, when you look into the face of Jesus.

Look into His eyes. What do you see?

Day 285/October 11 — Matthew 10-11

Take Your Cross. Take His Yoke.
Matthew 10:38; 11:29

His command is hard, but His yoke is easy. When you are willing to lose your life for His sake, you find rest for your soul.

These words of the Master, arguably contradictory at first blush, mesh together clearly as we follow Him. Yes, we must take up our own cross. This means that we have to lay aside our ambitions, goals, and desires when they clash with what He has for us. We crucify self-interest, losing our life for His sake, in order to take up His burden.

Jesus calls for us to give up everything.

And then we discover that His burden is easy. We discover that this cross we take up, even if it leads through the valley of the shadow of death, does not weigh us down.

A yoke is a means for sharing burdens. Two oxen or a team of mules are yoked together so they can share the burden in pulling a plow.

Jesus has a yoke that He places on us, and we are by no means equal in pulling with Him. We carry a cross, but the burden is light, for that Jesus carries our cross even as He carries His own.

In another place, Jesus tells us that when we sell all we have, we gain a pearl of great price, worth far more than what we leave behind. (Matthew 13:45-46)

Take up your cross. He shares the load. Your burden is light.

Even when carrying your cross, grace always comes.

Day 286 / October 12 – Matthew 12-13

Something Greater
Matthew 12:6, 41, 42

Jesus is not like anyone else, ever. Prophets have come and gone. Would-be messiahs have appeared repeatedly throughout Middle Eastern history. Leaders rise and fall. Religious figures dot the landscape of history like so many pushpins on a political map. Presidents, premiers, royals, and generals fade into obscure history.

Jesus is different. Jesus is better. Jesus is greater.

Jesus is greater than the temple, the centuries-long center of Jewish religious life. Jesus knows that His audience reveres this building where Sabbath observances take place and the law is taught. He is not denigrating their belief; He is explaining that what they have been awaiting so long has arrived.

Jesus is greater than Jonah, and to extend the metaphor, He is greater than all of the Old Testament prophets. He is not saying that they were wrong or insignificant. His point is that He is the one to whom they were pointing.

Jesus is greater that Solomon. The wise king, builder of the great temple and author of key books of the Bible, is a figure in history to be admired and studied with a level of awe, but even he was waiting on someone greater, and that someone is Jesus.

When we spend our lives chasing dreams and ideas, we eventually discover that they disappoint. We look around and say, "There must be something greater."

There is.

Jesus is greater than your problems, your temptations, and your weaknesses. Jesus is greater than anything you can imagine.

Jesus is something greater.

Day 287/October 13 – Matthew 14-17

The Son of God
Matthew 16:16; 17:5

The people look for a sign. They want proof of who Jesus is. Peter understands, perhaps before anyone else does, declaring that Jesus is the Messiah, calling Jesus the "Son of God."

Signs are everywhere in these chapters. Jesus feeds five thousand with five loaves and two fish, walks on water, and calms a storm. He heals sick strangers who touch His clothes. He teaches with authority and wisdom that no mortal can possess. He feeds another multitude on another hillside from another small lunch. Then He produces a coin in a fish's mouth.

If all that were not enough, He ascends a mountain and is transfigured—His form alters into something heavenly before three apostles' eyes—as He stands with Elijah and Moses. A bright cloud envelops Him, and these three disciples hear the voice of God Himself call Jesus His son, announce that He is well pleased with Him, and command them to listen to Him.

What has come before is never enough. People today demand still more signs, reasoning that if God would now simply show Himself and announce clearly who He is, then they will believe and follow. Signs are still all around, from childbirth to sunrise to healed disease, from the split atom to the blooming jonquil to the changed life.

Jesus is still the Messiah, and the Father is still well pleased. Waiting for yet another sign is simply an act of delay and denial.

The Son of God is here. Listen to Him.

Day 288 / October 14 – Matthew 18-20

Possible
Matthew 19:26

Ⓗ ow can it be done?

How can this world have been created from nothing?

How can a seed fall into the dirt, get wet, and break apart as tendrils of new life slowly creep from its center, pushing their way through the ground until they are introduced to sunshine and form a plant that bears fruits, leaves, flowers, and—yes—new seeds?

How can a person be born again?

How can a ninety-year-old woman or a teenage virgin give birth to a healthy human child?

How can the sick be healed, the blind be given sight, the lame made to walk, the dead given new life?

How can thousands be fed from one boy's lunch box?

How can one planet whirl through space at precisely the right distance from the sun to sustain life at livable temperatures, with rainfall and seasons that "just happen" to create growing seasons necessary to feed that life?

When you answer these and thousands more questions just like them with the only two answers you honestly can give—"I don't know" and "God"—then the question of the apostles in Matthew 19 is not difficult. We once again answer "how" with "Who."

So it is harder for a camel to go through the eye of a needle than for a rich man to enter into heaven… So what? Is solving this problem harder than designing the double helix or forming a tadpole that will metamorphose into a bullfrog?

Nothing is impossible for God. Grace always comes.

Wearing Your Wedding Clothes
Matthew 22:11-13

J esus is in the last week of His earthly human life, and as crucifixion approaches, His words take on a decidedly more solemn tone.

The parable of the wedding banquet wonderfully and cleverly mixes the astounding love and welcome of God with a crystal clear explanation of the choice left to each of us.

God does the inviting, and when the expected attendees do not show up, God's call turns out to be far broader than anyone expected. The invitation is for those on the street corners, along the highways, in the far countries, and from the undeserving families of earth. In other words, God asks all of us to join Him for His eternal feast.

As the host of the party, God even lays out the wedding clothes. We are invited to the party as we are, but we cannot come in as we are, for our clothes are dirty. Dressed in His righteousness, though, we are welcome at the table.

The clothes are offered, and we pay no price for them. But we do have to put them on. We have to take on the grace and forgiveness of Jesus Christ, for otherwise, we are rejecting the invitation to the wedding.

This is a story about one who is invited to change her clothes but who thinks she deserves to get in as she is. Grace has come, and she has said, "No, thank you."

Put on your wedding clothes that the Master has laid out for you.

Day 290/October 16 – Matthew 23-24

We Are All Pharisees
Matthew 23:12

There is a temptation to categorize the Pharisees of first century Jerusalem as the villains of scripture. Truthfully, the Pharisees were not by and large bad people. They strove to follow what they understood of God's plan. They cared deeply about their religion. They wanted others to walk the walk. Where they failed was in setting up something besides the word of God as the standard by which they judged themselves and others.

Many who reject Christ set themselves up as the deciders of what is right and wrong, making themselves and their philosophies and understandings the masters of their destiny.

More disturbing, however, is the pharisaical nature of those of us who are Christians. Too often and too easily, we slip into a pattern of doing things for people to see—church attendance, community service, monetary giving—as we look for our places of honor in the marketplace. Too often and too easily, we do not practice what we preach. Too often and too easily, we are whitewashed tombs, prettying up the outside while rotting away on the inside.

Too often and too easily, we exalt ourselves, setting ourselves up for the fall. We try to set out our own agenda, and we are all Pharisees.

We will be humbled.

Jesus loves us and would gather us as a hen gathers her chicks, but we do not come to Him easily. We choose the way that looks good to the world.

And so Jesus walks toward His cross.

Betraying, Denying, and Falling Away
Matthew 26:31

We do not like the scriptures that finger us so clearly. Judas Iscariot is the betrayer. He approaches the enemy and offers up Jesus in exchange for money. He feigns innocence at the Last Supper when Jesus calls him out. He carries out the scheme by identifying Jesus with a kiss.

Simon Peter is the denier. Sitting in the courtyard, too cowardly even to be near Jesus after his arrest, Peter is accused of being a follower of Christ. Three times, as predicted, Peter denies even knowing Jesus.

Judas and Peter are the most famous of the failing apostles on this terrible night, but we cannot miss Jesus' words when He says, "[t]his very night, you will all fall away…"

Not one of them steps up to help him. The best they can do is to raise a sword to maim a servant of a priest, but Jesus quickly puts an end to such nonsense. None of them is willing even to walk with Jesus, to stand next to Him. Instead, they desert and flee. (Matthew 26:56)

It is easy to point our finger at one whose betrayal is more obvious than our own or whose denial is repeated and poignant. We can all find a Judas whose sin is flagrant and a Peter whose failure is magnified. We compare ourselves and decide we are not so bad.

But we all fall away. We desert the master and flee from His side when He needs us most.

God forgive us.

Day 294/October 18 – Matthew 27-28

He Is Risen!
Matthew 28:6

Because Matthew's gospel is the first to appear in scripture, this announcement of the resurrection of Christ is the first time we see the Easter miracle proclaimed as we read through the Bible.

What a moment! There have been prophecies. Jesus has tried to tell His followers that He will be killed and then raised to life on the third day. (Matthew 16:21; 17:23; 20:19)

Now, of course, it is neither prophecy nor prediction. It is history. It is fact.

He is risen, just as He said.

Death cannot defeat Jesus, who is God on earth and who holds the keys to life itself.

The grave cannot hold Him. They can drive nails in His hands, pierce His side with a spear, beat Him, and whip Him. They can abandon Him. They can make Him bleed. They can suffocate Him. They can make Him die and put His body in a sealed tomb… But they cannot hold Him.

The crucifixion is a critical event as Jesus takes our sins away, but the crucifixion alone leaves us saddened and defeated. The resurrection means that the story is not ultimately about sin and punishment but about life and victory. The resurrection means that the one who promises eternal life actually knows what eternal life is and has it to give.

We are on the side of the one who has walked through the door of death and now calls us to follow. This is triumph. This is grace.

He is risen! Hallelujah.

Jesus Comes to Sinners
Mark 2:17

It is convenient to think of Jesus as we first pictured Him when we were children—preaching to believers, teaching in the synagogues, walking with His apostles, and talking to good people about the Kingdom.

Considering Jesus with prostitutes is not so popular. Thinking of Jesus interacting with the criminals, the greedy, and the mean is bracing. Picturing the Son of God sharing a meal with the organized crime syndicate, the corporate pillagers, and the foulest humanity we can describe is typically far from our minds.

To whom did Jesus—God come to earth—come? Did Jesus come for Adolph Hitler, for Pol Pot, for Ceauşescu? Did Jesus come for the gangbangers and the rapists? Did Jesus come to spend time with those who abuse and steal and kill?

The answer, of course, is yes. And if Jesus came to speak to those folks, to offer a cup of cold water to the thirsty no matter who they are and what they have done, then those of us who claim to follow Him must walk the same paths. If He is the doctor to the sick, then we are the orderlies, nurses, and technicians among the same patients. We cannot turn our back on the ones with whom Jesus sat down to dine.

Too many of us like the grace that has come to us but do not want to extend the grace to all. With or without us, grace always comes. Will we be a part?

Day 294/October 20 – Mark 4-5

Time to Plow
Mark 4:9

There are at least three views of this parable of the sower. First is the deterministic idea that the parable is simply about God's sovereignty: people are born different kinds of soil, and there is nothing we can do about it. When we come across those who are pathways, rocky places, or thorny ground, we simply have to understand that what we offer will not last long, if at all, with them.

The second response is to see this parable as Jesus' way of letting us off the hook. We do our best to share the gospel where we can, but many will not receive the message; if they do, they do not stick with it. There is nothing we can do about that. We are responsible only for trying. What happens afterwards is not up to us, and Jesus smiles at our efforts.

The third view of this parable is more nuanced. Holders to this view see the parable not as about the ground but instead as the story of Jesus, the sower who needs workers to help. Some ground is already prepared to receive the seed, but most soil is not. Much ground is hard, rocky, and full of thorns, much like uncultivated farmland in late winter. The farmer's blood, sweat, and tears make the earth fertile and ready for planting.

The harvest is plentiful, but the workers are few. We can conclude that our efforts do not matter, or we can decide it is time to plow.

Don't Be Afraid
Mark 6:50

When there is something real to fear, Christ is there. Knowing the apostles are terrified—whether because they think they have seen a ghost or because they are in a little boat in a big storm—Jesus tells them not to be afraid.

Why? Does He inform them that He is going to calm the storm? Does he recap His recent miracle feeding of five thousand and His awe-inspiring power over all of the elements of earth? Does He remind them of their own skills as handlers of boats?

No.

Jesus tells them not to be afraid for one reason: He is there.

The other reasons are true—He will calm the storm, and He is a doer of miracles, and they have sailed through storms before. But those reasons do not matter when they are in the storm. What they—and we—need in the storm is to know that Jesus is in the storm too.

God tells Isaac not to be afraid "for I am with you." (Genesis 26:24) God tells Joshua to be strong and courageous, "for the Lord your God will be with you wherever you go." (Joshua 1:9) The Psalmist says he will not fear because the Lord is His light. (Psalm 27:1) And the prophet reminds us that when we walk through the floods and fire, we must not be afraid, for God is with us. (Isaiah 43:2)

Now, as then, Jesus says to us, "Take courage, it is I. Do not be afraid."

Why Don't You Learn?
Mark 8:4-5

The Feeding of the Four Thousand is the second of the mass feeding miracles of the gospels, and while it is less famous than its predecessor, the Feeding of the Five Thousand, it is perhaps more important.

The first miracle is a surprise. How are the disciples to know how much Jesus can do with so little? Why should they expect Him to serve a meal to multitudes, and have twelve baskets full of left-overs, out of one boy's lunch? Truly, this miracle is a sight to behold.

The second miracle, however, should not come as a bomb-shell. After all, they have seen Jesus do this once before, not really all that long ago. So when Jesus points out that the crowd is hungry, the disciples should be prepared for Jesus to feed them all, right?

Instead, their response is as predictable as it is repetitive: "Where are we going to find enough food?" Jesus responds slow-ly, using small words and enunciating clearly, because for them He needs to explain it extra plainly: "How... many... loaves... do... you... have?"

The miracle is repeated, and the followers are just as flabbergast-ed as they were the first time.

Are we the same? No matter how many times we have seen God act, no matter the miracles of Christ we have seen performed in our life and in the lives of others, has our faith grown to expect the power of God? Have you learned to trust Him yet?

Coming to Die
Mark 10:45

Jesus is a performer of astounding miracles, but miraculous deeds are not why He is here.

Jesus is a model of organizational leadership, a friend, a challenger of religious and political principles, and a behavioral example for everyone. But none of those things is the reason He walks here among us.

Jesus is a phenomenal imparter of truth and learning, and many religions—and those who hold to no religion at all—acknowledge Him as a great teacher. But reducing the reason He has come to teaching misses the point.

Jesus walks the earth to love, to give, to seek, to serve, and to die. He says as much again and again: "The Son of man has come… to serve and to give his life as a ransom for many."

We must never minimize the extent of the sacrifice that God makes in becoming a human being with a body that can die. Jesus comes here in order to give His life, to bleed and suffer and fulfill the sentence that our sin demands.

Of course His teachings are monumental. It goes without saying that His behavior should be followed and imitated wherever possible. His principles should be embraced.

But God takes on the form of a servant in order to do what has to be done for a sinful people. He is more than a teacher, more than a model, more than a healer. Jesus is the one who comes to give Himself away. He comes to die.

Day 298/October 24 – Mark 12-13

Wise Answers
Mark 12:34

Many people think that having the right answers to key inquiries is the formula for salvation. Their answers will get them close, but only close.

To be sure, Jesus never denigrates wisdom. He teaches complicated ideas and encourages questions as His followers learn about the kingdom of God.

But even as Christ commends learning and investigation, He also makes it clear that intellect and understanding and wisdom, standing alone, are not enough. Indeed, wise answers demonstrate that we are, in Jesus' words, "not far from the kingdom of God."

In other words, what we know will get us close. Reasoning through conundrums and finding solutions to difficult questions can bring us to the doorstep of God.

Still, knowing what something is and understanding how to do it are not the same things as actually doing it. When Jesus is telling people how to become a part of the kingdom of God, His answer is never for them to investigate, learn, study, memorize, and recite an answer. His answer then, as now, is to follow Him.

For a rich young man, that following requires selling all that he has. For a tax collector, it means climbing down from his perch. For two brothers, it means leaving their family business. For all of us, it means walking in His steps.

Truly, we are saved by grace through our faith. That faith is more than knowledge, which gets us "not far" from the goal.

Faith means taking up a cross and following Jesus.

The Unnamed Witness
Mark 14:51

It is an odd entry into the narrative of the Book of Mark. Here —in the midst of the familiar stories of the Last Supper, the Garden of Gethsemane, and arrest of Jesus—we have two verses dedicated to an unnamed boy who witnesses these events.

This nameless boy may well be Mark, the author of this gospel; or he may instead be someone whose anonymity is striking to the apostles remembering that night, and the story of his fleeing into the night is an important tidbit to pass on to Mark, who is collecting biographical data about Jesus that will later form his gospel.

We all know, when we stop to think about it, that the events of our lives are observed by countless nameless faces. Some of those doubtless are uninterested in what we do and pay us no heed; but we never know about the one, or the few, who see and hear us and never forget.

We do not know the names of countless bystanders and spectators who come into contact with Jesus and take that experience home with them, to share it behind closed doors with friends or family.

Why does the unnamed witness, the fleeing boy, make it past the editors into the gospel? Why did Mark share this detail? Maybe it is to make us aware of those watching us, to keep us on our toes. Perhaps it is to remind us how many lives Jesus touches that we will never know.

Day 300/October 26 – Mark 16 – Luke 1

He Is Risen?
Mark 16:8

The empty tomb story in Mark is different from the triumphant story of resurrection we read in Matthew. Here, we find not excitement but instead ambivalence, confusion, and fright.

The resurrection of Christ raises questions for many good people. If Jesus really has died, then how can He return? Was His death some sort of joke, a masquerade pulled off by the divine who really was too immortal to die?

How can Jesus be like us, completely human, if He has this incredible power over death?

If I have seen Him die… if I know that my sins put Him on that cross… how can I face Him now that He is risen?

If I do not understand all of the details, what am I supposed to say about this?

The climax of Mark's gospel, just as in Matthew's, is a powerful declaration that Jesus is risen. He is not to be found in the tomb. Do not make the mistake of thinking that Mark is in any way cheapening this most important of messages, for he does no such thing. Resurrection is proclaimed.

But not everyone hears that message the same way. For some, it is confusing and even scary. It is a ghost story, an incredible event that just makes no sense.

That is ok. Believe anyway. Even if you do not understand how Jesus can conquer death itself, understand the words of the young man by the tomb: He is not here; He is risen.

My Eyes Have Seen Your Salvation
Luke 2:30

Reading this passage in October, of all times, allows a different perspective on the Christmas story: seeing Jesus is a powerful thing.

Seeing this incredible baby's face, Simeon divines the fulfillment of God's promise and the salvation of God's people.

Thomas is a doubter, saying he will not believe Jesus has been resurrected unless he can touch the actual wounds. When he sees Jesus, though, he no longer has to touch anything; seeing Jesus is enough to send him to his knees, proclaiming, "My Lord and my God!" (John 20:28)

When Jesus appears to a woman at a well, she runs to tell her friends. After they see Jesus, they tell her they no longer believe just because of what she has said; having seen and heard for themselves, they know that Jesus is the savior of the world. (John 4:42)

It is the same time and again through the gospels. When individuals see Jesus, they leave what they are doing to follow Him.

It has been the same throughout history. Truly seeing Jesus is what people need. They may have questions, and they often pose daunting philosophical challenges to the idea of faith. They may be dyed-in-the-wool agnostics or atheists, certain that they will never place their trust in the first century Galilean carpenter.

But when people meet Jesus, their world changes. That is why Jesus says, "If I be lifted up, I will draw all men to me." (John 12:32)

See Jesus again. See the salvation of God.

Day 302/October 28 – Luke 4-6

The Corruption of Scripture
Luke 4:9-11

If this passage does not give you pause and even scare you just a little, you are not fully involved. The temptation of Jesus is intimidating enough when we see that our Leader and Hero is subject to the wiles of Satan, albeit with the ability to withstand the tricks and snares of the evil one.

But this third temptation is particularly alarming, because in it we see the devil using scripture to his advantage. Note that the quotation is taken directly from Psalm 91. Satan neither misquotes nor massages scripture. He simply quotes it as support for what he is trying to lure Jesus to do.

Jesus fights fire with fire, using scripture Himself to aid His resistance.

Pay heed: the forces of evil know the Bible as well as we do, and they will try to misuse it for wicked purposes.

Simply quoting Bible verses is not a sign of anything. Anyone, on any side of the cosmic battle, can learn and cite scripture. Memorizing verses and tossing them into a conversation when it suits is not a mark of deep faith or religious conviction; it is merely an indication of a good memory and persuasive rhetoric. At times, it may be a signal of clever deception.

The key is to understand the context and true meaning of Bible verses. That is one reason we are reading all the way through scripture together, to get the whole picture. The Bible is God's story. Understand the whole story well.

Day 303 / October 29 – Luke 7-8

Who Touched Me?
Luke 8:45-46

As Jesus is on His way to raise the important man's daughter from the dead, His clothes are touched by a sick woman. She is immediately healed. Jesus asks, "Who touched me?" Why does Jesus ask?

Is Jesus is confused? Is He perplexed by the crowd?

Of course Jesus knows immediately who has touched Him. The healings of Jesus are personal extensions of Himself. Jesus does not act randomly. The control of the whens and hows of His miraculous work is not ceded by Jesus to a person who happens to reach out and touch Him at a coincidentally fortunate moment.

Jesus asks the question to make the point that **only He** had noticed her. "Did you notice? Of this whole crowd, who reached out to me? Whom did I heal? In this group, did you see the power of God displayed?

The same question could be asked today. We rush around on crucial errands. We direct Jesus in the way we want Him to go, aiming for the *right* person who has asked for *proper* help. On the way, we are surrounded by countless others who desperately need the touch of the Master. Triumphantly, Jesus sees their faith and responds as only He can. Tragically, we never notice.

"Who touched me?" is not a request for information—Jesus already knows the answer. "Who touched me?" is a quiz, a wakeup call to followers of Jesus who don't notice a miracle when it happens in front of their face.

Day 304/October 30 – Luke 9-10

Give Them Something To Eat
Luke 9:13

The apostles point out to Jesus that the hour is late and it is time to dismiss the hungry crowds. Not content simply to identify the people's need to Jesus ("they are hungry"), the apostles proceed to tell Jesus what to do ("send them away so they can go to the villages and buy food"). How often we do the same—going to Jesus with our own program and expecting Him to bless our choice of how to address the need. How often we pray just as an excuse to tell God what needs to happen.

Jesus surprises the apostles. He has no intention of sending the crowds away. Jesus tells those saying the prayer that they are the answer: "You give them something to eat."

Jesus does not explain what they are to do. The apostles do not know what Jesus is going to do. They have only five loaves and two fish, and they have their relationship with Jesus. Jesus gives them an instruction that has no apparent chance of success: there are insufficient raw materials available, and the apostles have no ability to make what Jesus wants happen. All they have is Jesus and their faith. Faith says to follow Jesus. Jesus has told them to feed the crowds.

The apostles answer as we would: "We don't have enough food." Jesus blesses what the apostles bring, and there is more than enough.

Faith knows this: the recipe of whatever we have added to Jesus is enough.

Day 305/October 31 – Luke 11-12

Bigger Barns
Luke 12:21

J esus' statements about possessions are complicated. He tells at least one person to sell all he has, yet He spends time with many other rich people without ever suggesting that they divest themselves of their wealth. He celebrates one widow's offering of her last mite as a great gift; yet He expects another widow to have a party when she finds her lost coin.

Jesus' attitude, however, is consistent. What He always models is that we must never value what we own above the kingdom of God. It is hard for the wealthy to enter heaven. The wealthy man in this parable is a "fool" not because he owns a lot but because his goal in life is to revel in his prosperity, to "eat, drink, and be merry," to build bigger barns to store even more treasure.

Jesus' unfailing rebuke of people like this character is that they are not "rich toward God." Jesus regularly preaches the need to give to those who ask, to use worldly goods to gain friends and strengthen kingdom goals, to feed the poor, to give extravagantly to God, and to repay those whom we have wronged.

The danger of wealth is not in the having; it is in the prioritizing. Paul famously writes it is not money itself but the love of money that is a root of all sorts of evil. (1 Timothy 6:10)

Examine your motives. Why do you gather? Are you using what you have for the kingdom of God?

November

Day 306/November 1 — Luke 13-14

Giving Up Everything
Luke 14:33

Following Jesus demands so much of us that Jesus calls it "giving up everything" we have. Like James and John who leave their work and their father and their boat to follow, or like Matthew who leaves his workplace in the middle of a shift, we are expected to be willing to give up all we know to follow Jesus. Even family and home have to be expendable.

This concept is known as "surrender." Whatever we have—wealth, relationships, plans, hobbies, or promises to keep—must be of lower priority than the road Jesus has laid out for us.

Jesus speaks in these stark terms to be clear. He demands first place in our lives. What Luke calls "discipleship" is the act of learning, following, emulating the teacher, and leaving behind what was so important just the day before.

In fact, of course, Jesus does not usually actually call us away from all we love. James and John remain fishermen, while Matthew does not really want to stay a tax collector. The teaching here is not that most of us will be forced to leave all that we know but rather that we must be willing to forsake all, to surrender, if Christ demands it.

To be sure, some are called to leave home and serve on the other side of the world, literally and figuratively.

All of us are called to surrender, to place Christ as the undisputed priority of our lives. Are you willing to give up everything?

The Father Runs
Luke 15:20

The Prodigal Son parable features three characters. The younger son gets the lion's share of the lines until the older son takes the spotlight at the end.

The true centerpiece of Jesus' story, however, is the father, who embodies the true nature of God. To begin with, he is generous, giving the son what he asks long before it is actually due. Then, he is forgiving, throwing a party for his returning son. Finally, he is patient and kind, explaining himself to the older brother and finding room in the family for both of these siblings.

Most important in this story is the father's defining action that marks God's distinctiveness. The father does not simply wait for the son. This father, filled with compassion, straining to see who is coming up the road, runs to meet the son.

The father does not wait for the son to come all the way to the estate, begging to be allowed to come back and offering himself as a servant. No, the father sees the son while still a long way off and runs to meet him.

This is our God. Unlike the so-called deities of other religions who wait to be found and demand complicated ritual before they can be approached, God seeks us out. God looks for us while we are still a long way off and reaches out. He seeks us, proclaims His gospel to the whole world, and sends His son.

Our Father runs to us. Grace always comes.

Day 308/November 3 – Luke 17-18

As a Little Child
Luke 18:17

Jesus says that only those who become like little children will
enter the kingdom.

The characteristics of a child—what Jesus must have in mind
—include openness, confident reliance, acceptance of gifts, candor,
affectionate love, dependence, honest curiosity, and energy. A child
comes into Christ's kingdom trusting and accepting what the Lord
offers, loving God and God's people, innocently depending on God
for everything, looking around with open eyes to take it all in and
find a place to serve. Children are unpretentious, loving and praying
and helping without stopping to look at themselves to see if they are
doing it right. They do not withhold trust until all of their possible
problems are solved.

What does it mean for us become more childlike? We cannot
just quit our jobs. We cannot abandon our responsibilities, for we
have children of our own and elderly parents and employees and
customers and clients and bosses and many others who depend on
us. These words of Jesus' can become a problem. We cannot become a little child. It is impossible.

Fortunately, what is impossible with us is God's specialty. God,
our father, offers us the right—and the ability—to become His children.

Now, that child that Jesus brings among us shows us what our
guarded, adult selves cannot see through our responsibilities and
prejudices and education. There is a miracle going on - God is accepting us, adopting us, rebirthing us as His children. Once again,
grace always comes.

Day 309/November 4 – Luke 19-20

Have You Come Down?
Luke 19:6

Zaccheus is a cheat. He is a despised chief tax collector, robbing the people to feather his own nest. Now, wanting to see Jesus who is hidden by the crowd, short Zaccheus climbs the nearest tree to get a good view.

Jesus stops under the tree, looks up, and invites Zaccheus to come down so they can eat together.

And at this point we come to the crux of the story. The turning point occurs while Zaccheus is still perched on the branch, as Jesus is waiting for him. The invitation has been given, and the choice is Zaccheus's. Will he come down? Will he stay in the tree?

We know what Zaccheus does. Having met Jesus, he rushes down, repents of his cheating, and offers to pay his victims back fourfold.

What about you? Have you come down from the tree, or are you still comfortably balanced on a limb, weighing your options? Jesus will not force you. He has sought you out, coming to your personal tree and finding you hidden among the leaves. He has called you by name, showing no discomfort with your problems and your failures. He wants to be with you, to enjoy a time of fellowship with you. He wants you. He stands at the roots and looks up, waiting.

Behold, He stands at the door and knocks. (Revelation 3:20)

The choice is yours. You, up on your perch, hear Him calling you. You are invited. Grace has come. Have you come down?

False Messiahs
Luke 21:8

It is an admonition as old as time itself: watch out for fakes. Since the serpent slithered into the garden, claiming to offer truth, many pretend to be what they are not. When the stakes are eternal, the temptation to come out of the woodwork is irresistible for some charlatans.

Jesus knows they are out there. He warns us to be careful so that we are not deceived. Notice that He does not caution us about those who teach a very different religion; no, His counsel concerns those who pretend to be the Christ, the anointed messiah sent by God to save us at the end of time.

You know they are all around us, don't you? You see them offering a too-good-to-be-true lifestyle just for the asking, ignoring Jesus' call for surrender. You hear them promising prosperity and freedom from sickness and defeat, no matter how obvious it is to all that illness and loss are a part of life on earth. You notice them offering themselves, albeit at a price, as the answer for whatever problem presents itself to you.

Jesus warns all of us to be discerning, to recognize these impostors for the swindlers they are.

How do we recognize them? Jesus tells us that we will know them by their fruit. Analyze what they do. Compare their words to the scripture you have been so carefully reading. Pray for guidance. Rely on the Holy Spirit within you to help you distinguish. Rely on Christ.

Be careful.

Day 311/November 6 – Luke 23-24

He Is Risen...
Luke 24:34

Luke's telling of the resurrection story is in many ways as triumphant as Matthew's and as full of questions as Mark's, but Luke takes the story a step further.

Like Matthew, Luke victoriously reports the statement to the women at the tomb that they must stop looking for Jesus among the dead, for He has risen just He has said he would

Like Mark, Luke reports confusion and disbelief at the news.

What Luke goes on to tell us, though, is of great importance, for Luke explains that the message is not simply Jesus has risen; instead, it is that Jesus has indeed risen, that He has appeared to numerous others, and that there is no reason to be troubled.

This is the best of news! The message of resurrection is validated by Jesus' repeated appearances to different people. The two sad disciples who are walking to Emmaus are transformed into joyful followers running exuberantly back to Jerusalem. They are there to verify this almost-but-not-quite unbelievable tale told by Mary Magdalene and the other women who visited the tomb. Peter's uncertainty after seeing the empty graveclothes on the ground becomes jubilant acknowledgment of the miracle of Christ, the conquering of death by the Son of God.

Then Jesus appears again, this time to the group of them, and he begins to open their minds. They understand, finally.

Resurrection means something more. What comes next is victory.

Resurrection is the great miracle. Death is not final. Grace comes, and grace wins.

Day 312/November 7 – John 1-2

Grace Comes Through Jesus
John 1:17

Without mentioning Mary, shepherds, magi, or angels, John starts his gospel far before Bethlehem, for Jesus begins long before Bethlehem. John starts "in the beginning," because Jesus, the very Word of God, is in the beginning. Jesus is God, the creator and sustainer, who becomes flesh to show us the glory of God and to become the savior of us all.

The theology in this opening of John's gospel is deep and profound, but it need not be confusing. John calls Jesus "the Word" to illustrate that everything there is to know about God – everything that God has to say to us – is found, seen, and heard in Jesus. Jesus has been alive since the beginning, because Jesus is God. When Jesus becomes human, the Word becomes flesh.

Those who pay attention reading through scripture know that grace always comes—clothes in the garden, the ark in the storm, water from the rock, never-ending flour in the widow's pantry, defense against attacking Assyrians, the lion and the lamb lying together on God's holy mountain, a New Covenant written on our hearts, the remnant protected during exile, Hosea's love for Gomer, one who takes up a cross and conquers death. John's message for us is that this grace, this manifestation of God, has a name. Grace comes in the person of Jesus, the Word.

Yes, the one behind what we have read all year is here! He is the one who has always been. He is the Word. He is grace.

Day 313 / November 8 – John 3-4

Whoever Believes In Him
John 3:16

John 3:16 encapsulates the gospel. God loves the whole world. God gives His only son. Whoever believes in Him will not perish but will have eternal life.

Incredible words: Love... Gift... Whoever... Eternal life.

The most critical phrase in this verse, however, is "believes in." Salvation comes to those who "believe in" Christ. Not to those who "believe what" Jesus says. Not to those who "believe the truth of" scripture. Not even to those who "believe that" Jesus performed miracles and rose from the dead. All of those kinds of "belief" are important, but none of them is what Jesus is talking about. "Believing in" something is more than recognition of fact, more even than acknowledgment of the truth of something.

Belief in someone requires commitment and surrender. It requires faith.

A woman looks up daily and sees airplanes. She knows that airplanes can fly because she watches them. She goes to the airport and sees family members get off planes that have just landed.

A man studies the physics of aerodynamics and jet propulsion and knows everything there is to know about air travel. He learns about fuselages and fueling and wings and landing procedures and announces himself as an expert in the field.

But neither that man nor that woman will set foot on board an airplane. They believe plenty about airplanes, but neither of them believes in airplanes. They know about airplanes but have no faith in them.

Everlasting life comes to those who believe in Jesus.

Day 314/November 9 – John 5-6

The Bread of Life
John 6:35

The people listening to Jesus preach know about manna, the bread from heaven provided by God to Moses and the Israelites as a miraculous means of keeping them alive as they wander the desert.

Many of the people have seen Jesus perform His feeding miracle with bread, turning five loaves into enough to feed thousands.

They all, of course, rely on bread for sustenance and nutrition. They break bread around tables as their primary means of fellowship. They bake bread and sell it or give it to their families for long journeys. In many ways, their lives—like ours—revolve around bread.

It is no accident that the metaphor Jesus chooses for Himself is bread. He is not suggesting that anyone take a bite out of Him any more than He is hinting that someone actually ingest His physical blood. He is making a far more important point: He is what is necessary for life.

Jesus is the miraculous gift of God, sent from heaven to us who would wander to our deaths without Him.

Jesus is the wondrously shared gift who is enough for all of us. Jesus sustains us. Jesus brings us together in fellowshipping community. Jesus is our livelihood, our shared bond as we travel the roads of life.

Jesus says that He is living bread, come from heaven so that we may not die. He gives life. He offers Himself to each one of us.

Jesus presents the bread of life to you. Come and eat.

Day 315/November 10 – John 7-8

Knowledge. Truth. Freedom.
John 8:32

They are carved on the outside of courthouses and printed on courtroom walls across the United States. Scandal-ridden celebrities use these words as part of come-clean interviews. Psychologists argue whether they are a guide for the value of honesty. Movies and books use the phrase, or variations of it, often.

These words that seem to pop up everywhere are: "The truth shall set you free."

Jesus is not talking about law, courtrooms, psychology, televised confession, drama, or personal relationships. He is talking about something completely different. He says that if we hold to his teaching and continue in His Word, then we are His disciples; only then do we know the truth. And that truth sets us free. And if Jesus sets you free, you are free indeed.

Popular spiritual discussion holds that we cannot really "know" anything about God. Rather, we are told, we "project" or "feel" or "reach our own place" with God. The world tells us that there is no absolute truth, that rules and morality and commandments are passé, that ethical calls are situational, and that claiming to know the truth is arrogant and misguided.

Freedom is a concept that has been relegated to historical discussions, categorized to apply to narrow classifications of needy groups across the world, or trivialized to discussions of things like "freedom from high interest rates."

Jesus is bringing a powerful message. Follow Him. Be His disciple. And you will know. You will know truth. And that truth will set you free.

What Has Happened to You?
John 9:25

Even when we cannot provide the answers or convince the skeptical, we all have a story. Answering all the theological questions of the philosophers of the age is beyond any of us. Debating with the one who is stymied by what happens when the irresistible force meets the immovable object is fruitless. Sophistry and pointless discussion will not lead anyone to an understanding of why you believe what you believe, why you follow whom you follow, or why your faith is where it is.

The man in the story in John 9 does not know the answers. He does not even know Jesus' name. He has no idea how mud on his eyes has had any healing powers. He does not understand the political and religious intricacies of the Pharisees' tricky, spiteful questions. He does not get any backup from his parents.

He has only one thing going for him. He knows that he was blind and now he is not. He could not see, and now he can.

Your story is your own. People can argue your theology and debate your points, but unless they simply discount you as psychotic or as a pathological liar, they cannot discount your experience. What you have to offer to the world's greatest discussion is simply this: What has happened in your life? How has faith in Jesus changed you? What do you care about and do now?

Tell your version of this great testimony: "I once was blind, but now I see."

Day 317/November 12 – John 11-12

Some Will Never See
John 12:37

Some, like Thomas, see Jesus and believe. Some, like the formerly blind man of John 9, experience the power of Christ in their own life and worship. Some, like the woman at the well, meet Jesus and tell everyone they know about Him. Some, like James and John and Nathanael and Matthew and Zacchaeus and many others, hear Him call, and they immediately leave what they are doing and follow. And some, like those at Lazarus's tomb and those disciples in the boat after Jesus has walked on the water and calmed the storm, see the miracles of God played out in the life of Jesus and come to faith in Him.

But there are others who never believe. They refuse to see Jesus, accept that there is truth of God that could be contained in this Nazarene carpenter, or hear His voice. They see miracles and pass them off as everyday science or optical illusion, or worse, they discount the stories of the miracles as the demented meanderings of misled pitiful people.

Sometimes, these people meet Jesus Himself and will not accept His claim as their savior. The preaching of the Apostle Paul was so ineffective to some that he had to flee out a window to avoid being killed (Acts 9:20-25). We should not be surprised when our words are not always persuasive.

Jesus does not abandon those who hear Him without response. Neither should we. Follow Jesus' and Paul's example, and keep telling people the good news.

Day 318/November 13 – John 13-15

Peace
John 14:27

Not as the world gives.

The world has always cried out "peace" when there is no peace. (Jeremiah 6:14; Jeremiah 8:11; Ezekiel 13:10). Some do it as an intentional deception, a diversion from their true activities; Ezekiel calls this a "whitewash." Others declare victory in the quest for what they believe to be peace, shutting their eyes to continuing discord all around. Still others notice that the current neighborhood squabble has ended and declare that peace has come.

Jesus brings peace that the world knows nothing about. He is not talking about an absence of war, a cessation of bullets, a slowing of hostilities, or an absence of anger. When Jesus says he brings peace, He is not suggesting that He is subtracting anything from the world. Jesus comes that we can have abundant life to the full (John 10:10), and abundance necessarily involves augmentation, enlargement, and intensification. Jesus does not come to subtract anything. Jesus adds to the world.

What is it that Jesus brings that qualifies as peace?

Jesus enters our world, our relationships, our churches, and our individual hearts with His presence, His comfort, His purposeful direction, and His saving mercy. What was there before – sin, with its entrapments; loss, with its uncertainty and meaninglessness; and fear, with its heartbreaking and backbreaking burden – is covered and replaced and expelled by the incredible love and power of God Himself. The storm is calmed. Our past is forgiven. Our future is guaranteed.

Grace always comes, and there is peace.

Day 319/November 14 – John 16-18

Overcoming the World
John 16:33

In this world, we have sadness. But grace always comes.

    In this world, there are disease and terrorism and despair. But grace still always comes. In this world, evil sends deceit and hatred and meanness. We are beset with those who seem to find no greater pleasure than to make us miserable. Still, grace keeps coming.

Storms rage. Drunks drive. Thieves steal. Crops fail. Savings accounts vanish.

In this world, we are scattered. In this world, we will have troubles. And yet, grace always comes. How? Why?

Grace always comes because grace and truth come through Jesus Christ, and Jesus has overcome the world.

In the short term, our own troubles are dwarfed by what will beset Jesus in the coming reports we are about to read: betrayal, denial, abandonment, arrest, beating, thorns, accusation, trial, spittle, exhaustion, exposure, weariness, pain, suffocation, crucifixion, death. He who knows no sin will take the sin of the world on Himself. He will be devastated.

The world will take its best shot at Jesus. And then the long term happens. Despite torture and punishment, Jesus overcomes. After crucifixion, there is resurrection.

Jesus says that, yes, there is trouble in this world, but take heart: He has overcome the world.

What does the world have to throw at you today? What demon is lurking in the shadows? Who will strike your cheek? What will challenge your integrity? From where does the next pain come?

    Take heart! Jesus has overcome the world. Grace still always comes.

Uncontainable
John 21:25

The last verse of the Gospel of John is wonderful and mysterious. The idea that we have read through four gospels of Jesus' biography and have not yet scratched the surface of what He said and did during His time on earth is a puzzle. The promise that everything about Jesus could not be contained in all the books of the world is John's way of saying that we cannot know all there is to know about Jesus. We cannot put Jesus in a box. Even those who walk with Him are not capable of encapsulating everything about Him in what they write.

We can become guilty of thinking we fully comprehend Jesus. We become comfortable that we know all His words and thoughts. We confidently face questions, either asserting that we know all He says about them or declaring that He has never said anything about them.

John tells us to step back and think again. We know what the Bible has told us. We know the nature of Christ. We know God is fully revealed in Jesus.

But to think we know it all, that we have understood everything that Jesus is, says, and wants is to approach a level of arrogance that our human knowledge does not support. We do not know it all.

The end of Chapter 20 tells us that the Bible tells us what we need to know for now. The end of Chapter 21 tells us that there is much still to learn.

Day 321/November 16 – Acts 1-2

The Birth of the Church
Acts 2:41

The Book of Acts is often called "The Acts of the Apostles." Some call it "The Acts of the Holy Spirit" or "The Acts of the Church." It is often considered to be the "fifth gospel." This book is history. This book tells a never-ending story.

This Book of Acts tells of the work of God carried out through His people, the apostles and disciples and earliest followers of Jesus, after Jesus' ascension to the right hand of the Father.

As the Old Testament tells of God the Father's work in the world and as the gospels display the work of God the Son, now Acts focuses on God the Spirit. The people's actions begin when the Holy Spirit comes to them, bringing power. (Acts 1:8) The Spirit strengthens and emboldens Peter, the recent denier, and the upshot is Peter's incredible sermon of Acts 2 that results in the conversion and baptism of thousands.

So begins what the world knows as "church." These followers of Christ receive and accept the message of salvation and commit themselves to following Christ, to fellowshipping with one another, and to carrying out the ministry of the gospel. They praise God together daily, and their numbers grow.

Jesus has earlier told Peter that He will build His church on what Peter has confessed—that Jesus is the Christ, the Son of the living God – and that the gates of hell itself shall not prevail against the church. (Matthew 16:18) Now, this church has begun.

Day 322/November 17 – Acts 3-4

No Other Name
Acts 4:12

How Jesus saves is miraculous and mysterious. How does the cross apply to me? How can Jesus hold me safe even when I reject His words?

We cannot unravel all of these mysteries logically or scientifically, but we know the answers nonetheless. The cross, the empty tomb, and the power of God have changed us.

Similarly, we cannot answer all of the questions that surround the grace of God. Our faith tells us that this work of Christ extends to all who receive it. What about those who have never heard the Word? How can God save those who do not know His name or those who worship God as they know Him but do not use the language we use for His love and grace?

These questions are worthy of debate and consideration, but they do not change the unalterable truth of the New Testament: Regardless of how salvation is understood and irrespective of what words are used, there is one savior. Jesus Christ, the Son of God, is the expression of God's grace in the world. Jesus is the way, the truth, and the life; no one comes to the Father except through Him. (John 14:6) Jesus is the resurrection, and those who believe in Him will not die. (John 11:25) Indeed, Jesus' name means "the Lord saves."

There may be room to access grace in different ways, but no matter how people receive God's gift, that grace has come through Jesus Christ.

Jesus saves, and grace comes.

Day 323/November 18 – Acts 5-7

We Must Obey God
Acts 5:29

Peter's reply—that the apostles "must obey God" rather than doing what they are told by the local controlling authorities—may be something dismissed as "Bible talk." Looking behind this statement, though, we see Peter and John demonstrating a commitment that deserves our study and our praise.

These followers of Christ have already been thrown in jail. Now they are hauled in front of the Sanhedrin, the local supreme court with religious and political powers no other Jews hold, and ordered to cease their preaching. These Sanhedrin members are some of the same people who called for the crucifixion of Jesus. If there is any question about the atmosphere surrounding this order not to preach, that doubt is erased by the story of chapters 6 and 7, where we see Stephen stoned to death. The world around the apostles is tense with hostility, violence, and intolerance.

The easy thing to do… the politically practical thing to do… what most would say the only thing to do… is to obey the rule set down by the powers that be.

Peter and the other apostles, however, cannot do the expedient thing, because they are guided by a single watchword: We must obey God.

Your circumstances may be difficult. Following your faith will cause you problems. You may be surrounded by those who, unimpressed with your faith, want to encourage you to take the easy road or order you to do their bidding.

You know better. We must obey God.

Conversion
Acts 9:17-22

These two chapters tell of people whose lives are literally converted—transformed by the power of God.

There are Simon the sorcerer (Acts 8:13) and the Ethiopian eunuch (Acts 8:36), who believe and are baptized. To be sure, they both still have a lot to learn, but their basic paths are changed.

There are the stories of the healing of Aeneas, the raising of Tabitha, and the salvation of hundreds of others as the church grows in Jerusalem.

Amidst these other stories, of course, is the central conversion story of the New Testament. It is the story of Saul, who is to become Paul. When Saul first appears in Acts, he is holding the coats of those who throw stones at Stephen, aiding and abetting the execution of this faithful deacon. Then, Saul sets off to destroy the church. (Acts 8:1-3) Amazingly, it is Saul whom God chooses as the one who is to take the gospel to "the Gentiles and their kings." (Acts 9:15)

After he is converted, Saul becomes Paul, who will write most of the rest of the New Testament. He becomes the great Apostle, more responsible for the growth of the church than anyone else.

The gospel changes lives. We do not obey in order to impress God. Like Paul, we obey because we have been changed.

Like a sorcerer, a foreign dignitary, a paralytic, new church members, and the one who would destroy the church itself, we have been converted into children of God.

Day 325/November 20 – Acts 10-11

What God Has Made Clean
Acts 10:15

Because Peter's dream about the sheet full of animals is told in the context of going to the house of a Gentile, it is often used as the primary Biblical lesson against discrimination on the basis of race. To be sure, that is a proper understanding of this story, for Peter has to learn the hard lesson that God's message is not limited to the Jewish race but indeed is for all.

The story, however, goes beyond ethnic discrimination. Read carefully what the voice of Christ says to Peter out of the trance in which the apostle finds himself: Do not call anything impure that God has made clean.

This commandment has no limit on it save this: what God has made clean. In other words, the one who decides who and what are clean is God. And if God has reached down and shared the freeing, cleansing, saving grace of Jesus Christ with a person, we have no business at all declaring that person to be unclean.

In their heritage and law, first century Jews have reason to think that Gentiles are unclean. Based on what they know, first century Christians have reason to stay away from Saul, and from Ethiopian eunuchs, and from sorcerers... and women... and lepers. But God says do not call them unclean. It is not for us to declare God's converted to be unworthy.

God cleanses. Grace makes pure. We embrace our brothers and sisters. Do not mix up your role with God's.

What the Law Cannot Do
Acts 13:39

Paul's message isolates the New Testament solution to the Old Testament problem.

The Old Testament is the story of how God deals with God's people, who repeatedly, stubbornly break God's law. Commandments are routinely ignored. God's will is not sought or is bent to the shape of the wants of the people. Over and over again, the covenant is renewed, as God calls on His people to keep His commandments. Time and again, the people violate the covenant. And so people—in the Old Testament and today—have a problem.

The problem is not the law. God's law is perfect. The problem is the people. We simply do not keep the law. We give in to temptation. We follow the offerings of the world. We do evil. We fail to do good. We follow other gods and create worthless idols. We dishonor the name of God. We do not love our neighbors.

There is none righteous. No, not one. (Ecclesiastes 7:20; Romans 3:10)

Fortunately, grace always comes. Paul explains how God reaches down to solve the ultimate problem of our separation from God that results from our interminable failure to keep God's laws: all who have faith in Christ are justified by that faith, even when, and because, they could not achieve justification through following the law. "Justification" is a crucial concept, because it explains how the unmerited gift of grace allows us to stand innocent, in spite of ourselves, before God as judge. Jesus solves our unsolvable problem.

Day 327/November 22 – Acts 14-16

Prayers and Hymns
Acts 16:25

Is it hard for you to picture Paul and Silas in jail? Do you laugh—or shudder—at the idea of being surrounded by those with whom you imagine you would share a cell and deciding to start a hymn sing and a prayer meeting?

Paul and Silas model for Christians the way to approach crisis. They are imprisoned, having been flogged and put into the stocks. This is not their first time in a cell, and they know the extremes of the feelings against them. Neither freedom nor escape is a likely outcome, when the situation is examined through human eyes. Jail is demeaning, dangerous, and perhaps final.

Paul and Silas, fresh from the whip and chained to the wall, choose to pray and sing hymns. Their praying and singing lead the jailer to Christ.

Prayer is talking with God. Paul and Silas are sharing their feelings, their needs, and their praises with their heavenly Father. They are no doubt asking for deliverance and sharing their faith in God's sovereignty.

Hymns are songs in praise and honor of God. The use of music throughout scripture is intentional—God is creator of beauty and art, of measured symmetry, of soaring notes and precise rhythms, of words of praise and worship and confession that we see throughout the Bible. To sing hymns is to give back to God that which He has bestowed, to praise and to honor Him.

No matter where you are, pray your prayers and sing your hymns.

Keep It Up; God Is with You
Acts 18:9-10

God is with us.

Paul is discouraged. He has matched wits with the best and the brightest that Athens has to offer, the Jews in the synagogue, and the heathens on the street. He has done his best to follow Christ.

Not only is he not being rewarded or even seeing the conversion of many to whom he is preaching, but he is also facing active opposition and abuse. The call from God surely seems far away at times. Paul must wonder if it is time to move on.

One night, God comes to him with this direct message: Do not be afraid. Keep speaking. Do not be silent. I am with you. No one will harm you. I have many allies in this city.

This is the word that Jacob receives at Bethel: I am the God of your father, and I will be with you wherever you go. (Genesis 28:13-15) It is the message God brings to Moses: Go, and I will help you. (Exodus 4:10) It is the same message God speaks through Elisha when the servant's eyes are opened to see the chariots of fire full of angels all around them: There are more who stand on our side than those who stand against us. (2 Kings 6:16)

Despair and discouragement come to us all. When we see odds stacked against us. God says to us all: Keep at it. I am with you, and there are many more on our side. Do not be afraid.

Day 329/November 24 — Acts 19-20

Finishing the Race
Acts 20:24

Heading into the stronghold of the enemy, where arrest and execution likely await, Paul tells the elders of the church that preserving his life at any cost is not the goal; he has a calling. He has been appointed by God to be the apostle to the Gentiles, and he intends to carry out the mission.

His metaphor is telling. He intends to "finish the race" and complete the task.

Notice that Paul does not set out to win the race. His job is not to compare how he does his task with how others complete theirs. He is not timing himself. He is not looking to do better than anyone else. His goal is to finish.

Each of us has a calling from God. Our lives as Christians are based on following Jesus, and the paths on which He leads each of us individually differ greatly. One follower may face steep drops and difficult turns, while another may navigate a simpler road that calls for consistency but not dramatic challenge. Still another may be called to a single task that takes years to accomplish.

Courage in the face of the enemy is based on the recognition that Christ is with us, for Jesus consistently teaches us, "Be not afraid. It is I."

Paul goes where the enemy is, following his lord. At the end of his life, Paul will write, "I have fought the good fight. I have finished the race. I have kept the faith." (2 Timothy 4:7)

Day 330/November 25 – Acts 21-23

As in Jerusalem, So in Rome
Acts 23:11

As predicted, Paul's arrival in Jerusalem is quickly followed by his arrest. Reminiscent of the trials of Jesus, Paul's path goes through a series of kangaroo courts before magistrates who have no idea what to make of him, his sermons, or his accusers. Ultimately, the Jewish leaders form an active conspiracy to kill him. His status as a citizen of Rome complicates things for his captors, who decide to take him to the local Roman authority.

Paul's prayer must be for relief. Surely, Paul asks the Lord to rescue him from his jailers.

Jesus comes to Paul, but instead of breaking his chains and opening his prison cell, He calls on Paul to continue to be courageous. "Just as you have testified about me in Jerusalem, so you must also testify in Rome."

At a base human level, Paul must be devastated to hear this command. Surely he has hoped for deliverance, for escape, for the Holy Spirit to punish his accusers for wrongly interfering with Paul's mission. Not only does he not receive a promise of relief, he is assured continued captivity, taking him all the way to Rome.

Relinquishing control of our life to Christ requires us to accept God's mission for us. If we follow only so long as we get the path we choose and the answers we desire, we do what anyone would do. When the path leads not to rest but to Rome, we face true surrender. Are you willing to follow Him there?

Day 331/November 26 – Acts 24-26

I Have Had God's Help to This Very Day
Acts 26:22

Paul's words before King Agrippa include, once again, the story of his dramatic Damascus Road conversion experience. Paul then argues that the charges brought against him are unproveable.

Noteworthy in Paul's defense is his testimony that he has "had God's help to this very day." Paul has been in jail for two years, has been flogged, has been prevented from traveling to Spain as he desired, and is now destined to be taken to trial in Rome itself. It could easily be taken as empty religious blather when Paul uses language like this. After all, how can he possibly see these hardships and roadblocks as anything but evidence that God has abandoned him?

The truth we learn from Paul's words and his experience is that God's help comes through, and despite, our problems. God's presence does not mean the problems and evils of this world are avoided. Daniel has to go into the lion's den. Shadrach and his friends are thrown into the fiery furnace. Jeremiah is tortured in the town square.

And Jesus dies on a cross.

The promise is that God helps us despite what comes. We walk though the floods, but we are not swept away. (Isaiah 43:2) The arrow flies and the plague strikes, but we do not fear. (Psalm 91:5)

And we can spend years in jail and still understand that God's help is always with us. God's amazing grace has led us "through many dangers, toils, and snares."

Even in prison, grace always comes.

Courage through Shipwreck
Acts 27:25

Living in fear is epidemic. It does not take a great deal of imagination or education to see shipwreck coming. We watch the news and understand that terrorism is blossoming and war is growing nearer. We listen to weather reports and learn of dramatic changes and immediate storms that bring their watches and warnings. Political debate is filled with cautions and advice about coming perils that threaten our way of life. Schools, churches, nightclubs, and shopping centers are targets of madmen. Disaster, it seems, awaits.

On an individual level, health and job and relationships and finances can all be far less secure than they were yesterday, for disease and unemployment and betrayal and poverty are very real menaces for us and our loved ones.

We can all understand the foreboding sense that a crash is looming.

Paul knows that shipwreck is literally on the horizon, but he also knows that God has a message of hope and promise. Paul knows that a messenger has come to him with the assurance of living through the coming disaster.

We too understand this point. We know that grace always comes, and so we do not have to live in fear. We who have accepted the gift of everlasting life know our eternity is assured. We resonate with Paul, because we live without being afraid.

We have a message for the world. The Prince of Peace has come. The Wonderful Counselor, who overcomes the world, is here. We do not have to be afraid.

Day 333/November 28 – Romans 1-4

Justified
Romans 3:22-24

Scripture now takes a turn, a change in tone and structure, a different form. The gospels and Acts have been historical and biographical in nature, recounting stories and presenting a narrative of the words and actions of Jesus, of the apostles led by Peter, and of Paul.

Now, we begin a series of letters, mostly written by this same Paul, that lay out the basics of our faith from the perspectives of those who have experienced the work and walk of Christ.

The first of these letters, Romans, spells out our situation.

Romans begins Paul's argument that we are all sinners under the law. The "law" in question may be the Ten Commandments, with the subsequent Old Testament requirements that the Jews recognize, or different but authoritative series of moral and ethical expectations that other societies, including our own, follow. Whatever "law" applies, none of us keeps it. The list of violations in Romans 1 is not exhaustive but instead is illustrative of the many ways in which we human beings fail. If your failing is not in one specific, it is in another.

We are not innocent people, and the judge of the universe cannot accept us. We need to be justified before this judge.

That is Paul's argument. Standing unjust, we are justified—made just—by Christ's grace. We are made worthy of the love of God. We are declared not guilty. Grace comes through our faith in Christ. Jesus makes us righteous before God. We are justified.

Adopted, Never Condemned
Romans 8:1, 15-17

These four chapters are rich with understanding of our lives now that we have been justified by Christ. Our old natures still lead us to do things we should not, but we now go through this familiar struggle as children of God. Our place in God's family is secure. There is no condemnation for those who are in Christ Jesus.

Paul says we are adopted into God's family, and his description of adoption mirrors Jesus' language to Nicodemus about the need to be born again or born from above. (John 3:3) "Adoption" and "rebirth" are two ways of saying the same thing: we become the children of God, permanently a part of the divine, eternal family.

Becoming a child of God does not instantaneously end temptation, nor does it immediately eliminate our human failings. We know what the Father wants, but we still do things we ought not to do. Yet we are no longer slaves to sin, and we have the Holy Spirit fighting for us to help us in our weakness. (Romans 8:26)

Paul finishes this section by giving us a preview of the end of the story: despite our individual failings, we are on the winning side of this cosmic battle. We are more than conquerors because of the power of Jesus Christ. If God is for us, who can be against us?

There is no condemnation for us, even when we fail. Nothing can separate us from God. We are a part of God's family forever.

Day 335/November 30 – Romans 9-12

Transformed
Romans 12:2

B e transformed by the renewing of your mind.
What a challenge Paul lays before us: the opportunity to allow our minds to be changed by Christ so that we can be revolutionized into something powerful.

We do not understand all that God has in mind. His ways are unsearchable. The depths of His wisdom cannot be approached by us, but we do not have to stay in the dark. God offers us the chance to transform, to convert, to become more and more like Him. The old-fashioned term for this process—sanctification—describes a lifelong progression from one condition to another.

Paul follows this challenge with the extended metaphor of the body, making the point that none of us is fully developed as a Christian so long as we walk on this earth; instead, we are a specific body part, we fulfill certain roles, and we should not think of ourselves more highly than we deserve.

Still, we are different than we used to be, and if we allow the Holy Spirit to work, we are transformed, changed from what we were to what we will be.

This transformation begins with our minds. To renew our minds is to take away old thoughts, intentions, goals, and ideas; our minds are newly filled with contemplations, concepts, plans, and aspirations that are placed by the Holy Spirit. When our minds, the control center of our lives, are newly formed, we are ready to be what God wants us to be.

December

As Christ Accepted You
Romans 15:7

What binds us together is our common faith in Christ Jesus.

Tragically, we allow many other things to divide us. Rituals and traditions can result is disunity and separation. Disagreements over specific issues drive wedges between us.

Using issues of eating certain foods or venerating certain days as examples, Paul urges us Christians to accept and live with each other despite our differences in practices and orthodoxy.

Notice that Paul does not say that holding and teaching correct beliefs or rigorously knowing and maintaining correct doctrine are wrong. Paul, himself a vigorous defender of his own principles and careful belief, is terribly concerned that we not become stumbling blocks for one another. As far as it is up to each of us, we are to live in peace, accepting the differences of our Christian sisters and brothers. What is most important is that we, with one heart and mouth, glorify the Father and Son together.

How can we accept such differences? How can we worship with those whose behavior is inexplicable to us? How are we supposed to be unified with those who do not accept tenets we believe are basic? The answer is found in emulating the way Jesus Himself accepts us. While we were yet sinners, Christ died for us. (Romans 5:8) Jesus does not wait for us to line up with Him on every issue, and neither must we expect others to be in agreement with us. Instead, make every effort to do what leads to peace.

Day 337/December 2 – 1 Corinthians 1-4

The Mind of Christ
1 Corinthians 2:16

The contrast between the "wisdom" of our age and the "foolishness of God" has been misunderstood by many as some sort of pathetic defense of unreasonable belief in silliness. We are ridiculed for reading the writings of ancient shepherds and fishermen. Doubters, agnostics, and questioners accuse faithful Christians of relying on childish tales that cannot possibly be true. Post-modernists go even further, declaring that there is no permanent truth and that those who claim to approach and understand truth are misguided, if not outright stupid.

Paul has a different approach. His use of the term "the foolishness of God" is ironic, for he teaches that wisdom comes to the mature from the Holy Spirit. Some can see God's word and plan as foolish not because they are too simple but because they are far too complex. No human mind can conceive what God has prepared.

Our puny human minds cannot comprehend the vastness of the creator of the universe. It is the mind of Christ that sets the waves pounding in lunar rhythm. It is Jesus who holds the secrets of black holes and quantum physics in the same mind that sees Moses and Genghis Khan and you and me and our great-great-grandchildren simultaneously.

We can all describe the visible fact that rain makes the flowers grow, but the wisest person will never satisfactorily explain how it works. Instead, we rely on the "foolishness of God," the mind of Christ.

The Spirit gives this mind to us. Truth is ours.

That Is What You Were
1 Corinthians 6:11

S exual immorality is only one of many seedy examples in this
discussion of behavior that should be foreign to Christians.
Paul provides laundry lists of characters—idolaters, thieves, drunk-
ards, materialists, slanders, and swindlers among them—to make the
case that none of is worthy to inherit the kingdom of God.

Fortunately, we are saved despite our unworthiness, for Jesus
comes to us while we are sinners. That is the point of the cross.

Paul makes the point that some of us were guilty of the very sins
on his list in this chapter before Christ washed us clean. All of us,
of course, are guilty of our own set of sins, even if our list does not
appear in these chapters.

Paul's thrust is that these lists describe what we were; they should
not describe what we are. Christ lovingly welcomes the adulterous
woman, and then He tells her to sin no more. (John 8:11)

We are changed. We are washed. We are transformed. We have
the Holy Spirit at our side, fighting for us as we struggle against
temptation. We do not have to stay the same. We are no longer slaves
to sin. We should behave as those claimed and changed by Jesus.

When sexual immorality—or anything else on Paul's lists—re-
appears in the life of the Christian, our human nature is gravitating
back to its pre-Christ history.

Keep your past in the past. Strive to be what Christ wants you to
be. You have been sanctified.

Day 339/December 4 – 1 Corinthians 9-13

I Am Nothing If I Do Not Love
1 Corinthians 13:2

Chapter 13 is known in many circles as "the love chapter." Its famous description of *agape*—the love of God mirrored in our lives as Christians—is really a description of God, who is agape. (1 John 4:8) When we try to measure up, we will of course fail, for we are unholy and imperfect. Try as we might, we can never be God.

Still, Paul teaches that we must "have love" in our lives. We must strive to reflect this perfect charity, this holy *agape* that Christ has laid out for us. We are called to love one another.

It is a worthy list of adjectives we want to describe our lives: Patient. Kind. Not envying, boastful, rude, proud, or self-seeking. Not easily angered. Keeping no record of wrongs. Rejoicing in truth, not in evil.

Bearing all things. Believing all things. Hoping all things. Bearing all things.

Never failing.

When we decide that this list is beyond us because we are sinful Christians, we can become satisfied in settling with something less than love in our lives. We can decide that speaking great words and clinging to our doctrine are what make us really excellent Christians.

Paul has an unsettling word for us. Though we prophesy with the best of them, though we understand the deepest religious mysteries, though we know our Bibles, and though we have a faith that can move mountains… if we do not have love, we are nothing.

Jesus' commandment is this: Love one another.

Day 340/December 5 – 1 Corinthians 14-16

Death: The Last Enemy to be Defeated
1 Corinthians 15:26

Most of us face death with varying degrees of uncertainty, fear, and loathing. We are uncertain because those who have passed before us do not come back to tell us what to expect. We fear because it is essentially human to be scared of the dark, and death presents a closing off of whatever life and light we understand in this world. We loathe death both because we all know too many people taken from us by death too early for our liking, and because we ourselves are never quite ready to go.

Paul understands our natural perception of and reaction to death, and he is not trying to talk us out of that uncertainty and distaste. Instead, he moves beyond the natural, telling us that death does not have the final word. Our corruptible body's physical death is as necessary to our spiritual beings as planting is to the seed. It is only through this death that our immortal, imperishable persons will be released to our eternal life.

This is, as Paul says, a mystery, but the picture is glorious. The trumpet will sound! We will be raised incorruptible. We will then scoff at death and its ultimate toothlessness.

We may not read Chapter 15 and eliminate our fear of death, but we should read it with an understanding of the triumph to follow. Overcoming the power and sting of death is child's play for Jesus, who gives us the great victory. Even at the end, grace always comes.

Day 341 / December 6 – 2 Corinthians 1-4

Hard Pressed; Not Crushed
2 Corinthians 4:8-9

Scripture is full of promises to us. We are promised the presence of Christ and the love of God. We are promised the indwelling Holy Spirit to fight for us and pray for us when we are at a loss. We have the rainbow and the empty tomb.

There are other, less gratifying, promises in scripture. We are promised that many in the world will hate us because they hated Jesus first. We are promised that we will have troubles in life. We are promised that the rain will fall on the just and on the unjust in equal amounts.

Here, Paul recognizes one of the immutable promises of living in this fallen world. We Christians will be hard pressed. We will be perplexed. We will be persecuted and struck down. Paul talks about our mortal bodies as "jars of clay" to emphasize that we are mortal, breakable, imperfect vessels through whom Jesus works, and our fallibility stays put to emphasize that we are not the source of our own power; Christ is. We are breakable. We crack. We do not always hold water.

Thanks be to God that these promises do not stop there. Paul also guarantees that because of the love and power of Christ, despite being hard pressed, we will not be crushed. We will never be in despair. The children of God are never abandoned.

It is a promise: Despite persecution, confusion, attack, and our own human weakness, we will not be destroyed. Grace always comes.

By Faith, Not By Sight
2 Corinthians 5:7

What is it to live by sight?

Living by sight means following what our eyes can actually see before us, so we pursue those things that catch our attention. Today, that may be a political leader who offers prosperity; tomorrow, we have to find someone else to follow. For today, that may mean pursuing a career that makes us the most money; if we later get burned out or bored, we will find a new job. For today, it may mean hating the people who, we are told, present the current threat.

Living by sight means focusing on the concrete, the mathematically provable, and the safe. It means following styles and relying on popular wisdom.

Most of all, living by sight is self-reliance. It trusts, ultimately, only the self. What do I know? What can I see? What makes sense to me? What sounds right to me?

Living by sight abhors death, for death enters us into an unseen world. Paul explains that we Christians would rather be away from our bodies, because then we will be at home with the Lord. Those who live by sight cannot understand that idea, and it frightens them.

What, then, is living by faith?

Faith follows neither the shiny, the prudent, or the natural. Living by faith is following the One whom we know, relying on His leadership, His knowledge, His plan, and His grace. It is neither safe, popular, nor scientifically testable... but it is the way to life, abundant and eternal.

Day 343/December 8 – 2 Corinthians 9-13

Sufficient Grace
2 Corinthians 12:9

God's gift of peace to the Christian flows from the promise of sufficient grace. God gives us what we need, and so we are at peace.

Despite terror and destruction and anger that flare all around us, Christ bestows hope and assurance and comfort—in short, the grace that always comes—to provide us peace in the midst of the world's hubbub. Human history teaches us that violence and anger are endemic and epidemic in our fallen world. In the holy mountain of the lord, the lion and the lamb will lie down together, but until we arrive there, battles will rage on.

Peace is not the absence of internal turmoil. Like Paul, we want things we cannot have. Like Paul, we are tortured by something that nobody else seems to understand, our own personal thorns in the flesh. We may not be flogged and shipwrecked as Paul was, but we have our own collection of afflictions, whether they be related to health or finances or age or relationships. We are weak. We get sad.

The world fights on. Terrorism erupts. Recession insidiously returns like clockwork. Vitriol and hatred spew from our television sets.

And yet, scripture promises peace.

Jesus makes clear to Paul that, despite whatever he is going through at the moment, "My grace is sufficient for you." The sufficiency of grace calms the mature Christian, for we know that no one can snatch us from His hand. We can totally rely on the grace that always comes.

We Are Israel
Galatians 3:29

In Genesis, when Jacob's name is changed to Israel, we recognize that Israel's story is our story. We too are unworthy, deceiving and being deceived and wandering in our own ways, wrestling with God.

Reading through the Old Testament, we see ourselves repeatedly in the adventures and antics of Israel. We turn to burnished idols before the ink is dry on what God has promised for us. We joyously accept God's covenant, only to violate it once more. With our sin and disobedience, we back ourselves into a corner, where exile is the only realistic option for us.

Throughout the Old Testament, we see God's promise to His people, beginning with Abraham, repeated again and again as the covenant is renewed. As the New Testament opens, we see Jesus heartbroken for Jerusalem as He tells of coming to the Jews. We note Paul's repeated plea for all Israel to be saved. Over and over, we see that Israel's story is our story.

Now, we understand our identification with Israel. "Israel" here is not a political nation. Paul tells us in Galatians that we who are Christ's are Israel, Abraham's offspring, because we are children of the promise. Chapter four explains the metaphor, contrasting the offspring of Hagar with the offspring of Sarah.

The blessing of Israel is not a legalistic thing based on race, geography, heritage, or tradition. It is the promise of God to His people, the faithful, who follow Christ. We are Israel, and grace is our story.

Just Because You Can Does Not Mean You Should – Galatians 5:13

We know that Christ sets us free. We are free from the slavery of sin. We are free from binding tradition and the unnecessary need to please anyone other than God. As disciples, we know the truth, and that truth has set us free. (John 8:31-32) We have eternal life and can do nothing to stop being children of God.

We are free. Our actions cannot affect our eternal security. Yet God is still intimately concerned with our behavior.

Freedom, like any other gift, can be abused and misused. Whether the issue is what food to eat, what ritual to keep, or what law to follow, Paul has consistently written to churches in Rome, Corinth, and Galatia that their exercise of freedom must be tempered by their concern for and leadership of others. The guiding principle for how to exercise freedom is the Golden Rule, the command to love your neighbor as you love yourself.

Exercise of our rights and freedoms has become an excuse for all sorts of misbehavior. Jesus has freed us from what bound us before, but the fact that we can do anything without risking condemnation does not make anything we do right.

Paul is not teaching that you must follow whatever restrictions the local regulators set. This chapter is not a new legalistic rule to bind us again. Instead, we are to act in love, knowing that what we do and say is seen and heard.

Use your head. Know that your actions have consequences.

By... Through... To...
Ephesians 2:8-10

Prepositions. Infinitives. Little words in a specific order to define how Jesus has worked in us and how Jesus will work in us.

By Grace. Through faith. To do good works.

Paul uses what we now think of as an old-fashioned word when he talks about our being saved. "Saved from what?," you may ask. Earlier in chapter 2, he explains that our disobedience and transgressions left us "dead," subject to the wrath that comes from being a part of the kingdom of the air. It is from this death and wrath that we are saved.

But by what?

We are saved by Grace, the unmerited favor of God bestowed on us because He loves us. We do nothing to deserve Grace. We cannot work hard enough, jump high enough, learn enough, or love enough to earn Grace.

How?

What we can do is have faith in God through His son Jesus Christ. Jesus calls that "believing in" Him. (John 3:16) The Grace that saves us, which has existed long before we walked the earth, comes to us through our faith.

For what purpose? We are saved to a new life, a life of obedience and addressing the needs of a hurting world. We are created in this new eternal life to do good works.

Do not get these backwards. God's Grace always comes first. We then believe, walking in faith, and are saved. Then, as God's great works of art, we accomplish what He has for us to do.

Day 347 / December 12 —Ephesians 6; Philippians 1-2

Humility
Philippians 2:3

In humility, consider others better than yourself.

The essence of our sinful nature is not simply selfishness; it is self-aggrandizement. It is not just pleasing ourselves; it is worshiping ourselves. Our tendency is to be certain we know best, we are best equipped to solve problems, and we deserve the choicest of the world's offerings.

The archetype Paul sets before us is Christ Himself. Paul tells us to have the same attitude as Christ.

How does Christ model humility? Paul spells it out through the words of an ancient hymn. Jesus has to steal or claim or grasp nothing to be equal with God because Jesus is the Son of God, part of the trinity, the divine one through whom the world has been created. Coming to earth to wear skin and breathe air and drink water is not simply a role for the Christ to play; it is a lowering of self to a degree that none of us can begin to comprehend. The agent of creation becomes the creature. God becomes man. Holiness becomes servitude.

What attitude must Jesus have to take on this form?

It is an attitude first and foremost of love. Jesus takes whatever step He must to give those whom He loves what they must have.

It is an attitude of submission, of setting aside all to which He has a right in order to do what must be done. Even to die.

Jesus is the epitome of humility. Let your attitude be His.

Day 348/December 13 –Philippians 3-4; Colossians 1

Jesus: All the Fullness of God
Colossians 1:19

If you ever find yourself the least bit unsure of who and what Jesus is, Colossians 1 is for you. This chapter is as good a basis of Christology—what to believe about Jesus—as there is.

Jesus is God. Make no mistake about it.

Scripture gives us descriptions of God as the Father and Creator, the Son and Savior, and the Holy Spirit and Comforter. These three manifestations of God—called by the hymn writer "God in three persons"—lead some to order Father, Son, and Spirit in some sort of hierarchy to try to understand the trinity better.

Scripture does not lower Jesus below God the Father. On the contrary, Paul explains to us that Jesus is God. All the fullness of God—everything that there is of God—dwells in Jesus.

Jesus is the image of the invisible God. In other words, the way we see God is to look at Jesus.

Jesus is the creator. All things in heaven and on earth were created by Him and for Him.

Jesus is sustainer. In Him, all things hold together.

Do not worry that you cannot explicate the details of all of the trinity, for none of us can, just as we cannot fully explain the pollywog's metamorphosis into the toad. The wonders of God are beyond our ken. What we can understand—indeed, what we know—is that Jesus, God in the form of human servant, draws near and saves us. Through Jesus, God's grace always comes.

Things Above
Colossians 3:1-2

This world is not our home. We are aliens, passing though this human existence in a temporary human form. Our kingdom and our life are in another place.

We have died to this life, and our existence is now hidden with Christ.

It is no wonder, then, that our minds are elsewhere, that we find ourselves longing for what we cannot fully comprehend. We set our hearts on "things above" because our destiny is not here. We are citizens of heaven.

That sounds poetic, but what does it really mean as we walk this earth?

It means the cares of this world are not of ultimate importance to us. Oh, we still put money in the bank and obey the laws. We continue to go to our jobs and shop at the grocery store. We still strive to make the best decisions we can about where to go to college and with whom to spend our days.

But with our minds set on things above, we know that the bank accounts and the careers and the diplomas are not what count. We know that things can go wrong with a job or a relationship and, while we will hurt and suffer as any denizen of this place will, our eternity is unchanged.

It also means that our goals and our actions are shaped by things above. We act for an audience of One, and it is His approval only we seek. He is our hope, and He is what matters.

Always/Never
1 Thessalonians 5:17; 2 Thessalonians 3:13

Paul writes in what seem to be extremes. "Always rejoice." "Have the same attitude as Jesus." "Be transformed." "Avoid every kind of evil." "Pray continually." "Be anxious for nothing." "Never tire of doing what is right." Simply giving a decent effort falls woefully short.

Paul does not allow for gray areas. He sets out targets for life that require full and never-ceasing commitment. There is no hint of trying hard here.

Is it unrealistic to tell us never to tire of doing what is right? Is it a bridge too far to call on us to avoid every kind of evil?

We are only human. Isn't getting close good enough?

God does not think so when He tells Moses to tell the people to be holy.

Jesus does not think so when he tells the disciples to be perfect.

Christianity is not a compromise. Faith is not graded on some sort of percentile score where we measure ourselves against others and feel good because we have done reasonably well.

True faith in the One who gave His all—who went to the cross for us—demands that we give Him our all. He demands that we take up our own cross. He tells the rich young ruler to sell all he has. He commends the woman who uses up the extravagant jar of perfume for His anointing. He praises the widow who gives all she has.

Paul knows and imitates His master, and so Paul speaks in superlatives.

Walk worthy of the Lord. Always rejoice. Never tire.

Day 351 / December 16 –1 Timothy 1-5

Invisible God
1 Timothy 1:17

Why does scripture say that God is invisible?

God is not transparent. He is not some gossamer being of so little substance that we can visualize things through Him as though He were not there.

God is not a vapor, lacking any real presence in our lives.

God is not a Dickensian ghost, appearing to teach us a lesson and then sinking back into our subconscious as though no more than a dream.

God is not a magician's illusion, conjured out of oblivion to entertain and amaze and then destined to return to nothingness.

And God is not in disguise so that He can sneak in unseen when we are committing a sin and catch us red-handed.

No, God is invisible to us only because we are human. God is so magnificent, so multi-dimensional, so beyond our comprehension that our puny human eyes cannot begin to capture Him. God is invisible in the literal sense: He is unseeable.

We cannot see the face of God because we cannot survive exposure to that level of holiness. (Exodus 33:20-24)

God will not always be invisible to us. One of the greatest benefits of heaven will be that we will get to see God face to face, as He is. (1 John 3:2; 1 Corinthians 13:12)

For now, we are limited by our fall, and God is invisible. We are not yet able or worthy to see Him. Thanks be to God that we have met Jesus, the image of the invisible God.

Day 352/December 17 –1 Timothy 6; 2 Timothy 1-4

Bring Mark with You
2 Timothy 4:11

Paul is nearing the end, and he wants to see his true friends. He urges Timothy to make plans to "come before winter." (2 Timothy 4:21)

Among those other friends whom he wants to see is Mark, author of the gospel and former missionary traveler with Paul.

Paul and Mark have had a falling out. For reasons historians can only guess, the man known then as John Mark leaves Paul in Perga in the middle of his First Missionary Journey. (Acts 13:13) Whether Mark is homesick, upset over changes in leadership, or just frustrated with Paul, his leaving results in Paul's loss of trust in him. (Acts 15:37-38)

The story of Paul and Mark thankfully does not end there. By the time Paul writes his later letters, Mark is back with him and in his good graces. (Colossians 4:10; Philemon 24) And now, writing to Timothy from Nero's dungeon, Paul asks for his friend Mark.

A feel-good story? Yes, but it is more than that. Looking at the relationship over time teaches us the reality of Christian reconciliation. Since we do not know the reasons for their parting, we can only speculate as to who forgives whom; the reality is that they each undoubtedly have need to forgive the other. We do not need to know that detail to understand the truth that, in Christ, we are reconciled to our Christian brother.

As you continue through life, do not leave your friends behind. Be sure to bring Mark with you.

Eight Names for Jesus
Hebrews 1:2-3

Jesus is:

The Son. He is the only begotten of God, the firstfruit of the children of god, Son of God and Son of Man.

Heir of All Things. All that God has is His. He is the model for us, His joint-heirs.

Maker of the Universe. Jesus is the agent of creation. All things were made through Him. Without Him, nothing that has been made was made.

Radiance of God's Glory. When we see Jesus, we will see God. The glory of God that is too magnificent for human eyes to see will be beheld, fully for the first time, when we see Jesus as He is.

Exact Representation of God's Being. There is nothing about God that we cannot see in Jesus. Jesus is God, exactly and completely. He makes the invisible visible.

Sustainer of All Things. Not only has Jesus created all things, but He is also the one who holds all things together. We go on because of Christ. Working through and as His Holy Spirit, Jesus is the bonding glue of the world and of His people.

Purifier of Sins. His true loves—you and I—are incapable of communing with God because we are stained indelibly by our sins. So Jesus purifies us, paying the price for and erasing our sins.

The One Seated at God's Right Hand. He is God. He is with God. He is the one we will see at the judgment, and He is there when our prayers are heard.

The Anchor for Our Souls
Hebrews 6:19

Hope is the anchor for the soul.

Hope is not a wish, a longing, a fantasy, or a mere goal. Hope, whenever it is mentioned in scripture, is what we know to be true. Hope is that to which we cling, not just a possibility.

No one whose hope is in God will be put to shame. (Psalm 25:3) The eyes of the Lord are on those whose hope is in His unfailing love. (Psalm 33:18) Those who hope in the Lord shall renew their strength. (Isaiah 40:31) Our hope springs from the plans of the Lord. (Jeremiah 29:11) When we remember the great love of the Lord, we have hope. (Lamentations 3:21-22) Paul is willing to stand trial because of this hope. (Acts 26:6) All that is written in the scripture is there so we might have hope. (Romans 15:4) We wait for Christ's return, which is the hope of glory. (Titus 2:13)

The nations of the world put their hope in the name of Christ. (Matthew 12:21) Hope does not disappoint. (Romans 5:5) We wait with perseverance for the hope we do not see. (Romans 8:24-25) The one in whom we have set our hope will deliver us. (2 Corinthians 1:10) The hope of salvation is our protective helmet. (1 Thessalonians 5:8)

Why can we approach the throne of grace with confidence? (Hebrews 4:16) It is because of hope, because we know the one who has walked before us, the one who keeps our souls firm and secure.

Day 355 / December 20 – Hebrews 7-10

Incarnation
Hebrews 10:5

I f you are using this book on the calendar year plan, you are now finalizing your preparation for Christmas. Here, in the midst of Advent, Hebrews emphasizes the fact of the physical body of Jesus.

Incarnation literally means "being in a body." Christmas is the celebration of the incarnation, the coming of God into the body of a human baby.

There are two real tipping points for most people when it comes to faith:

First, for the atheist and doubter, is belief in any god at all. For this person, the idea that maybe our lives and the uniqueness of earth with its placement just the right distance from the sun, its livable temperatures, its miracles—like the transformation of the caterpillar and the water cycle—are all just coincidence, a series of random results of chaos theory.

Second, for the seeker whose eyes are open enough to understand that life cannot exist without a supreme designing hand, there is still the issue of the incarnation. Other religions are based on books, laws, customs, rituals, and ideas; the seeker recognizes Christianity is none of that but rather presents a relationship. Relationship can only exist if there is someone with whom we have relationship, if God has taken the form of a human being with whom we have that relationship.

Jesus is not just another useless sacrifice and offering. He is God in a body. When you come face to face with the incarnation, you cannot leave the same.

Certainty
Hebrews 11:1

In this post-modern world, where truth is considered to be relative, this bedrock certainty of Christianity surprises many non-believers.

We are sure of what we hope for. We are certain of what we do not yet see.

We continue in the Word, we are disciples, and we know the truth that sets us free.

We walk by faith, not by sight.

We know whom we have believed, and we are persuaded that He is able to keep what we have committed to Him.

The knowledge of the mysteries of heaven has been opened to us. We are enriched in that knowledge to know the mysteries of God's will.

We are given the Holy Spirit, a deposit guaranteeing our inheritance, by whom we know what Christ has told us is true.

With the apostles on the newly-calmed lake and with the Centurion at the cross, we say, "Surely, this is the Son of God."

Our faith is not a guess. We do not cross our fingers and dream that the pretty words of the church might be true. We have not pledged our lives to a hunch.

We are not presenting a point of view, a suggestion, or our perspective on the world.

Faith is being sure of what we hope for. It is being certain of what we do not see. Of course, we see through a glass darkly. We do not know Christ now as we will know Him one day. Still, we are certain. That is faith.

Day 357/December 22 – James 1-5

Unpolluted
James 1:27

G od is looking for those who remain unpolluted by the world.

Christians are not called to avoid the world. Believers are follow-ers of Jesus, who ate with despised thieves, befriended prostitutes, and generally spent his time among the sinners around Him, wheth-er they were poor beggars or powerful Pharisees. Followers cannot influence those whom they never see or hear.

Christians are also not called to live a life devoid of temptation. To the contrary, temptation is a guarantee. The devil prowls around us, and the world is crawling with allure and suggestion. Temptation cannot always be avoided.

What believers are called to do is to come out of the world, to be in the world without being of the world, to avoid falling into temptation. It is the great accomplishment of the disciple to walk in the world and to stay pure.

Aristotle famously said that it is the mark of an educated mind to be able to entertain a thought without accepting it. James is rea-soning along the same lines when he advises Christ's followers to consider the world, to be a part of it and walk in it, without becom-ing polluted by it.

James articulates this truth in a number of ways. He tells us dis-ciples to show our faith by our actions, to discern the gifts of God from the temptations of the world, and to rely continually on the grace of God, which always comes.

Do not reflect the world. Be holy, as God is holy.

Day 358/December 23 – 1 Peter 1-4

Ready to Answer
1 Peter 3:15

The time comes to all who claim to be followers of Jesus when someone asks why they are believers. Somebody raises inevitable questions about why evil exists if God is omnipotent and all-knowing and truly loving. Another will complain about troubles that have come despite her earnest prayers. Still others will ask how the disciple can possibly believe in a God who cannot be seen.

Those who do not hear these questions are either not letting anyone know they are Christians or are closing themselves off to those around them, shielding themselves from vulnerability to the very questions that plague the minds of seekers everywhere.

It is true that followers can often, in the words attributed to St. Francis, preach a sermon using words only when necessary. Our actions can point the way to Christ for many without our saying anything.

But Peter warns away from relying totally on a silent demonstration. With all gentleness and respect, Christians are called to be ready to answer the questions.

Doubters will argue the Christian's logic all day long. The authority of scripture is a topic for debate at all levels of society.

What the skeptic cannot do is wish away any Christian's personal experience. The Christian who says, "This is what has happened to me, and this is why I have the hope of eternal life..." can be written off as a liar or a lunatic, or else the listener has to consider the story told. Always be ready to give your answer.

Day 359/December 24 – 1 Peter 5; 2 Peter 1-3

Grow
2 Peter 1:5-8

The moment of salvation, when Christ enters into the Christian and the Holy Spirit begins working on the heart, is not an end but a beginning. Becoming a Christian should not be the goal, as though the brand new Christian has finished a race. To the contrary, the very phrase "becoming a Christian" implies change in order to be and do new and better things.

So what comes next? The Apostle Peter teaches us to add to faith. Start the process with goodness. Saved by faith, now begin becoming a good person. Change. Reflect Christ. Grow. Become. Add to the foundation, for our character must be built.

To goodness, add knowledge. Read scripture. Discuss great ideas with smarter people. Pay attention to others. Learn. Study literature. Know the philosophies and economics and politics and psychology of the world.

To knowledge, add self-control. A faithful, good, smart Christian who is overbearing and boorish accomplishes little for Christ.

To self-control, add perseverance. There will be troubles for all Christians, and standing firm demonstrates a power and a resolve that are reserved for those who are certain of what they cannot see.

To perseverance, add godliness. Be holy, as God is holy.

To godliness, add brotherly kindness. Care for one another, and then care for those who cannot do anything in return.

To kindness, add love. Bear all things. Believe all things. Hope all things. Endure all things. Never fail.

These attributes do not come immediately or easily. You must grow in Christ.

Extravagant Love
1 John 3:1

O n this Christmas, we read of God's extravagant love. God has not parceled grace out to us in rations but instead has overwhelmed us with His love so much that we can see ourselves only as His children.

He lavishes love on us in creation, in giving us a world of beauty and provision and wonder. He places us here to work and to enjoy, to observe and to love, to discover and to understand.

He lavishes us with love with beautiful gardens, with protective skins and protective arks, with dreams interpreted and schemes uncovered, with unexpected blessings and promises kept.

He lavishes us with love by teaching us a law that will keep us alive when we keep it and then by forgiving our failings when we do not keep it.

He lavishes us with love by speaking to us through prophet, poet, teacher, and singer. Words of Psalms, Proverbs, the Song of Songs, and the prophecies are gifts from God, showing us again and again that we are the apple of His eye.

Today, we revel in the love lavished on us by God's sending His only begotten Son to teach us how to live and then to show us how to die, only to rise again and conquer the very death that threatens and frightens us.

He lavishes us out of His nature. John says it over and over again: God is love.

Our response? Love one another because He first loved us. Love extravagantly.

Merry Christmas.

Day 361/December 26 – 1 John 5; 2 John; 3 John; Jude

Able to Keep You from Falling
Jude 24

Life is treacherous. Temptation is around every corner. Pitfalls and trapdoors await. People will—intentionally or not—lead you off a cliff.

We can fall because we stumble.

We can fall because we are pushed.

We can fall because we step in a hole we do not see.

We can fall because we are weak.

We can fall because our fallen world is rife with snares and trip-wires and bullies.

We can fall because we are human, because we have a nature that gives in to the temptations of the flesh and to the allures of the world.

We can fall because falling is often easier than standing up straight and marching forward.

Falling seems so natural that many simply do not try not to fall. They focus instead on dusting themselves off and getting back up. Phrases like "I'm only human" or "the devil made me do it" serve as excuses for falling.

To be clear, scripture is explicit that we will all fall. None of us is righteous. None of us is immortal in this earthly body. None of us is immune from disease and hidden deception.

Yet, grace always comes. We do not have to fall. We serve one who is able to keep us from falling. He walks beside us to hold our hand and walks above us to show our way and walks beneath us to uphold us when we are unsteady. What can keep us from falling is Christ, for He is always able.

Holy and Worthy
Revelation 4:8,11

The Book of Revelation is filled with figures and mysteries. Reading through this essay, written from exile to churches under persecution, requires an understanding of its makeup of codes and representations meant to be grasped by some readers but simultaneously indecipherable to prying Roman eyes. Reading it is more satisfying when approached with the acceptance that not everything will be understood.

Stars, lampstands, scrolls, time periods, numbers, creatures, and angels all find their place in this apocalyptic scripture. John writes as emperor worship is being enforced. Opposition to Christian faith is arising on every side.

Now John, probably the last of the original twelve apostles to still be alive, is given a revelation, perhaps as a vision or a dream. He receives specific instructions about writing to seven churches, and he is shown a series of pictures and told to record some and to remain silent about others.

The language and the style of Revelation are different from the rest of scripture, and the themes and symbolism can discourage and even aggravate many readers.

Amid the frustrating words, though, is scripture's primary character who continues from the beginning to the end of the Bible: Jesus is the hero of the story. Jesus is holy, eternal, and almighty. Jesus is worthy to be worshiped and to receive all glory and honor and power due the creator or the world.

These are powerful words. As we travel through Revelation, remember this main them: we worship Lord Jesus—holy and worthy —alone.

Day 363/December 28 – Revelation 5-9

No More Tears
Revelation 7:17

These chapters include more symbols, the beginning of tales of woe and destruction, and cautions of the highest order for those who are not God's children.

But for those who are Christ's, for those who are marked with the seal of the Lamb, for the ones gathered in from all the tribes of the people of God… what a glory awaits!

Worship in eternity will not be a picture of drudgery, as though heaven were every seventh grader's worst nightmare: some kind of forced sitting in hard-backed pews while a boring minister intones lessons and homilies. No, what awaits God's people is celebration before the throne of the one who has collected His people to Him. What awaits is satisfaction. What awaits is comfort.

What awaits is a world where God has wiped away every tear.

Ponder for a moment all the things that have brought you sadness, defeat, and pain in your life. Catalog for one minute the tear-causers of your existence.

Now, turn your attention to what is to come. No aging. No hurt. No setbacks. No loss. No more discouragement or exhaustion. No grief or sorrow. Not a hint of melancholy. Every possible thing that could lead to gloom erased.

What we call heaven has many descriptions in art and literature. What our bodily forms will be and "where" heaven is are subjects not to be comprehended until those gates themselves are opened.

But one thing is abundantly clear. There will be no tears. Grace always comes.

Woman, Dragon, Beast, and Lamb
Revelation 14:8

The dragon delegates power to the beast. These are the villains of Revelation. The woman, hero of these chapters, is pursued by Satan, who knows his ultimate defeat is sure. The Lamb of God—Jesus the Lord—watches and protects her.

Like a modern cinema blockbuster, this tale lays out scenes of war and destruction, counter-intelligence and tactics, battles and retreats. The writer of Revelation never lets the story go too long before stepping back from the front to remind the reader who the winners are.

The kingdom of this world is become the kingdom of our Lord and of His Christ, and He shall reign forever and ever. The dragon is not strong enough to defeat the angelic hosts. Now have come the salvation and the power and kingdom of our God.

Fallen is the great evil city. Fallen is the source of pain and hatred. Fallen is she who would lead the world to slavery and destruction.

The end will come when it comes. The woman-church will doubtless face attacks from Satan and from those who are unwittingly led along by sly servants of evil. Christ, who is patient and wants no one to perish, will wait and watch and endure great destruction as humanity continues its pattern of unrepentant failure to accept the covenant of God.

But in the end, as at the beginning and throughout history, God will be on His throne. The creator, who was before, will be after.

The victory is decided and secure.

Day 365/December 30 – Revelation 15-19

The Word of God
Revelation 19:13

We are almost finished reading through scripture. Have you understood the Word?

In the beginning was the Word. The Word was with God, and the Word was God. (John 1:1) The Word is a lamp to my feet and light for my path. (Psalm 119:105) The Word of God is living and active, sharper than any double-edged sword, judging thoughts and attitudes of the heart. (Hebrews 4:12) Blessed are those who hear the Word of God and obey. (Luke 11:28) You have been born again, not of perishable seed, but of imperishable, through the living and enduring Word of God. (1 Peter 1:23) You are strong, the Word of God lives in you, and you have overcome the evil one. (1 John 2:4)

The Word became flesh and dwelt among us. (John 1:14)

The word of God is in scripture's prophecy, poetry, law, psalm, gospel, and history. God speaks through prayer, study, and experience, all substantiated by our basis in scripture.

Ultimately, though, scripture is a record of Jesus, who is the Word of God. If you want to know what God says, how God thinks, or what God wants, you need to watch and listen to Jesus, for He is the Word of God.

The one whose name is King of Kings and Lord of Lords also bears the name The Word of God as He mounts His white steed and leads His people to their final victory.

When evil falls, it will fall to the Word of God.

Day 366/December 31 – Revelation 20-22

Take the Free Gift
Revelation 22:17

The Bible ends with these two triumphant final chapters of Revelation. Here, we find the familiar descriptions of heaven, with foundations of precious stones, gates of pearl, and streets of gold. Not only are there no more tears, we are assured that there is no more night, for the presence of God and of Jesus provides eternal light, overcoming all hint of darkness. For good measure, we are assured that there is no more curse, for Satan and evil and their servants have been defeated and dispelled.

Scripture does not, however, end with this glorious description of victory. There are still a couple of more critical points to be made.

The first is Jesus' promise of return. He is both the Beginning—the agent of creation—and the End. He is Alpha and Omega. He is First and Last. His return will mark the end of what we know and understand of this place, this time, this existence even as He brings the beginning of eternity.

The second is the invitation of Christ to everyone, expressed by John, by the Sprit of God, and by Christ's bride, the church.

That invitation is this: Come.

If you are thirsty, come to the water. Take the free gift of life.

All we have read together amounts to this: Come to Jesus. Accept the free gift. Quench your thirst.

Come, Lord Jesus!

Scripture ends as it began, with grace. John extends "the grace of the Lord Jesus" to his readers.

Grace always comes.

About the Author

Lyn Robbins is a practicing attorney with twenty-five years of experience in a wide range of legal matters. He has tried more than fifty cases to verdict and has been involved in dozens of appeals. He spent more than twelve years as the senior general attorney for one of America's largest railroads.

He was National Debate Champion and the first person ever named the top individual college debater in the nation for two consecutive years, and he later coached the national championship team. He graduated cum laude from Baylor University School of Law, where he was the Lead Articles Editor of the Baylor Law Review and was a member of the Order of the Barristers.

Lyn is also a Sunday School teacher and deacon at his church. He is active in the community where he has appeared in occasional community theatre productions and coached both baseball and softball for many years. He was a long-time member of the Board of Directors of an NGO dedicated to promoting sustainable growth among some of the world's poorest and most challenged populations.

His first book, *In the Court of the Master: An Ordinary Man's Walk With An Extraordinary God* is a vibrant description of the Christian life from the perspective of an experienced believer.

Lyn's books are available at
www.LynRobbins.com

www.ingramcontent.com/pod-product-compliance
Lightning Source LLC
Chambersburg PA
CBHW060237100426
42742CB00011B/1557